Mircea Eliade

Mircea Eliade

MYTH, RELIGION, AND HISTORY

Edited by

Nicolae Babuts

Transaction Publishers

New Brunswick (U.S.A.) and London (U.K.)

Library of Congress Catalog Number: 2013030956
ISBN: 978-1-4128-5299-9
Printed in the United States of America

Library of Congress Cataloging-in-Publication Data

Mircea Eliade : myth, religion, and history / edited and with an introduction by Nicolae Babuts.
    pages cm
  Includes bibliographical references and index.
  ISBN 978-1-4128-5299-9
  1. Eliade, Mircea, 1907-1986. I. Babuts, Nicolae.
  BL43.E4M585 2014
  200.92--dc23

                                                        2013030956

In Memory of Irving Louis Horowitz

Contents

Acknowledgments

The project to prepare a volume on Mircea Eliade began on the initiative of Dr. Irving Louis Horowitz, chairman of the board of Transaction Publishers. Initially the collection of essays was meant to belong to the series titled Culture and Civilization, whose scope was and is a critical examination of "the continuing relevance and importance of religion." "Indeed," writes Irving Louis Horowitz, "I see Culture and Civilization as the best way to move beyond the malaise of the new and the old or is it the good and the evil!" (in a January 17, 2012, letter). In March of 2012, Professor Horowitz passed away, and it was left to Mary E. Curtis, his wife and the president of Transaction Publishers, to consolidate and continue his legacy. Although the aims of the Eliade volume have not changed, the decision was made to have it stand alone.

I wish to acknowledge here the invaluable help and guidance given to the project by Mary Curtis. Thanks are also due to Professor Howard Schneiderman of Lafayette College, editorial consultant with Transaction Publishers, for his oversight of the review process. In like manner, I wish to thank Jeffrey Stetz in the editorial department of Transaction Publishers for his help. Finally, I wish to express my appreciation to Jennifer A. Nippins, the managing editor, for her help during proofreading.

Eliade's "Theös Éghènou" first appeared in *Gândirea* [*Thought*] 7, December 12, 1927; the Romanian version was republished in *Mircea Eliade, Itinerariu Spiritual. Scrieri de tinerețe* [*The Spiritual Itinerary: Writings of Youth*], 1927 (Bucharest: Humanitas, 2003, 392–397, edited by Mircea Handoca).

Mircea Eliade:
Biographical Note

Mircea Eliade (pronounced *Meer*-ch'a Eli-*a*-de) was born in 1907 in Bucharest, Romania, and died in 1986 in Chicago, Illinois, at age seventy-nine. He was known in his homeland as a novelist, journalist, and educator, and in his later life, universally, as a historian of religions who wrote and taught a distinctive approach to the study of "comparative religion."

He began to write and publish in school newspapers while in high school, and wrote professionally throughout his university years. Many of his articles appeared in the newspaper, *Cuvântul,* where his favorite professor, Nae Ionescu, was to become editor in late 1927. Eliade was called the "Chief of the Young Generation" in college because he made himself spokesman for his colleagues. In 1928, he graduated from the University of Bucharest with a thesis on Italian Renaissance philosophy. Drawn to oriental studies, he had the good fortune to obtain a scholarship from a Maharaja for period of residence in India. He studied Sanskrit and Yoga philosophy at the University of Calcutta and practiced yoga in a Himalayan hermitage. His stay was cut short after three years by the ruler's death and obligatory military duty at home. Returning at the end of 1931, he wrote his dissertation on Yoga and was awarded a doctorate from the University of Bucharest in June, 1933.

Nae Ionescu invited Eliade to be his assistant at the university in November of 1933, and he continued in that capacity until 1938, teaching various courses in religion and philosophy. In 1932, Eliade and some of the leaders of the "young generation," representing various ideological stripes, formed a group called "Criterion" that gave public lectures on timely cultural and political topics. This era of "good feeling" was not to last for long and the group broke up in 1935. In January1934 Eliade wed Nina Mareş, a member of Criterion who was divorced and had a child, in what proved to be an ideal marriage. While still in India Eliade had begun writing novels, and he continued to do so after his return. His best-known novel was *Maitreyi* (1933). He also wrote newspaper and magazine articles and several scholarly books, foreshadowing his later history of religions works.

In the summer of 1938 he was arrested without charge, held at the police station and later sent to an internment camp for members and suspected members of the Legion of the Archangel Michael (or Iron Guard). A semi-religious, anti-Semitic, militaristic, organization, the Legion was much feared by the government. After four months of confinement and showing signs of tuberculosis, he was simply released. He resumed his writing and founded a journal of religion and folklore, *Zalmoxis*. Unfortunately, the journal saw only three issues before succumbing to the war.

On Diplomatic Service

In April, 1940, Eliade was appointed by King Carol II (who had imprisoned him) cultural secretary to the Romanian Legation in London. There he experienced the terrors of the first "Blitz" and other air raids, before the legation moved to Oxford. When England and Romania broke off diplomatic relations in February1941, he was transferred to Lisbon. That position was nullified when the Russians occupied Bucharest in August 1944. Soon after, on October 20 1944, his wife died of cancer. Eliade remained in Lisbon until September 1945. Meanwhile, all his works were banned in Communist Romania.

Parisian Years

As soon as he could obtain a passport and visa, Eliade together with his step-daughter, Giza, emigrated to Paris, where many Romanians had taken refuge. There he renewed friendships with fellow-countrymen E.M. Cioran and Eugène Ionesco. His financial existence was precarious. After teaching one course at the Sorbonne, he undertook to write articles and books on the history of religions while becoming fluent in French. His basic Works date from this period (1946–1956): *Traité de l'histoire des religions, Le mythe de l'éternel retour, Le Chamanisme et les techniques archaïques de l'extase,* and *Le Yoga, immortalité et liberté.* In 1950, he married a Romanian living in Paris, Christinel Cotescu. That same year his association with Eranos and the Bollingen Foundation began.

At the University of Chicago

At a History of Religions Conference in Rome, 1955, Joachim Wach, chair of History of Religions at the University of Chicago Divinity School, invited him to come there as lecturer and visiting professor for 1956–1957. But Wach died suddenly a few weeks later, leaving a vacancy on the faculty. The position had not been filled when Eliade and his wife arrived the following year. After one term, Eliade was offered Wach's post, which he tentatively accepted. Thus began an association that lasted nearly three decades, since he retained his Chicago residence adjacent to the campus even after his retirement at age 75.

In his Chicago years, his renown reached its acme. His French academic books were translated into English (and other languages). He wrote many new titles in the history of religions including the masterful three-volume *A History of Religious Ideas*, plus many smaller texts on myth, symbol, initiation rites, alchemy, witchcraft and more. He edited a sixteen-volume *Encyclopedia of Religions* and founded a quarterly journal, *The History of Religions*. His books and theories have exerted a continuing influence on the way in which "comparative religion" is taught in American colleges and universities.

He also published personal books (*Autobiography* and *Journal*). He wrote, in his native Romanian, a large number of short stories in the fantastic genre. Only a few of these have been translated into English but many are available and admired in other languages (French, Italian, German, and Japanese, among others). His literary masterpiece, the novel *Noaptea de Sânziene* (Night of St. John), written in Paris, exists in English translation as *The Forbidden Forest*.

—Mac Linscott Ricketts

Introduction

The aim of the present volume is to study the emergence, function, and value of religion and myth in the work of Mircea Eliade (1907–1986), one of twentieth century's foremost students of religions and of cultural environments. For Irving Louis Horowitz, as for many of us, Eliade is "a scholar who lived a long, complicated and creative life on two continents" (February 8, 2012, letter). The task of studying his work is rendered difficult because of his vast and varied production and also by the fact that his ideas and concepts may have undergone an evolution during his lifetime. In his March 16, 2012, e-mail, Mac Ricketts writes about Eliade's use of the terms "sacred" and "profane":

> I believe the first usage of these terms is in *Mitul Reintegrarii* (1942)—3 or 4 times. This book is partly about the coincidence of opposites, and he says that the sacred and the profane are such a pair. But the volume published in 1942, *Comentarii la Legenda Meşterului Manole*, is filled with references to the sacred and the profane. References to Jung are frequent, and "archetype" occurs several times—in such a way that it is clear Eliade has not yet understood what Jung meant by it, and thinks he and Jung share the same idea. This book grew out of a course Eliade taught in 1936–37, but how much of the original course remains is impossible to say. (He finished the book hurriedly in 1942 in Portugal.)

What emerges from Professor Ricketts's clarification is that terms and concepts in Eliade's work do acquire additional connotations and references and perhaps that this implies an evolutionary trajectory. In any case, the task is to study the texts to understand his concepts, their meaning and import, as well as what they could signify for our time. There are in fact several semantic centers in Eliade's cosmogony, which are not easy to decipher, but which carry within their conceptual network profound insights.[1]

For what is becoming clear the more one delves into the life and works of Mircea Eliade is that he was a complex person willing to bring into his perimeter of vision and engage many conceptions of the world, many worldviews, and many experiences from the Romanian roots and folklore to the Indian philosophical systems, Indian epics, folklore and myths to the Australian, African, and Iranian myths. Ricketts rightfully points out that "Eliade read widely and eclectically, in Eastern and Western religions and philosophies, ancient and modern, as well as other fields!" (March 16, 2012, e-mail). And John C. Holt points to the vast scope of his project: "In describing and analyzing the patterns and meanings of myths, rituals, symbols, and types of religious experiences, Eliade seemingly moved effortlessly from his knowledge of one religious culture to another" (xiii). No doubt also, he does engage in a dialectic dialogue with other students of religion in modern era and assigns an important place to Christian and Jewish views of the sacred. Holt also indicates that Eliade's overriding concern is to describe and understand religion "on its own terms, or within its own planes of reference" (xii). What strikes me is the interdependence, almost interpenetrability, of Eliade's concepts that appears as a compelling argument in favor of the unity and harmony of his thought. In view of his insights into the essence of religious experience, I do not see a reason to call into question his methodology. Douglas Allen says it succinctly: "Mircea Eliade will be seen as a generalist who uses a phenomenological approach" (*Structure*, 70). And further: "Eliade wants to deal faithfully with his phenomena as phenomena, to see just what his data reveal" (114). "By insisting on the irreducibility of the sacred, Eliade attempts sympathetically to place himself within the perspective of *homo religiosus* and to grasp the meaning of the religious phenomena" (115). There is no better way to put it.

What I would like to add, however, is that no matter what the historical context of one's methodology, no matter how closely a scholar follows a given direction in his or her approach, the ultimate product will still reflect an individual interpretation and will be in harmony with the inner vision. That is universally true. To believe that one can rise above one's own vision in a stratosphere of pure rational objectivity is just not humanly possible. In this regard, W. C. Beane's reminder is pertinent: "we are obligated to realize that even when we make it our aim to allow the ciphers to speak for themselves, we must accept the practical paradox of knowing that those ciphers are really speaking through us (=*re*-presentation); and this marks the inevitable but formidable presence of the task of creative hermeneutics" (187).

However, another error, one that has spawned political criticisms of Eliade, is to assume that no degree of objectivity is possible and that Eliade's views of religion have been influenced by his early Legionary sympathies. I believe that among the best sources of information to assess the validity of this criticism are Mac Linscott Ricketts's comprehensive biography, *Mircea Eliade: The Romanian Roots* (especially volume 2, chapter 22, "Nationalism and the Primacy of the Spiritual," 881–930); Ricketts's article on Eliade's *Ifigenia* and *Comentarii la legenda Meșterului Manole*; and Bryan Rennie's *Reconstructing Eliade* (in particular the chapters "Eliade's Political Involvement," 143–177, and "Scholarly Criticism of Eliade," 174–194). Norman Girardot, in his nostalgic look at the past, both Eliade's and his own, refers to the charges heaped upon Eliade and believes that they "do not fit with [the] man [he] had known." He adds: "Nor do I think that a compromised political past necessarily or completely invalidates all of one's life work as a scholar. Somewhere in the course of these heated accusations, we need to remember the initiatory nature of a human life—that youthful transgressions can lead to atoning emotional and intellectual transformations in later life" ("Nostalgic," 158). Similarly, Bryan Rennie writes:

> I would suggest that Eliade's brush with totalitarian ideologies in the 30s influenced his theoretical position as expressed in his later books as a reaction *against* such tendencies; that his perilous attraction to the extreme right in his younger years led to a far more mature position; that, in its own way, his later works were a repudiation of the exclusivism and ethnic superiority of the later Iron Guard. (*Reconstructing*, 165)

Moreover, in assessing Eliade's position and his sympathies for the Legionary movement, one has to take into account some factors that militate in his favor. Ricketts reminds us that "Eliade finds in this philosophy of living in the 'now' a theoretical justification also for his disinterest in politics" (*Romanian*, volume 1, 588). And as far as the accusation of anti-Semitism, is concerned, again Ricketts points out the following: "Eliade seems to have been keenly sensitive to racial or religious prejudice. His testimony to his 'suffering' on learning about the expulsion of two outstanding Jewish scholars indicates this, as does also another column from about this time on 'Racism and the Cinema'" (*Romanian*, volume 1, 628).

In his scholarly work, the statements about the terror of history that have political implications corroborate Girardot's and Rennie's conclusions. The following passage is an example of the views of a mature Eliade: "And in our day . . . how can man tolerate the catastrophes and horrors of history—from collective deportations and massacres to atomic bombings—if beyond them he can glimpse no sign, no transhistorical meaning . . .?" (*Myth of Eternal* 151). It is a poignant reminder of what ideology and hatred have done in Europe, both during the war and afterward. The Jews suffered the most; but the Romanians, the Poles, the Czechs, the Slovaks, and others in the same geographical area and elsewhere also endured hardships. Clearly, beliefs, religious or not, can veer into ideologies. There is a difference between patriotism on the one hand and ideologies like Nazism or Marxism on the other, and the difference is precisely ideological hatred. Religions are not exempt and neither are some of Eliade's critics. We need help to promote more friendships among peoples; the purveyors of hate sprout by themselves.[2]

It is significant then that in an article, published in *Credința*, February 14, 1934, and cited by Ricketts, Eliade casts a plague on both Communism and Nazism:

> "How can we imitate Hitlerism which persecutes Christianity or Communism which burns cathedrals?" he asks. "The Communist arsonists of churches are hooligans—and so are the Fascist persecutors of Jews. Both of them trample humaneness and personal faith—which are the freedoms of every individual." (*Romanian*, volume 2, 893)

He warns of the danger for Romania:

> No, gentlemen, do not be deceived by words. Just as much innocent blood will flow on our streets whichever "power" wins, whether it be the "left" or the "right." We shall see old men with heads split open, young men stood before firing squads, and the women raped—and in either case we shall awake to find ourselves more wretched, more oppressed by this sad life, on the morning of the red flag or the morning of the black shirts. (*Romanian*, volume 2, 893)

And Eliade wrote this prophetic warning in 1934 when the worst was still to come. Perhaps, while criticized for his faults, he has not been given enough credit for his insights.

On another level, some critics say that Eliade's religious structures are "atemporal and ahistorical" (see Chung Chin-Hong, 197), and yet this may be misleading. Because the concept of the sacred is so united to the concept of sacred time, one cannot separate the two. It is just that we are dealing with a different kind of time, which nevertheless has an ontological existence. The idea that Eliade's structures are ahistorical is similarly incomplete if not misleading. The author who spoke so eloquently about the "terror of history" can hardly be accused of neglecting the historical dimension of reality. But again we have to clarify his awareness of the determining influence of history. Chin-Hong himself observes that "The structure or meaning Eliade finds is not the least bit ahistorical or antihistorical" (199). And he explains:

> This is to affirm that without historical time there could be no manifestation of structure. But Eliade also argues that even though this may be so, history in this sense does not fundamentally modify or determine symbolic structure. Of course, history invests the symbolic with value and thus the reevaluation of the symbolic arises in historical circumstances. (198)

What Chin-Hong says remains valid to the extent that it shows the interdependence between history and symbolic structures. And in this context, Douglas Allen sees some ambiguity in Eliade's phenomenological analysis. On the one hand, "By means of the basic nontemporal and nonhistorical religious structures, especially the archetypal systems of religious symbols, Mircea Eliade is making significant claims about human beings and their existential situation, about the human mode of being in the world and the human condition" (*Structure*, 180). On the other hand, he emphasizes "the extreme importance of the particular and the historical conditionings of the revelatory experiences" (182). He thus emphasizes "a sense of *activity* and *creativity* on the part of homo *religiosus*" (181). Again, there is a dialectical interplay between the historical and the universal. One does not negate the other. These issues are at the center of Eliade's thought and constitute a challenge to our critical enterprise.

It is essential then to clarify the dimension of the field we explore in search for answers. We have to bring in as evidence from Eliade's texts themselves to make a compelling argument about his views before we compare them with the views of other students of religion and place his views in a modern phenomenological context. In cautioning against using a vocabulary of other critics to determine one's own interpretation, Rennie specifies: "Eliade's own vocabulary and terminology must be used to understand his intentionality" (*Reconstructing*, 187–188). In other words, we can let Eliade himself speak. In his "Notes for a Dialogue," published on the web, while responding to Thomas Altizer's book *Mircea Eliade and the Dialectics of the Sacred*, Eliade says that he is grateful to Altizer for "understanding so well, and expressing so sympathetically my endeavor to disclose the coherence and richness of primitive and Asiatic religions." But Eliade detects a kind of *malentendu*, and adds, "Altizer appears to be convinced that I present the 'situation' of the shaman, the yogi, the alchemist, and particularly the 'archaic mode of being in the world' as models for the modern man" (2). Eliade categorically denies that such was his intention: "I never suggested that we must go back to the archaic or Oriental modes of existence in order to recapture the sacred" (3).[3] Douglas Allen echoes the thought:

> Once again, Eliade is not advocating that Western philosophy "return" to pre-Socratic archaic ontologies so that contemporary philosophers can reestablish premodern philosophies.... Rather, he advocates that philosophers "return" to the archaic other ... in order to revalorize and reconstitute transhistorical mythic and symbolic religious structures and archaic primordial metaphysical insights into the human condition as part of new philosophical reflections and creativity. ("Mircea Eliade's," 226)

It is perhaps understandable that one may be led astray by Eliade's sympathetic treatment of the archaic mentality that valorizes the sacred, and the coherence he attributes to the archaic man's views of time and of the beginning of the world. But his goal is not to offer the archaic mode of existence as a model for our times. His goal is for all intents and purposes even more ambitious. What is that goal? Eliade defined it more than once and in terms that aim to create "a new humanism": "For whatever its role has been in the past, the comparative study of religions is destined to assume a cultural role of the first importance in the near future" (*Quest*, 2). And he explains:

> This is not only because an understanding of exotic and archaic religions will significantly assist in a cultural dialogue with the representatives of such religions. It is more especially because, by attempting to understand the existential situations expressed by the documents he is studying, the historian of religions will inevitably attain to a deeper knowledge of man. It is on the basis of such knowledge that a new humanism, on a world-wide scale, could develop. (*Quest*, 3)

One discovery that emerges from the studies of "Indian thought or certain 'primitive' mythologies," is "that the decisive act which determined the present condition of man took place in a primordial past, and that therefore the *essential precedes the actual human condition"* (*The Two*, 14). Or as Eliade explains it elsewhere, "that *the essential human condition precedes the actual human condition,* that the decisive deed took place before us, and even before our parents: that decisive deed having been done by the mythic ancestor (Adam, in the Judaeo-Christian context)" (*Myths, Dreams,* 54–55). Eliade immediately points out the relevance of this claim for the Western philosopher. Indeed, this claim is undoubtedly responsible for the accusation of essentialism leveled against him. One might wish to have this sentence repeated. "Essentialism," meaning what? And then we remember the great vogue of existentialism in Western philosophy and the prestige of authors like Sartre and others, who claimed that on the contrary existence precedes essence. Of course, we have to understand in what sense one precedes the other. Both assertions can be justified and can have validity. Individuals grow and change all their lives, and only at the end can they offer their essence. On the other hand, however, certain events at the beginnings of humanity were of such magnitude that they have determined the course of our history. Those events have essential attributes that modulated our evolution in a decisive way, in a way that defines our essence as human beings. But to understand this, we need to engage in a *bona fide* dialogue. We conclude that Eliade is not offering an answer, but *proposing a dialogue,* which would be the equivalent to a key to lead us to the hoped for new humanism. He is perhaps justified in pointing to the danger of provincialism that the Western world faces, if it simply looks at other cultures with disdain, considering them inferior or irrational, and refuses to engage in a needed dialogue: "Western man will not be able to live indefinitely cut off from an important part of himself" (*The Two* 14).

History and the Proximity of Death

The issue, then, is not just a matter of particular ideas that have to be accepted or rejected; rather, it is also important to develop a hermeneutics that would produce insights. One example is Eliade's suggested dialogue to compare the Western view of history and the views of other cultures. He points out that the Western man, who is not religious and who defines himself by his role in history, has a passion for historiography. But while he may not be aware of it, his attachment to history, to a time that has a necessary end in death, involves an anxiety at the proximity of death. This understanding could come from a comparison of one who is not religious with any men or women who have religious beliefs. Eliade begins by pointing out that in the Western world, "the discovery of historicity, as the specific mode of being of man in the world, corresponds to what the Indians have long called our situation in Mâyâ" (*Myths* 239). And he explains:

> Rather than an invitation to renounce History what is revealed to us in the *Bhagavad Gîtâ* is a warning against the *idolatry* of History. All Indian thought is insistent upon this very point, that the state of ignorance and illusion is not that of *living* in History, but of *believing* in its ontological reality.... The ignorance, and hence the anxiety and the suffering, are perpetuated by the absurd belief that this perishable and illusory world represents the ultimate reality. (*Myths*, 242)

Moreover:

> The Indian, then, would agree with us inasmuch as he admits that anguish in face of the Nothingness of our existence is homologous with the anguish of facing Death—but, he would immediately add, this Death that fills you with such anxiety is only the death of your illusions and your ignorance: it will be followed by a rebirth, by the realisation of your real identity, your true mode of being: that of unconditioned and free being. (*Myths*, 240)

The Western man would perhaps answer that we have no assurance that death would be followed by a rebirth; and that would be a reasonable answer. Nevertheless, there is no one who could be sure that our world represents the ultimate reality, because that is precisely what we do not know. It is significant, then, to note Eliade's statement, that in observing

> the general behavior of archaic man: we are struck by the following fact: neither the objects of external world nor human acts, properly speaking, have any autonomous intrinsic value. Objects or acts acquire a value, and in so doing become real, because they participate, after one fashion or another, in a reality that transcends them. (*Myth of Eternal*, 3–4)

As "receptacle of an exterior force," the object or fact becomes sacred. And it is the dimension of the sacred that is real and the profane, the brute material aspect, illusory. The sacred time of the beginning is real; the profane time of history is illusory. If this notion of archaic man sounds to us, well, "illusory," it may not sound so if we consider the following. Describing the difference between imaginary time and real time, Stephen Hawking writes:

This might suggest that the so-called imaginary time is really the real time, and that what we call real time is just a figment of our imaginations. In real time, the universe has a beginning and an end at singularities that form a boundary to space-time and at which the laws of science break down. But in imaginary time, there are no singularities or boundaries. So maybe what we call imaginary time is really more basic, and what we call real is just an idea that we invent to help us describe what we think the universe is like. But according to the approach I describe in chapter 1, a scientific theory is just a mathematical model we make to describe our observations: it exists only in our minds. So it is meaningless to ask: which is real, "real" or "imaginary" time? It is simply a matter of which is the more useful description. (*A Brief*, 144)

This astonishing declaration and confession of difficulty coming from one of the foremost scientists of our time should certainly give us pause. What is at stake here is how to deal with a reality that may be beyond the ability of our minds to comprehend. Perhaps we were not created for this universe or the universe was not created for us. The reason it is hard if not impossible for us to imagine that time began with the Big Bang is that we always come back to the question what was before that singularity. Was it Nothingness? The laws of physics fail us.

In the following passage, it is as if Eliade were attempting to give an answer to the dilemma of the Western world:

For Mâyâ is not an absurd and gratuitous cosmic illusion, it knows nothing of the absurdity that certain European philosophers ascribe to human existence as they conceive it, issuing out of Nothingness and proceeding to Nothingness. For Indian thought Mâyâ is a divine creation, a cosmic *play*, of which the end and aim is human experience, as well as deliverance from that experience. It follows that to become conscious of the cosmic illusion does not mean, in India, the discovery that all is Nothingness, but simply that no experience in the world or of History has any ontological validity and, therefore, that our human condition ought not to be regarded as an end in itself. (Myths, 241)

Thus, if Mâyâ is a cosmic play, it must have had a beginning and also it must have an end. And just as we have no answer as to what was before the Big Bang, we have no answer as to what happened before the play. Or perhaps Hindu mythology tells us. Judaism and Christianity certainly do. If God is eternal then the question as to what happened before the creation of Adam and Eve is no longer relevant. And Eliade emphasizes what is relevant and is a new element in Judaism and Christianity, and that is faith "in the sense inaugurated by Abraham—as a unique means of salvation." The specificity of Christianity "is guaranteed by *faith* as the category *sui generis* of religious experience, and by its valorization in *history*" (*Myths*, 29).[4] Eliade points to Judaism, Christianity, Indian thought, and the paradigmatic gestures of the archaic man as dimensions of our minds to be explored. And that may be part of his legacy.

The *Illud Tempus*

What we begin to know, and that in part thanks to Eliade's hermeneutics, is that the vast literature comprising myths, in almost every archaic culture, represents the human endeavor to go back to a time at the beginning when the world was created by the gods and was benefitting from the energy and freshness of the just created. Eliade emphasizes that among the primitives this was part of a nostalgia for the lost paradise. The mythical memories of paradise present "the image of an ideal humanity enjoying a beatitude and spiritual plenitude forever unrealizable in the present state of 'fallen man'" (*Myth of Eternal*, 91). For a man who belongs to a traditional culture, this going back is linked to the belief that "Living in conformity with the archetypes amounted to respecting the 'law,' since the law was only a primordial hierophany, the revelation *in illo tempore* of the norms of existence, a disclosure by a divinity or a mystical being" (95). Moreover "the repetition of paradigmatic gestures" executed *in illo tempore* by the gods or the mythical heroes is equivalent not just to remembering but to reliving the cosmogonic beginning. And "any meaningful act . . . any repetition of an archetypal gesture, suspends duration, abolishes profane time, and participates in mythical time" (36).

But the fact that the individual and the group are completely under the ascendancy of the sacred time, does not imply that profane time is destroyed: it simply means that the participants are leaving the profane time and entering a new time that has been regenerated, being now identified with the time of the original creation. As Robert Segal puts it, speaking about the imitation of the archetypal deeds: "Humans are rejuvenated by *encountering* the sacred not by *becoming* sacred" ("Are There," 26). Yet, in explaining the symbolism of the New Year, Eliade does believe that ritual rejuvenation involves an act of transcendence. He writes: "Nature recovers only itself, whereas archaic man recovers the possibility of definitively transcending time and living in eternity" (*Myth of the Eternal*, 158). However, "Insofar as he fails to do so, insofar as he 'sins,' that is, falls into historical existence, into time, he each year thwarts the possibility" (158). Archaic man wishes to pay scant attention to the historical time that is irreversible, and places his hopes on the reliving of the mythical time. While Eliade extols the value of the archaic man's hopes, nowhere does he suggest that we adopt them.

The Sacred and the Profane

We can begin with the manner in which myths reveal their sacredness. Eliade writes: "myths describe the various and dramatic breakthroughs of the sacred (or the supernatural) into the World. It is this sudden breakthrough of the sacred that really establishes the World and makes it what it is today" (*Myth and Reality*, 6). How should we understand this foundational concept of myth and religion? Clearly to understand myths we have both to interpret the symbolism of their archetypes and to focus on the value of the concept of the sacred. Eliade offers the following definition of what is involved in the archaic man's experience when he attempts to go back to the mythic times: "we might say that by 'living' the myths one emerges from profane, chronological Time and enters a time that is of a different quality, a 'sacred' time at once primordial and indefinitely recoverable" (18). We have now reached the center of Eliade's ontology, that is to say, reached his conception of the two aspects of the world: the sacred and the profane. Understanding the two elements that appear to define reality would clarify the goals of Eliade's hermeneutics. It is remarkable then that some scholars have misunderstood the two concepts. Eliade has this to say about it:

> Altizer's most serious criticism concerns my understanding of the dialectic of the sacred as a hierophany. He interprets this as meaning that the *sacred* abolishes the *profane* object in which it manifests itself. But I have repeatedly pointed out that, for example, a *sacred* stone does not cease to be a *stone*; in other words, it preserves its place and function in the cosmic environment. In fact, hierophanies could not abolish the profane world, for it is the very manifestation of the sacred that establishes the world, i.e., transforms a formless, unintelligible, and terrifying chaos into a cosmos. ("Notes," 3)

One can see above that Eliade himself used the words "abolishes profane time" (*Myth of the Eternal*, 36) and that this may be the source of the misunderstanding. But in light of the dialectical movement of the two forces and of their intertwining strands, it becomes clear that neither one nor the other can disappear. The sacred is defined precisely by what is wholly other, the *ganz andere*, which is opposed to the profane. It is the opposite of the profane. "Whatever the historical context in which he is placed, *homo religiosus* always believes that there is an absolute reality, *the sacred*, which transcends this world but manifests itself in this world, thereby sanctifying it and making it real" (*The Sacred*, 202). And to repeat, "It is this sudden breakthrough of the sacred that establishes the World." Perhaps we may have to understand that the sacred does not promulgate the world in its material identity, but that it establishes its structure and organization, endows it with value, and gives it its meaning. And it certainly does not annihilate it or delete it. Guilford Dudley III encapsulates Eliade's view: "The experience of the sacred in the hierophany confers value and meaning on objects in the phenomenal world that otherwise would have no value or meaning" (87). In his remarkable analysis of the concept of hierophany, Bryan Rennie concludes "that it *must* be perception which makes the event a hierophany." And he explains: "Thus the *object* [a stone for example] is not actually changed; from the profane point of view nothing distinguishes it. Rather it must be the *awareness* of its sacrality, the perception of the sacred as manifest in that particular object which has wrought the transformation" (*Reconstructing*, 14, 19). All of which means that the process of the breakthrough, the interpretation of the world that gives it value and meaning, takes place in the mind.

Nevertheless, the relation between what is in the mind and outside the mind is difficult to interpret. Elsewhere I have stressed that there is no meaning without an observer and something to be observed.[5] Others have said that this is "a reciprocal affair."[6] And Robert Ellwood is justified in asking a crucial question: "whether the structures—sacred and profane, cosmos and history—are out there in some ontological sense, or in the minds of individuals and societies?" (March 13, 2012, e-mail). We can answer that, at least in an archaic culture, the structures of the world, both sacred and profane, are out there, have an objective ontological existence, but that their experience, interpretation, and meaning occur in the minds of individuals. A believer and a nonbeliever would differ in their interpretations. A believer, experiencing the presence of the sacred, will believe in its ontological reality. Eliade employs so many times the term *homo religiosus*. But what does it mean? My answer is that *homo religiosus*, while it may have other secondary meanings, primarily means one who believes. Because humans are used to the equation that posits a relation between our interpretation and an outside event, it is not surprising that for a believer the presence of the sacred is a reflection of an outside reality. In his remarkable analysis, Bryan Rennie writes: "Only by taking seriously . . . the various beliefs of a religion might one succeed in comprehending the existential situation of the people who hold those beliefs" (*Reconstructing*, 253).

One revealing example is that offered by experiences of the mystic Light. Such experience of the Light

> always evolves into a religious experience. All types of experience of the light that we have quoted have this factor in common: they bring a man out of his worldly Universe or historical situation, and project him into a Universe different in quality, an entirely different world, transcendent and holy. The structure of this holy and transcendent Universe varies according to a man's culture and religion. . . . Nevertheless they share this element in common: the Universe revealed on a meeting with the Light contrasts with the worldly Universe—or transcends it—by the fact that it is spiritual in its essence, in other words only accessible to those for whom the Spirit exists. (*The Two*, 76–77)

One can assume then that the Spirit exists for those who have the experience. The experience itself leads to an interpretation, and both happen in their minds and are a function of their beliefs. Moreover, for them, precisely because they have the experience, the transcendent universe into which the individual is projected, has an ontological reality. The general tendency to believe that the inner structures reflect the outer reality is strengthened by their religious beliefs. Of course, one may choose not to believe. And that is legitimate, but it does not lead us to an answer. Not to an answer that Michel Meslin's expects when he writes: "Even if one adopts such a view of matters, it must be emphasized that the continuous re-presentation of the origin can only be actualized through a tradition that transmits myths, symbols, and rites, and that every tradition is always interpretive" (18). And he adds: "If, as has been said (*Patterns*, 397), the time that one can repeat by ritual reenactment is sacred, then these same times[sic] cannot be situated outside the duration of the contingent, because it is humanity that effects the representation that, through ritual, makes primordial time present once more" (19). Again, as in the case of Altizer, Meslin's difficulty is with the dialectical movement of the sacred and the profane. The fact that tradition prepares the group or individuals to experience the sacred does in no way justify glossing over its character and attributes. Bryan Rennie says it as well as can be said: "The potential to detect, to apprehend, the real, the sacred, in a particular object or event is culturally conditioned, but it is also affected by, and effected through, the creativity of the human imagination, and thus it is not culturally *determined*" (*Reconstructing*, 130). A Lourdes pilgrim coming face to face with the statue of Our Lady in the Grotto would certainly be prepared by tradition to see the material statue as sacred. However, there are several things to be noted: The first is that, prepared or not, the human mind needs the material presence of the statue (outside it) in order to experience the hierophany. The second is that it is the structure of human consciousness that facilitates the intervention of belief and the creation of mnemonic conditions for the hierophanic irruption to occur. This appears to be Eliade's foundational claim. And the third is that the time of that experience, the time of the hierophany, is a sacred time that unfolds its dimension in contradistinction to the profane time.

Again, neither the sacred time nor profane time is destroyed, but the ascendancy of the profane time is no longer in effect. This becomes very clear also from Eliade's description of the continuity between the Christian liturgy for a given Sunday and the Sunday following and the Sunday before: "The profane succession, on the other hand, which flows between two Masses, not being transformed into sacred time, cannot have any connection with the hierophanic time of the rite: it runs parallel, so to speak (*Patterns*, 391). Clearly, the sacred time has the power to intervene and impose its dominion within the human mind. And because the human mind is needed to receive the intervention of the sacred time, it has been conditioned to do so, but humanity is not the agent; it is the recipient of the outside force, of the numinous, of this *ganz andere* that is not human. Even clearer than in the rituals destined to relive the primordial time, the experience of the mystic light shows that the human being is not controlling the event; rather the individual is projected into "a Universe of different quality."

Things happen in the cosmos, in human history, and they also happen in human experience, as a reflection of the events outside the human mind. If, as Eliade says, the sudden breakthrough of the sacred establishes the world, it is the experience of that breakthrough that gives meaning to our view of the world. However, we have to stress, that this does not imply that human beings are completely passive. After all, they are needed to participate in the ritual to relive the events of primordial time. Douglas Allen explains: "The sacred may 'show itself,' but *homo religiosus* is not some passive receptor. The dialectic of the sacred is a dynamic complex process of transfiguration and transformation"

("Mircea Eliade's," 218). And indeed we find in *Patterns in Comparative Religion* this surprising admission, when Eliade states that the seasonal celebrations of vegetation cults must not be

> taken to mean some sort of pantheist experience, some mystical way of getting in touch with cosmic life. . . . It is not the natural phenomenon of spring, the actual occurrence itself which inspires the rituals of springtime, but it is, on the contrary, the ritual which confers its significance upon the coming spring. (325)

In the experience of the mystic light, we can see that the individual does not have the initiative. Similarly, when, as we shall see below, God tells Moses that he is on sacred ground, God has the initiative, and Moses is the recipient of the divine power. We may have to understand that the rituals themselves are inspired by the presence of the sacred. And that is because in the same book, in speaking about sacred places, Eliade explains: "a sacred place involves the notion of repeating the primeval hierophany which consecrated the place by marking it out, by cutting it off from the profane space around it" (*Patterns*, 368). Moreover, the fact that the sacredness of a place continues through time shows that hierophanies are autonomous: "the sacred expresses itself according to the laws of its own dialectic and this expression comes to man *from without*" (369). We have to understand, then, that while the group or individuals may take the initiative to begin a ritual, the need to do so comes from the knowledge that a certain place was chosen by the original hierophany. The choice of the sacred place is not left to man. Yet Eliade allows for a certain flexibility here. Thus, David Cave quotes the following: "We say a space can be consecrated by a hierophany, but man may also construct a sacred space by effecting certain rituals" (qtd. 237n7; from Eliade's, *Symbolism, The Sacred and the Arts*, 109). In any case, whether outside forces intervene or the group or the individuals have the initiative, it is clear that the sacred exercises its power of conferring significance on the events within the human mind. And the ascendancy of the sacred is a human experience. Eliade concludes a chapter in *Patterns* by stressing the human "longing for transcendent forms—in this instance, for sacred space" (385).

While that much is clear, understanding the relation between the sacred and the profane remains as the core of the problem. Eliade has attempted to use the philosophical concept of *coincidentia oppositiorum* to explain the opposition between the two. But as John Dadosky points out, he appears to have been misunderstood: "Altizer misinterprets Eliade by claiming that the existence of one excludes the existence of the other—the two cannot coincide." And he adds, "In contrast, for Eliade the sacred and the profane can coincide, but he explains this coincidence of opposites as paradoxical rather than contradictory" (*Structure*, 70). The difficulty is that *coincidentia oppositorum* is an abstract philosophical term and can be applied to many different encounters and can also be misread. Eliade himself agrees "that all expressions of the *coincidentia oppositorum* are not equivalent" (*The Two*, 123n1).

More than anything else, however, it is perhaps useful to recall, with Dadosky, that Eliade saw that the revelations of the history of religions are in need of "a new *Phenomenology of the Mind*" (*Quest*, 64). Why would this be needed? It is in part because both the manifestation of the sacred and the going back to the beginning require "an effort of thought" (*Myth and Reality*, 112). Hierophanies, the manifestations of the sacred, do represent experiences, either experiences of an individual or of a collective of individuals. In *The Sacred and the Profane* (20), Eliade gives the following example: Jehovah addresses Moses and tells him: "'Come no nearer; take off your sandals; the place where you are standing is holy ground'" (Exod. 3:5–6). The ground is sacred because it manifests itself so in Moses's mind. Just as in the case with those experiencing the Mystic Light in their own minds, God's words enter Moses's mind, and they are part of his experience, regardless of the objective form they might be supposed to take. Moses is projected into a sacred universe.

At the beginning of the book, Eliade offers what has to be one of the most compelling passages in his *oeuvre*:

> A *sacred* stone remains a stone; apparently (or, more precisely, from the profane point of view), nothing distinguishes it from all other stones. But for those to whom a stone reveals itself as sacred, its immediate reality is transmuted into a supernatural reality. In other words, for those who have a religious experience all nature is capable of revealing itself as cosmic sacrality. (*The Sacred*, 12)

This is Eliade's great insight, the extraordinary discovery that it is in human experience, whether individual or collective, that the sacred dimension of the world reveals itself. The reason this is crucial is that this circumstance explains how a stone and an event can at the same time be sacred for those who have the experience and remain without any significance beyond their material presence for those who are not capable or not willing to enter the sacred dimension. It can also explain what Altizer apparently did not see, that is, that the sacred and the profane can coexist in a paradoxical opposition, without destroying each other.

The dynamics of the coexistence of the two primary elements of reality, the sacred and the profane, is reflected on a nonreligious plane in the dialectical relation between objects that have a negligible value as material entities but have an enormous value as objects that have a history. The Associated Press reports the following story: "A century after it was minted, a humble 5-cent coin with a storied past is headed to auction, and bidding is expected to top $2 million." The story of the nickel is this: "The 1913 Liberty Head nickel . . . was surreptitiously and illegally cast, discovered in a car wreck that killed its owner, declared a fake, forgotten in a closet for decades and then found to be the real deal" ("Humble Nickel," A-1). A work of art that fetches millions at an auction is understandable: It has an aesthetic beauty and the reputation of the artist to vouch for its authenticity. But a nickel? An ordinary nickel? The explanation is clearly in keeping with Eliade's insight that an object can at the same time be materially indistinguishable from the others like it and yet acquire a sacred value, or, as in the case of the humble nickel, that it can be endowed with fame and monetary value by its history. It is within human memory that all this takes place.

It is not surprising, then, that for Eliade the drama of human hopes, desires, nostalgias, and beliefs, of human religion then, takes place on a mnemonic stage. Whether it is a ritual where the cosmic beginning is relived, a shaman's ecstatic bird calling, or the "remembered births" of Buddha and his disciples, in all cases it is the power of memory that is extolled. Thus "'absolute memory'—such as the Buddha's, for example—is equivalent to omniscience and gives the possessor the powers of Cosmocrator" (*Myth and Reality*, 90).

This is certainly crucial to any cognitive view of religion, literature, and the world. And it is a question that comes to mind when considering the "pan-Indian technique," "known to all sages and contemplatives of the Buddha's period . . . practiced and recommended by the Buddha himself." It states that "it is possible, starting from any moment of temporal duration, to exhaust that duration by retracing its course to the source and so come out into the Timeless, into eternity" (86).

> Hatha-yoga and certain Tantric schools employ the method called "going against the current" (ujāna sādhana) or the "regressive" (ulta)

technique to obtain the "inversion" of all the psycho-physiological processes. In the man who accomplishes it this "return" or "regression" finds expression in the annihilation of the Cosmos and hence brings about "emergence from Time," entrance into "immortality." (86–87)

The question remains: What is the relation of this "annihilation of the Cosmos" that presumably happens in the mind of the yogi to the objective reality of the cosmos? If the cosmos continues to exist in an objective dimension, how can the individual obtain immortality? Moreover, if as Eliade contends, reality, generally considered to have an objective existence, does in fact have no value except the value conferred on it by human consciousness, where does the sacred come from? And here is Eliade's answer: in discussing Rudolf Otto's book *The Holy* (*Das Heilige*), Eliade speaks of "the feeling of fear before what is sacred, before the mysterium tremendum" and adds: "Otto designates all these experiences numinous, for they are evoked by the same aspect of the divine power: the 'numinous' is distinguished by its being something 'wholly other' (*ganz andere*): radically and totally different; it resembles nothing either human or cosmic" (*Myths, Dreams*, 124). It appears, then, that the numinous is different both from the level of human intellect and from nature in its cosmic dimension. It can be approached neither by scientific inquiry nor by human reason. But if the source of the sacred or the numinous is outside human consciousness, where does it come from? The question is doubly relevant if we assume that the numinous has the power to supersede history or the world. Eliade offers a glimpse of where to look for it when he discusses the function of symbols and says that symbols reveal a hidden side of human life, which "is 'divine' in the sense that it is the work of Gods or supernatural Beings" (*Two and the One*, 202; see the quotation in full further down). Perhaps then we should look at the beginning, at the primordial time of creation, the *illud tempus*, when the creative energy of the supernatural beings was in its full vigor. Rennie suggests as much when he points out that "the sacred models do not belong to the profane, historical realm. . . . They issue from the alternative realm, considered to be the locus of the real and the true and the significant. This realm is *illud tempus*" (*Reconstructing*, 81). It is perhaps not without significance that today's science looks also to the beginning, to the explosion of the original singularity for answers. In any case, we are dealing with a numinous presence whose dimension has to be further explored.

Regardless how we imagine it, the source of the sacred power is outside the human mind. Nevertheless, as the case of Moses illustrates, while the words he hears come from Jehovah, it is Moses who hears them: they enter his mind and are part of his experience. Thus, while the sacred and its power come from the dimension of the divine, they are revealed in the human mind; they are part of human experience. Eliade believes that "the 'sacred' is an element in the structure of conscious-ness, not a stage in the history of consciousness" (Preface, *Quest*, i). And Douglas Allen stresses Eliade's point: "Modern persons have lost awareness of nontemporal, nonhistorical structures that are perma-nent essential structures of consciousness" ("Mircea Eliade's," 217). One can see again here the dialectical movement of the structural and the historical attributes of reality. It may be pertinent at this point to introduce what Eliade himself says about his experience:

> I am not a man with normal religious experiences; neither am I an agnostic or an anti-religious person. . . . I know the divine presence only in moments of great despair--but at all other time I ascertain this presence in any human act. More clearly, religion is for me the thirst for and intuition of the *real*, the absolute. I identify this thirst in any significant act of man, in all times. (*Journal*, December 23, 1942; quoted by Mac L. Ricketts, *A New*, 73)

Myth and Language

It appears, then, that there are three powers that operate on the stage of the world: the presence of the sacred (Gods or supernatural beings), the cosmos, and the human mind. The cosmos in its material identity represents the profane, the sacred represents the numinous state, and both, the cosmos and the sacred, are reflected and modulated in human experience. We have already seen the importance of human memory that gives such power to the yogi and to the Buddha himself. But Eliade appears to vaunt the power of language also. Dudley believes that in Eliade's view language itself has an autonomy, the power to establish certain structures like "*coincidentia oppositorum*," "divine polarity," "the sacred androgyne," and "the *axis mundi*." Duddley writes: "In short Eliade postulates something like Jung's 'collective unconscious.' In a very real sense, then, the history of religions for Eliade points to invariable structures and paradigms inherent in the human mind" (152).

However, according to Eliade, the archaic culture does not pos-sess theoretical terms that are characteristic of Western philosophy:

"Obviously, the metaphysical concepts of the archaic world were not always formulated in theoretical language; but the symbol, the myth, the rite, express, on different planes and through the means proper to them, a complex system of coherent affirmations about the ultimate reality of things" (*Myth of Eternal*, 3). Both Douglas Allen and Norman Girardot quote Eliade saying: "In the last analysis *the World reveals itself as language*" (from *Myth and Reality*, 141; quoted by Allen, *Structure*, 183; Girardot, "Nostalgic," 7). And Carl Olson believes that "For Eliade, the world reveals itself as language, which implies that it needs to be interpreted" (30). We are reminded here of Jacques Lacan's claim that the unconscious is structured as a language. We could say with equal justification that the mythic imagination, in its symbolic function, is structured as a language. Or, on the other hand, we could adopt John Holt's view that "myth, rite, and symbol" constitute "a grammar of religious culture" (e-mail, September 2, 2012). The term *grammar* would be more precise. In any case, language and grammar offer a metonymic relation that is not contradictory. Either one, or both, can function as an organizing principle.

One has to caution, however, against assuming that Eliade's archetypal structures are homologous to Jung's unconscious, for example (or to Lacan's, for that matter). Their sources are not the same. As Ricketts has pointed out, Eliade himself may have initially thought that they are, but as his thought evolved he realized the difference between his views and those of the proponents of what he calls "depth psychology." For Eliade, "the contents and structures of the unconscious are the result of immemorial existential situations, especially of critical situations, and this is why the unconscious has a religious aura" (*The Sacred*, 210). So if Eliade agrees that "the contents and structures of the unconscious" are "the results of immemorial experiences of critical situations" (*Myths, Dreams*, 17), why, then, are the mythical structures different from Jung's unconscious?

The problem with the proponents of depth psychology, in which Eliade, as far as I can tell, includes Jung and Freud, is the psychologist's reductive techniques. One could say that "A myth is produced by the unconscious in the same sense in which we can say that *Madame Bovary* is the 'product' of an adultery" (*The Sacred*, 210). But does such reduction advance us? It would be "equivalent to explaining *Madame Bovary* as an adultery." "But *Madame Bovary* has a unique existence in its own frame of reference, which is that of a literary creation, of a creation of the mind" (Preface, *Myths, Dreams*, 14). "It is when the psychologist 'explains' a mythological Figure or Event by reducing it to a process of the unconscious, that the historian of religions—and perhaps not he alone—hesitates to follow him" (14). The distinguishing mark of the religious experience of the symbolism of the tree, for example, is that in myth the image of the tree is "awakening the whole consciousness of the man and 'opening it to the universal'" (*Myths, Dreams*, 19). In myth, symbols are apprehended by intuition and understood in their totality, that is, in relation to each other. And in their reference to the cosmogonic beginning, they reflect a religious and universal significance. In dreams, the image of the tree does not reveal its universal significance. In that sense, perhaps, it remains incomplete.[7] In contrast to myths, which have an organizing function and which aim to represent the totality of the structure of the sacred and of its cosmic relevance, revelations of the unconscious do not represent a "total experience." Speaking about Eliade's understanding, John C. Holt succinctly defines the relation between this experience and the function of myths and symbols: "The function of narrative myths, then, is to link various symbols into a constellation or 'logic' expressive of a coherent world view responsive to the experience of the sacred" (xiv). Thus, in spite of his great admiration for both Jung and Freud, and in spite of admitting similarities, Eliade does not follow the psychologists in reducing myths to the structures of the unconscious. He envisages myths as the product of a creative imagination that favors certain structural possibilities or tendencies to endow symbols and multivalent images with religious (sacred) values and that eschews metaphysical abstractions while at the same time implying them. And it appears then that dreams and the contents of the unconscious do not reflect the totality of a worldview and, while gaining a certain religious aura, do not carry the whole value of the sacred. Symbols, on the other hand, because they are religious, are fraught with the mystery of the sacred.

Indeed, Eliade's pages describing this mystery of religious symbols, at the end of *The Two and the One*, remain among the most fascinating of his corpus. He begins by recalling Paul Tillich's statement: "This is the great function of symbols: to point beyond themselves . . . to open up levels of reality which otherwise are closed, and to open levels of human mind of which we otherwise are not aware" (*The Two*, 201n1). Then he proceeds to enlarge and modulate this definition, stating that a "symbol is not a replica of objective reality. It *reveals* something deeper and more fundamental" (201). The condition of the world it reveals "*is not evident on the plane of immediate experience*" (201), and the revelation is not "a matter of rational cognition" (202). Symbols are always religious because they point to something *real*, that is, something *sacred*:

> A corollary of the preceding observations: religious symbols which touch on the patterns of life reveal a deeper Life, more mysterious than that grasped by everyday experience. They reveal the miraculous, inexplicable side of Life, and at the same time the sacramental dimension of human existence. "Deciphered" in the light of religious symbols, human life itself reveals a hidden side: it comes from "elsewhere," from very far away; it is "divine" in the sense that it is the work of Gods or of supernatural Beings. (202)

As one can see, Eliade modifies Tillich's definition to endow symbols with the mystery of the sacred, their capacity to lead to an apprehension of "the sacramental dimension of human existence." There is no doubt that these new attributes only add to their potential to function as a language.

Indeed, like language, symbols are able to point to, identify, and valorize a structure of the world "that is not evident on the plane of immediate experience" (201). Moreover, again in keeping with their capacities of revealing and creating meaning, symbols do operate in the human mind. They represent a human experience. "It follows that the *man who understands a symbol not only 'opens himself' to the objective world, but at the same time succeeds in emerging from his personal situation and reaching a comprehension of the universal*" (207). And it is a spiritual experience: "Thanks to the symbol, individual experience is 'awoken' and transmuted into a spiritual act" (207). The experience is equivalent to a hierophany. The question that remains unanswered is the following: what about literary symbols? Deep down, Eliade appears to be convinced that all symbols are religious. And his strategy of co-opting literary symbols into religious ones seems in keeping with his analogy between archaic myths and some aspects of modern creative activities, like painting, writing, and reading. Is all creative activity in some sense symbolic?

Faith and Belief

The overriding characteristic of the mythic imagination, especially in the Indian religious practices is the belief that immortality can be achieved, belief that the processes taking place in the mind have validity over and above the material reality outside the mind. Of course,

Christianity also promises that history will come to an end and the kingdom of God will bring salvation to those who deserve it. One has to have faith. At this point, we may be prompted to ask if there is a difference between belief and faith. We may recall that Eliade stressed what was new in the Jewish religion:

> Moreover, the Mosaic dispensation laid the emphasis upon faith, upon a religious experience which implied an interiorisation of worship, and this was its greatest novelty. One might say that the discovery of faith as a religious category was the one novelty introduced into the history of religion since neolithic times. . . . The religious forces set in motion by Jahveh are *spiritual forces*. (*Myths, Dreams*, 143)

And elsewhere he writes: "Faith . . . means absolute emancipation from any kind of natural 'law' and hence the highest freedom that man can imagine: freedom to intervene even in the ontological constitution of the universe" (*Myth of Eternal*, 160–161). Eliade further elaborates this description with the example of the sacrifice that God asks of Abraham: "Whereas, for the entire Paleo-Semitic world, such a sacrifice, despite its religious function, was only a custom, a rite whose meaning was perfectly intelligible, in Abraham's case it is an act of faith" (109).

Two things appear with some degree of clarity: Abraham's faith was a personal spiritual force as opposed to the collective beliefs of the archaic cultures; and second, as a corollary of the first, there is a difference between faith as a spiritual force and belief as a sort of tacit agreement to accept as true the symbolic value of the mythical archetypes. It may also be the case that the former manifests itself by dominating the inner world of the individual, whereas the latter acts as a force within the precincts of the assembly of the group.[8]

Nevertheless, it also appears that the force of beliefs is just as great and can be just as personal as that of faith. For one cannot imagine a shaman in his ecstatic trance not believing in the visions of his experience or a yogi rejecting the accomplishments of his efforts to travel in time "against the current." In fact, without belief, our interpretation of our environment, of the world we observe, would not be coherent. The harmony and unity of the events in our memory and of our spiritual transfiguration of the world would not be possible. Whether they are right or wrong, or somewhere in between, our beliefs act as a unifying and meaning-giving agent within our mental world. They are the director of our inner drama. I do not believe that my interpretation is contrary to Eliade's central concepts, although I am sure he would have expressed and would have defined "belief" in different terms.

Myth, Religion, and the Terror of History

Conceptual differences between faith and belief also appear as reverberations in our modern world. Christianity defines itself by the value and characteristics it attaches to its faith. And just as coherently, the secular arm of our society offers its beliefs, beliefs whose foundation is historical, as a measure of its viability and strength. According to Eliade, modern man, Western man, defines himself by his passion for historiography, by his role and accomplishments in history. Eliade's criticism comes in the guise of an Indian philosophical stance and would say to us, Because you have to live in history you do not have to idolize it.

Historicity or the belief in the creative opportunities of the modern human beings opposes the cyclical theories of the archaic man. In Eliade's view, the central issue is modulated by the degree of freedom that modern individuals can obtain from believing in the linear advance of historical time. In comparing this freedom with the freedom of the archaic man who believes in the possibility of renewal by reliving the paradigmatic gestures of the gods in the mythical period of creation, Eliade thinks that the advantage belongs to the archaic man. This advantage consists in the means to combat or at least ward off the terror of history. Eliade asks:

> For our purpose, only one question concerns us: How can the "terror of history" be tolerated from the viewpoint of historicism? Justification of a historical event by the simple fact that it is a historical event, in other words, by the simple fact that it "happened that way," will not go far toward freeing humanity from the terror that the event inspires. . . . We should wish to know, for example, how it would be possible to tolerate, and to justify, the sufferings and annihilation of so many peoples who suffer and are annihilated for the simple reason that their geographical situation sets them in the pathway of history. (*Myth of Eternal*, 150–151)

Moreover, it is an illusion to believe that we in the modern world have the ability to make history. Eliade is skeptical. At most, a handful of people, some leaders, are in the position to influence the course of history. Faith in God and the belief that suffering has a meaning in the consequences that may follow after history has run its course are the only salvation. And to repeat what we have quoted earlier, "And in our

day ... how can man tolerate the catastrophes and horrors of history—
from collective deportations and massacres to atomic bombings—if
beyond them he can glimpse no sign, no transhistorical meaning ...?"
(151). Eliade's compelling question will remain without an answer, but
it will still preserve its urgency and its appeal.

Myth and Modern Imagination

One might think that the modern world has completely abandoned the
archaic beliefs in the mythical existence of archetypes that have inaugurated the cosmos. But Eliade argues that there are in our world certain
forms of activities and beliefs that hark back to the archaic beliefs and
approximate the mythic imagination. He emphasizes that they are not
the same; nevertheless, he gives the example of Marxian communism.
Marx's concept of classless society has its precedent in the myth of the
Golden Age. The Nazis' ideological formulations were an attempt "to
reanimate the [pagan] Germanic mythology" (*Myths*, 26).[9] Christianity
itself, while not a myth, does involve a "mythic attitude—the attitude
towards liturgical time; that is, the rejection of profane time and the periodical recovery of the Great Time, *illud tempus* [Nativity—Ascension]
of the beginnings'" (30).

Moreover, Eliade points to the fact that myths and mythological
images are everywhere in modern societies, even if by ancient mythical
standards they are degraded. The exemplary models that our education prescribes are such images. In addition, society fashions a "diffuse
mythology" and offers heroes, real or imaginary, heroes of war or of
adventure, who carry on "mythological traditions" (33). There is the
mythological basis of New Year celebrations aiming to reach a "world
reborn"; there are the images of the oceanic islands, suggesting the
myth of the lost paradise. In the final analysis, all spectacles, bullfight-
ing, racing, the theater, the cinema, and other spectacles, all take place
in a "time of heightened intensity; a residuum of, or a substitute for,
magico-religious time" (34). And this appears to be an important part
of Eliade's message: the mythical dimension still survives in the modern
world because it is part of the human condition.

Endowing modern beliefs and activities with at least some attributes
and values that appear to function in a way that is similar to the effects
of the sacred, Eliade leads us to a wholly new and unexplored territory.
What is very significant from a cognitive point of view is the fact that a
person can have a spiritual or quasi-spiritual experience on occasions
when he or she is alone or in social gatherings. While this experience

is not necessarily "sacred," it nevertheless shares with religious experiences a spiritual intensity that appears to spring from the very foundation of the mind and testifies to its capacity to transform the encounter with the new into a profoundly memorable and determining event. This capacity transforms what appears to be a mundane encounter into one of spiritual power.[11] We can adduce two compelling examples from Eliade's novel *The Forbidden Forest*. Stefan, the main character, tells his friends about his experience when he was five or six years old and entered the mysterious room *Sambo*, "a privileged space," "a place like a paradise." Stefan says:

> Later, when I would think about *Sambo* I was sure that God had been waiting for me there and had taken me in his arms as soon as I stepped across the threshold. I have never, at any place or any time, felt such happiness; not in any church or art museum—nowhere—ever." (75)

Notice the reference to a church and an art museum. The other example is an experience Stefan has in his adult life in Lisbon after a storm:

> The city disclosed itself to him as it had never done before. Every house, every window, every stone on the sidewalk seemed to come to meet him, displaying itself, revealing itself. He walked faster, feeling no want, no desire for anything. Suddenly all things around him seemed to be proffered in abundance. He was aware of traversing a *full* universe, one with no empty spaces, no voids or deficiencies. Seemingly all things were in their places, and all had been provided eternally. (308)

The significance of these events is in the fact that the individual who is experiencing them is not necessarily a *homo religiosus*, but a child or a man who from a profane universe, from the dimension of history, enters a world that possesses the attributes of the sacred, which in Eliadean ontology has the aura of "a *full* universe," like the one at the beginning of creation. Now these accounts are fictional. But I suspect that Eliade, as it was his wont, transfers real experiences onto the plane of the novel. We can infer that from an Eliade statement chiding Altizer for not consulting "*Forêt interdite* [*Forbidden Forest*] . . . which could have helped him grasp more acutely [Eliade's] personal ideas on time, history, destiny, etc." ("Notes for a Dialogue," 2).

In modern times, there are also stories that are actual not fictional and whose sources are religious but which again do not necessarily require those involved to be religious. I am thinking of present-day prophecies of an end of times, which just recently have inspired mass hysteria. Such was the rumor that according to the Mayan "Long Count" calendar, the long cycle of time would end, and on December 21, 2012, so would the world. In an excellent article, Hart Seely points out that the Mayans did not think of the end as a punishment for sins; rather, they thought of "cyclical creation and re-creation":

> One of the strong elements is that these creations come about because the deities are dissatisfied: People are not smart enough or articulate enough to worship in a proper way, or they are arrogant and too far-seeing, and they need to be remade. So you get this sort of progressive improvement of people, from the deity's point of view, until they get it right. What we're not so sure about is whether they've gotten it right yet. ("Cornell," A5)

What strikes me in this account is the idea of cyclical creation and re-creation that harks back to Eliade's understanding of myth. In describing the modern nostalgia for the "primordial totality," Eliade writes:

> Moreover, all the modern artistic movements seek, consciously or unconsciously, the destruction of the traditional aesthetic universes, the reduction of "forms" to elementary, germinal, larval states in the hope of re-creating "fresh worlds." . . . It is unnecessary to mention how all this should interest the historian of religions familiar with the rather well-known mythological system that involves the symbolic destruction and re-creation of the universe in order to periodically begin anew a "pure" existence in a fresh, strong, and fertile world. (*The Quest*, 65–66)

The similarity between Seely's interpretation and Eliade's leads us to a question. Seely does not supply any references, but we can ask, did he read Eliade? If he did, perhaps that shows that Elaide is still influential. That he may not have read him is even more significant: It means that Seely confirms that Eliade has been right all along. Despite the fact that modern myths are marked with a certain degradation, they survive today and appear to be revived by the same fear of destruction and of end of time as well as by a nostalgia for a better beginning, a purer world.

The impulse to be lured into the nostalgia of the beginning is characterized by our desire to escape from the domination of historical or linear time. Perhaps this desire explains why "the mythical archetypes survive to some degree in the great modern novels" (*Myths*, 35).

Eliade believes that literature and the arts in general can contribute to the knowledge of the human condition. By seeking to replace "the traditional aesthetic universes" "in the hope of re-creating 'fresh worlds,'" they recall the mythological system that, as we have seen in the quotation above, "involves the symbolic destruction and re-creation of the universe." Also, he points to the fact that literary critics have already shown a great deal of interest in "symbolisms and rituals of initiation" for the purpose of interpreting literary works.

What is significant is that Eliade includes reading in our mythical behavior, because reading like the other forms of entertainment represents an attempt to escape from Time: "reading, perhaps even more than visual entertainment, gives one a break in duration, and at the same time an 'escape from time'" (36). This strategy of defense against time is a mythological attitude and is part of the human condition. "Whether we are 'killing time' with a detective story, or entering into another temporal universe as we do in reading any kind of novel, we are taken out of our own duration to move in other rhythms, to live in a different history" (36). Eliade's description of reading offers a striking resemblance to Christopher Collins's concept of *kairos* (derived from the Greek). Collins speaks of repeatable units of time that characterize certain activities, time of ritual, drama, narrative, song, and dance. Each unit of time is a *kairos*. This is also equivalent to what the mother means when she begins her storytelling with "Once upon a time," and the child understands as "story time." Collins emphasizes the difference between this time of the story, both in telling and in listening, and the general flow of time that is abandoned by the act of stepping into the story time. Both Eliade and Collins mark the boundaries of the two durations: Eliade by pointing out the new rhythms of the novel's time with its liberating effect, that is, the capacity to liberate the reader from his or her history, the latter by emphasizing the nondescript character of the general flow of time as against the intimate and exciting time of storytelling. Both the archaic man and the modern man attempt to escape from historical time: one into the time of the beginning by living or reliving the paradigmatic events performed by the gods at the beginning, *in illo tempore*, the other into a magical time with its reinvigorating attributes. Perhaps Carl Olson is right: "In a sense, by means of his scholarly and literary works, Eliade transforms himself into a symbol of a pilgrim seeking the centre" (165). Perhaps one can detect the pilgrim impulse in Stefan, the main character in *The Forbidden Forest*, who tells the story of Anisie and interprets it in the following manner. For Anisie nothing counts "but cosmic time":

> Now he doesn't let anything distract him from living each essential moment of this cosmic time. For him the new moon or the full moon, the equinoxes and the solstices, dawns and twilights, don't have the simple function they do for us, of marking dates on a calendar. Each event reveals to him a new aspect of the whole, of the cosmos. He accepts no time other than cosmic time, and he especially rejects historic time; for example, the time during which parliamentary elections take place, or Hitler's arming of Germany, or the Spanish civil war. (69)

Moreover,

> He's discovered in Nature . . . the key to fundamental metaphysical revelations—the mystery of death and resurrection, of the passage from nonbeing to being. And this man, who is scarcely at the beginning of this experience, has already succeeded in escaping from time. (69–70)

We recognize here Eliade's movement against historical time and the concept of nostalgia for paradise and for the time when the world was new as it came out of the hands of the Creator. We may also understand why Eliade spoke of the terror of history. We are moving in the mythic dimension.

Robert Segal contrasts Eliade's concept of myths and those of Jung and Campbell and writes: "Where they [the latter] allow for fully secular myths, in which case modern adherents need not be religious to employ them, Eliade insists that seemingly secular myths are really religious, in which case modern adherents must themselves be religious to use them" ("Are There," 32). However, since by ancient mythic standards, modern myths are degraded and sometimes camouflaged, they may not require that "modern adherents" be religious.[10] Speaking of Eliade's "idea of *the presence of the sacred dimension* in ordinary man's being," Eugen Simion explains:

> There is a *concealed* mythology . . . , a system of signs, "*hiérophanies*" that welcome the non-religious man, completely lacking a sacred dimension, from the so-called profane societies. This man, despite what he has said and what he thinks about himself, *participates* in the experience of the sacred aspect through his waking-dreams, through certain aspects of his behavior (such as his love for nature), through his nostalgia, even through his *entertainment* (reading, attending shows). (149)

Segal asks, "does the modern spectator or reader travel to the time and place of the story?" ("Are There," 30) and answers negatively. But we have seen that both Eliade and Collins do speak of reading or listening as an experience of entering a different time, the time of the story. Moreover, in Eliade's novel *The Forbidden Forest* (which, as we recall, Eliade believed would help Altizer grasp his personal ideas on the concept of time), the playwright Dan Bibicescu explains his theory of the theater and says: "To exorcise Destiny—this is the function of the Theater. To force it to manifest itself in your presence, *on the stage*, in a concentrated time, so that *you escape, you remain a spectator, you go out of Time*" (492). There is no doubt that Eliade sees an affinity between the theater and the reenacting of the archetypal events in myth. The theater recalls the ancient myths and their capacity to offer a way to escape the historical time.

Again, I stress, Eliade does not claim that modern myths are equal to the archaic myths. What he does is attribute mythical dynamics to entertainment, especially reading, and implies, whether intentionally or not, a possible relation between the sacred character of the religious experience and the nonsacred but still spiritual experience of entering a different time flow and living in the intensity of the new rhythms of the story. This similarity or analogy between the myths of the past and modern imitations suggests again that in spite of their differences and their separate historical sources they represent basic structures of the human consciousness.

In the context of the relation between the encounter with the sacred and spiritual experiences that are not, strictly speaking, religious, I cite the analysis of William Paden, in which he speaks about Eliade's second model (the first being the sacred as wholly other): "Here [in the second model] is the language that every world is an 'ontology,' a 'universe,' a 'cultural creation' analogous to the thousands of imaginal universes of art. Here Eliade is not theological at all, but postfoundationalist and to some extent postmodern" (250). And further, "Eliade writes often of religious worlds as 'creations' analogous to those of artists and novelists" (253). Thus, we observe again an analogy between on the one hand the experience of the sacred, a hierophany, and the experience that novelists have in creating and readers in reading. Eugen Simion points out that the analogy holds for sculptors and painters as well:

> The sacred dimension is also represented by the attraction for substance that we find in the work of Brâncuşi and in all the European

avant-garde. According to Eliade, the 20th century artist's obsession
to penetrate the depths of the world and the depths of his own mind
suggests something more than a creative technique. (151)

For those who do not walk the mythic road, reading may offer
a way to imitate the mythic escape from historic time. In reading,
the individual shares in the passions of the heroes and knows at the
same time the cathartic effect of the spectator, to be at the same time
within the drama and have the freedom to observe from a distance.
We can note here Aristotle's extraordinary insight in offering us the
concept of catharsis. And perhaps we would not stray far in believing
that Eliade's "magico-religious time," "time of a heightened intensity,"
has some resemblance with Aristotle's catharsis and its curative
effect. The strength of Eliade's phenomenology is in the ability to
point to an affinity between the experiences of the sacred and experiences that emerge from nonreligious activities but are still spiritual.
In speaking about "the fundamental yearning of man to transcend the
human condition," Ricketts writes: "Eliade sees dreaming, art, dance,
magic, mysticism, and love as having their source in this sentiment"
(*Romanian*, volume 1, 577). And Ricketts explains that for Eliade there
are two spiritual planes: "One is multiple and complex." The other "is
single and transcendent." "The former is the plane reached by 'aesthetic
contemplation, logic, ethical experience, vitalistic exaltation.' The other
spiritual plane is one 'about which we know nothing, at which one
arrives through religious experience'" (*Romanian*, volume 1, 267; see
also hereinbelow, Eliade "Theös Éghènou"). And Ricketts points out
the role of consciousness: "'Consciousness,' Eliade contends, 'is only a
bridge for crossing over to the true spiritual worlds'"(267). Clearly, the
two planes "are of different essences"; nevertheless, they both share
the bridge of human consciousness to reach the spiritual realm. The
delineation of this primary capacity of human consciousness and mind
may be his greatest insight.

It is to dramatize the consequences of Eliade's insight that Robert
Ellwood offers his study, "Eliade: Essentialist or Postmodern?" Ellwood
begins by pointing out that Eliade, like Émile Durkheim and Claude
Lévy-Strauss, has stressed binary oppositions: good/evil, day/night,
male/female, and, of course, sacred/profane. But the center of his argument is that our modern world exhibits signs of millennialism and a
desire to transcend the human condition. The most compelling example
is the shrine dedicated to the long distance runner Steve Prefontaine,

who was killed in an auto accident on May 30, 1975. Fans and friends visit the site of the accident, the memorial rock, which became known as Pre's Rock. These visits are pilgrimages that are not unlike religious pilgrimages in the intensity of the spiritual experience. Significantly, Wojcik, the man who reported the events, was told that the rock was thought to house Pre's spirit while the grave contained his body. The example shows, as Eliade maintained, precisely how an ordinary rock or stone can become sacred while still being only a rock.

In "The Place of Literature in Eliade's 'Rediscovery' of the Archaic World," Eric Ziolkowski begins by highlighting Eliade's aim to "rediscover and make alive the pre-Socratic world." This ambition unfolds against the background of Eliade's struggle against time or, as Ziolkowski puts it, the intense "competition with time and finitude." According to Ziolkowski, Eliade felt in some respects an affinity with the Danish philosopher Kierkegaard. At the center of Ziolkowski's argument is the all-important relation between mythical imagination and literature in Eliade's hermeneutics. For example, in Eliade's view, the goddess Siduri in *Gilgamesh* represents a "primordial model" for a succession of other figures of goddesses or heroines. Gilgamesh requests from her immortality and similarly, Calypso in the *Odyssey* offers Odysseus immortality. The most striking example is Dante's ascension symbolism in *Paradiso*, recalling the Shamanic ascent by a ladder and also Jacob's dream of the heavenly ladder. For Eliade, the nineteenth-century novel is a repository of degraded myths. The positive side of the idea of the degradation of myths is that myths have survived in the role of precursors. Ziolkowski points to Eliade's controversial conclusion, namely, that "the metamorphosis of historical figures into a mythic or epic heroes typically conforms to a mythic paradigm."

In "Eliade and Girard on Myth," John Dadosky sheds new light on the two contrasting views of myths. He studies the mythic dimension against the background of nineteenth-century and twentieth-century views of myth. In Dadosky's study, Eliade considers myth to reflect the events that led to the creation of the world and believes that the mythic archetypes have the capacity to confer value and reality to the world. Girard, for his part, appears to agree that myths mark the beginning of society. But, according to Girard, "all pre-Christian myths contain the themes that embody and perpetuate the cycle of violence."

In "Eliade on Myth and Science," Robert Segal focuses on Eliade's conception of myth and its attributes. Segal believes that Eliade is "bolder than most of his fellow twentieth-century theorists because he refuses to concede the physical world to science exclusively." But Segal is rather critical of Eliade's claims about the status of modern myths. In Eliade's view, "Plays, movies, and books are the genres that express modern myths because they reveal the existence of another world." This belief explains the desire and the capacity of moderns to escape the time of history and enter a different time. And Segal's objection is that "moderns travel back in time only in their imagination not in reality." I believe, however, that Segal's criticism is only partially justified. For, here, the relation between imagination and reality is similar to the relation between the sacred and the profane: they both have ontological status. One does not abolish, delete, or destroy the other.

In "Eliade's Phenomenological Approach to Religion and Myth," Douglas Allen explores the metaphysical dimension of Eliade's claims "about the nonhistorical, nontemporal, nonmaterial sacred nature of reality." There are two aspects of Allen's presentation that are especially compelling. First, Allen points to the dialectic tension between the outside reality and human consciousness. The mythic sacred reality "has ontological and epistemological essentialized status of reality independent of our perceiving and constituting consciousness." However, the paradox is that "there are no religious phenomena without intuiting, sensing, perceiving, imagining, constituting human subjectivity." As a result the sacred structures are given to human subjects but always given partially, sometimes camouflaged, unfulfilled, "in need of our constituting their meanings." The second aspect is that "the sacred is an essential structure of human consciousness" and appears expressed indirectly "through structures of the unconscious, dreams, fantasies, nostalgias and yearnings, modern art and literature, films," and ideologies. I would relate this aspect to what I have mentioned above as an important affinity between the sacred and experiences that are not religious but are nevertheless spiritual.

For his part, Liviu Bordaş broaches the problem of the relation between the young Eliade and Julius Evola, pointing to the differences that distinguish their views. In this historical review of the European thought of the period between the two wars, especially 1926–1928, Bordaş places the young Eliade at the center of the exchanges of ideas among various scholars of the period. He clarifies the way that Eliade understands the dialectic relationship between the mystic and the magic dimensions of spiritual thought, a perspective that will dominate his first scholarly works.

The contributors to this volume believe that Eliade's views on religion and myth gain new relevance in that they explain modern spiritual manifestations in terms of their mythic predecessors. Robert Ellwood shows that moderns still experience the nostalgia for the lost paradise, have millennial aspirations, and engage in rites of initiation. Eric Ziolkowski points to the scaffold-like role of the premodern mythic structures in modern literature and art. John Dadosky illuminates Eliade's conception of myth by means of a comparison with René Girard's. Even Robert Segal, who is skeptical of Eliade's view on the status of modern myths, by his very criticism, identifies the fault lines of the issue of relevance. In his article translated by Mac Ricketts, Eliade indicates that he was aware, very early in his career, of the existence of the two planes of experience: a religious plane and a plane that is not religious but still spiritual involving aesthetic, ethical, and rational experiences. Using metaphysical tools, Douglas Allen shows the relevance today of the relation between the structures of the sacred within human consciousness and the structures revealed in the unconscious, dreams, fantasies, art and literature, films, and ideologies. And Bordaş stresses the young Eliade's understanding of the phenomena of magic and mysticism.

It is of no consequence to follow the fashion of the day and believe that Eliade belongs to the past, not if his insights reveal new structures of our human consciousness and add to the spiritual dimension of the modern world's new qualities and meanings. In my view, the greatest achievement of Eliade's phenomenological approach is revealing what we in the modern world have in common with the archaic or pre-Socratic man: *the mind's structural capacity to endow objects and events with spiritual values and meanings that may or may not be religious.* Eliade's theory of the dialectics of the sacred and the profane points to hierophanic or creative moments during which the activation of our symbolic impulse and the intensity of our beliefs transform a common, ordinary, blank reality into a meaningful, spiritual, and transcendent world.

—Nicolae Babuts

Notes

1. In a novel begun in June 1931(in Romanian) and titled *Întoarcerea din Rai: The Return from Paradise*, the monologue of the main character, Pavel Anicet, reveals these thoughts: "În sfîrşit, la 11 ani, cea dintîi cosmologie, religioasă sau laică, fundată pe axiome pe care nu le înţelege nimeni: creaţia cosmică, infinitul, atracţia unversală, neantul" (60). "Finally, at eleven, the first cosmology, religious or secular, founded on axioms that no one understands: cosmic creation, the infinite, universal attraction, the nothingness" (my translation).

It suggests that already in his youth Eliade began to explore the metaphysical dimension of the cosmic beginnings. This interest is confirmed in an "Autobiographical Fragment" that mentions an unpublished manuscript titled "The Memoirs of the Lead Soldier" with Eliade's explanation: "I proposed, purely and simply, to present the history of the Cosmos from the appearance of the first galaxies to our own day" (*Imagination*, Girardot and Ricketts, eds., 119). He was only fifteen.

2. Here is an example that illustrates the problem. When the Nobel committee gave the 2012 Peace Prize to the European Union, many thought that the prize was undeserved. But the committee's explanation is worth noting: "Members of the Nobel committee lauded six decades of reconciliation among enemies who fought Europe's bloodiest wars while simultaneously warning against the hazards of the present. The decision sounded like a plea to support the endangered institution at a difficult hour" (Alan Cowell and Nicholas Kulish, *New York Times*, October 12, 2012. Web). And so, if it supports peace and friendship, the award is justified.

3. Altizer appears to be aware of the complex relation of his ideas to Eliade's views. On the one hand, he professes "to be in large measure [Eliade's] disciple." He expresses his "profound sense of gratitude to Professor Eliade for the encouragement, the criticism and inspiration that he so freely gave [him]" (*Mircea Eliade and the Dialectics*, 20). At the same time, however, he says that it should be obvious "that I am employing Eliade as a route to a new form of theology" (18). This diverging goal may explain Altizer's misreading of the relation between the sacred and the profane in Eliade's writings. Adrian Boldişor asks, "Did Mircea Eliade's understanding of religion influence the 'death of God' theology of Thomas Altizer?" and answers, "My view is that he did not. Even if there are many links between them, I observe that Altizer, in his book about Eliade and in other books, did not clearly understand the meaning of Eliade's concepts" (277).

4. Carl Olson is somewhat critical of Eliade's idea of dialogue: "His dialogical encounter is too one-dimensional because Westerners have much to learn from other religious traditions, but there is nothing said about what the East might learn from the West" (78). Indeed the impression is there. However, Eliade points to the new values introduced by the Mosaic religion and by Christianity: the element of faith and the soteorological implications attributed to history by the appearance of Christ as a historical figure. Although Eliade does not say so, the idea that the East could consider these values may be an implied possibility. Moreover, Rennie adduces passages that show that Eliade was aware of weaknesses in the archaic attitude: "Both visions [archaic and modern] ultimately fail to 'maintain their position' independently of some concept of regeneration" (*Reconstructing*, 81).

5. For a discussion of the role of the observer, see *Mimesis*, xxxi–xxxii, 33–34, 66–67, and *Memory*, 50–51.

6. What I have been emphasizing is not new. Others have said it. Here is a remarkable example: "experience is a 'reciprocal affair' involving an 'organic togetherness of the experiencing self and the experienced world'; therefore, experience cannot be taken as the 'passive reception' of 'bare' or 'given' data and is 'impossible without interpretation from the side of self'" (John E. Smith, "The Experiential Foundations of Religion," *Reason and God*.

New Haven: Yale University Press, 1967, 173–183; cited by Douglas Allen, *Structure*, 187).

7. In making the distinction between the view of the unconscious proposed by the adherents of "depth psychology" and his own view of mythical imagination, Eliade gives two explanations: one is that the image of the tree in the unconscious does not display the same potential and value that it has in myths, and the other is that to reduce a mythological image or event to a process of the unconscious is like reducing *Madame Bovary* to an adultery. For a discussion of the difference between myths and private myths like those that play a role in Freudian and Jungian psychology, see Robert Segal, "Are There," 29).

8. Elsewhere Eliade appears to make a further distinction: there is the memory of "primordial events" (cosmogony, theogony, genealogy) and the memory of former lives, that is, of historical and personal events. (See *Myth and Reality*, 123.) But what interests us here is the fact that primordial events recalled in ritual are events that concern a people as a group; they are not personal memories. It would be interesting to speculate whether the fact that the modern world emphasizes the role and freedom of the individual may explain our cult of individual memory. But then we recall the grip that ideologies have on the consciousness (and conscience) of individuals as a group and realize that today, as in the past, the individual may get lost in the mentality of the masses.

9. Marxism and Nazism, I believe, are more aptly described as ideologies, characterized by fanaticism, as all ideologies are.

10. For a critique of Segal's view of Eliade's concept of myth, see Bryan Rennie, "The Meaning," 268–70.

11. W. C. Beane offers the following example of "otherwise 'profane' cultural moments" that underwent "vital religious valorizations": "For when my students are asked to ponder the significance of the reference of John the Baptist to Jesus of Nazareth as 'the *lamb* of God' . . . against the background of archaic-totemic legacy of their forebears—the radiance of their countenances as they make the cultural-religious connection (or 'revalorization' for Eliade) reminds one of nothing less than the amazement with which Helen Keller finally made the association between her experience of sonic vibrations and the miraculous 'feel' of water!" (175–76).

Works Cited

Allen, Douglas. *Structure and Creativity in Religion: Hermeneutics in Mircea Eliade's Phenomenology and New Directions*. Foreword by Mircea Eliade. The Hague: Mouton Publishers, 1978.

———. "Mircea Eliade's View of the Study of Religion as the Basis for Cultural and Spiritual Renewal." In *Changing Religious Worlds: The Meaning and End of Mircea Eliade*, edited by Bryan Rennie, 207–33. Albany: State University of New York Press, 2001.

Altizer, Thomas J. J. *Mircea Eliade and the Dialectic of the Sacred*. Philadelphia: Westminster Press, 1963.

Associated Press. "Humble Nickel from 1913 likely to Fetch a Pretty Penny." *Post-Standard* [Syracuse] (January 30, 2013):A-1.

Babuts, Nicolae. *Memory, Metaphors, and Meaning: Reading Literary Texts.* New Brunswick, NJ: Transaction Publishers, 2009.

———. *Mimesis in a Cognitive Perspective: Mallarmé, Flaubert, and Eminescu.* New Brunswick, NJ: Transaction Publishers, 2011.

Beane, Wendell Charles. "Eliade and History-of-Religions Methodology." In *Changing Religious Worlds: The Meaning and End of Mircea Eliade,* edited by Bryan Rennie, 165–89. Albany: State University of New York Press, 2001.

Boldişor, Adrian. "A Controversy: Eliade and Altizer." In *Mircea Eliade Once Again,* edited by Cristina Scarlat, 247–280. Iaşi, Ro: Lumen, 2011.

Cave, David. "Eliade's Interpretation of Sacred Space and Its Role toward the Cultivation of Virtue." In *Changing Religious Worlds: The Meaning and End of Mircea Eliade,* edited by Bryan Rennie, 235–248. Albany: State University of New York Press, 2001.

Chin-Hong, Chung. "Mircea Eliade's Dialectic of Sacred and Profane and Creative Hermeneutics." In *The International Eliade,* edited by Bryan Rennie, 187–205. Albany: State University of New York Press, 2007.

Collins, Christopher. *The Poetics of the Mind's Eye: Literature and the Psychology of Imagination.* Philadelphia: University of Pennsylvania Press, 1991.

Dadosky, John D. *The Structure of Religious Knowing: Encountering the Sacred in Eliade and Lonnergan.* Albany: State University of New York Press, 2004.

Dudley, Guilford, III. *Religion on Trial: Mircea Eliade and his Critics.* Philadelphia: Temple University Press,1977.

Eliade, Mircea. *The Myth of the Eternal Return: Or, Cosmos and History.* Translated from the French by Willard R. Trask. Princeton: Princeton University Press, 1954.

———. *Patterns in Comparative Religion.* Translated from the French (*Traité d'histoire des religions*) by Rosemary Sheed. Introduction by John Clifford Holt. New York: Sheed and Ward, 1958. Lincoln: University of Nebraska Press, 1996.

———. *The Sacred and the Profane: The Nature of Religion.* Translated from the French by Willard R. Trask. New York: Harcourt, Brace and World, 1959.

———. *Myths, Dreams and Mysteries: The Encounter between Contemporary Faiths and Archaic Realities.* Translated from the French by Philip Mairet. New York: Harper and Row, 1960.

———. *Myth and Reality.* Translated from the French by Willard R. Trask. New York: Harper and Row, 1963.

———. *The Two and the One.* Translated from the French (*Méphistophélès et l'Androgyne*) by J. M. Cohen. New York: Harper and Row, 1965.

———. *The Quest: History and Meaning in Religion.* Chicago: Chicago University Press, 1969.

———. *Zalmoxis: The Vanishing God. Comparative Studies in the Religions and Folklore of Dacia and Eastern Europe.* Translated from the French (*De Zalmoxis à Gengis-Khan*) by Willard R. Trask. Chicago: University of Chicago Press, 1972.

———. "Notes for a Dialogue by Mircea Eliade." In *The Theology of Altizer,* chapter 14. www.religion on line.org. August 2012. Web.

———. *The Forbidden Forest*. Translated by Mac Linscott Ricketts and Mary Park Stevenson. Notre Dame: University of Notre Dame Press, 1978.

———. *Întoarcerea din Rai*. Edited by Mircea Handoca. Bucharest: Rum-Irina, 1992.

Girardot, Norman J. "Nostalgic Reflections on Mircea Eliade's Significance for the Study of Religion." In *Changing Religious Worlds: The Meaning and End of Mircea Eliade*, edited by Bryan Rennie, 143–163. Albany: State University of New York Press, 2001.

Girardot, Norman J. and Mac Linscott Ricketts, eds. *Imagination and Meaning: The Scholarly and Literary Worlds of Mircea Eliade*. New York: Seabury Press, 1982.

Hawking, Stephen. *A Brief History of Time*. New York: Bantam Books, 1988, 1996

Holt, John Clifford. Introduction to *Patterns in Comparative Religion*, by Mircea Eliade, xi–xvi. Translated by Rosemary Sheed. Lincoln: University of Nebraska Press, 1996.

Meslin, Michel. "The Sacralization of Time in the Thought of Mircea Eliade." In *The International Eliade*, edited by Bryan Rennie, 15–22. Albany: State University of New York, 2007.

Olson, Carl. *The Theology and Philosophy of Eliade: A Search for the Centre*. New York: St. Martin's Press, 1992.

Paden, William E. "The Concept of World Habitation: Eliadean Linkages with a New Comparativism." In *Changing Religious Worlds: The Meaning and End of Mircea Eliade*, edited by Bryan Rennie, 249–59. Albany: State University of New York Press, 2001.

Rennie, Bryan. *Reconstructing Eliade: Making Sense of Religion*. Albany: State University of New York Press, 1996.

———. "The Meaning and End of Mircea Eliade." In *Changing Religious Worlds: The Meaning and End of Mircea Eliade*, 263–81. Albany: State University of New York Press, 2001.

———, ed. *The International Eliade*. Albany: State University of New York Press, 2007.

Ricketts, Mac Linscott. *Mircea Eliade: The Romanian Roots, 1907–1945*. 2 vols. Boulder, CO: East European Monographs, 1988. Distributed by Columbia University Press.

———. "A New Fragmentarium." In *Mircea Eliade Once Again*, edited by Cristina Scarlat. Iaşi, Ro: Lumen, 2011. Mirela Roznoveanu, Noi Aparitii. October 20, 2012. Web.

———. "Did Eliade Try to Conceal a Hidden Meaning in *Ifigenia* and *Comentarii la legenda Meşterului Manole*?" *Carmina Balcanica* 4.2 (7) (November 2011): 81–100.

Scarlat, Cristina, ed. *Mircea Eliade Once Again*. Iaşi, Ro: Lumen, 2011. Mirela Roznoveanu, Noi Aparitii. October 20, 2012. Web.

Seely, Hart. "Cornell Mayan Expert: Don't Expect 'Rain of Jaguars,' Other Catastrophes" and "A Time to Appreciate Mayan Culture." *Post Standard* [Syracuse] (December 21, 2012):A1 and A5.

Segal, Robert A. "Are There Modern Myths?" In *Changing Religious Worlds: The Meaning and End of Mircea Eliade,* edited by Bryan Rennie, 25–32. Albany: State University of New York Press, 2001.

Simion, Eugen. *Mircea Eliade: A Spirit of Amplitude.* Boulder, CO: East European Monographs, 2001. Distributed by Columbia University Press.

1

Eliade: Essentialist or Postmodern? The Sacred and an Unseen Order

Robert Ellwood

The title of one of Mircea Eliade's basic books, *The Sacred and the Profane*, offers a key to his thought about the nature of religion. Religion, in his view, is fundamentally a symbol and vehicle for humankind's profound yearning for transcendence of the ordinary, "profane" world of everyday space and time, to share in the mythic and absolute realm of origins, the "other time," *illud tempus*, when the gods made the world and heroes walked the earth. Times of religious rite and festival are sacred times that seek to offer means of access to, and temporary participation in, the strong primal time. Sacred space demarcates on the face of this earth, in the terrain of temples, shrines, pilgrimage sites, holy mountains and sacred trees, places offering entry to that level of reality; often they are at the site of a mythic event back then, or of a later hierophany or sacred manifestation of its personalities or powers.

Eliade never provided a simple, brief definition of religion, indeed writing in the Preface of *The Quest* that, "It is unfortunate that we do not have at our disposal a more precise word than 'religion' to denote the experience of the sacred" (Preface, n.p.). But clearly, according to him, religion is that in human culture which has to do with the sacred and our attempts to find access to it. The sacred is unseen of itself, perhaps, but must be given, or gives us, forms and instruments by which it can be seen and touched; these means are religion.

Religion, then, is that which shows ways in which *homo religiosus*, "religious man," "attempts to remain as long as possible in a sacred universe" (Eliade, *Sacred and Profane*, 13). This understanding of religion is in the spirit of William James, a very different kind of thinker,

1

when he said that religion "consists of the belief that there is an unseen order, and that our supreme good lies in harmoniously adjusting ourselves thereto" (James, 53). But Eliade was far more interested than the American psychologist, with his focus on religious subjectivity, in the external representation of sacred space and time in temple and rite, though he granted that the sacred could be internalized in such phenomena as shamanism, yoga, and mysticism. Whether within or without, he perceived such patterns or structures as sacred space and time, symbolic ways of transcendence.

Eliade was a structuralist. The overall outline of a place of pilgrimage, or a festival like New Year's, he saw as consistent through many religions though the names and externals change. Structuralism, following the linguist Ferdinand de Saussure and the anthropologists Émile Durkheim and Claude Lévi-Strauss, claimed particularly that structures declare their meaning through binary oppositions: good/evil, day/night, male/female, and of course Eliade's sacred and profane: the time of the festival versus ordinary time (Durkheim), and the shifting circumferences around sacred space. Always one finds interaction—dialectics—between the sacred and the profane in form and in psyche, but always both are there. It is worth noting that the structural, dialectical manifestations of religion, like that of culture generally, do not directly meet physical human needs, those for food, shelter, clothing, or reproduction. Rather, they clearly cater to another kind of need, one for harmony with an unseen order of which we are also a part.

The Sacred after the Death of God

What is the significance of this kind of thinking in our times? There are those who would say a central aspect of the world of Eliade's times and after—the modern world—was that it all became profane, or at best the sacred and profane were inextricably mixed, so that to speak of their "dialectics" no longer had meaning.

For Friedrich Nietzsche and his followers, the decisive event that separated the modern world from what went before was the death of God. "God is dead. God remains dead. And we have killed him" (181). However literally or metaphorically one were to take such a statement, the suggestion is certainly put forward that, for modern people, God—or his spokespersons—are no longer absolute sources of value, whether or not people remain nominally religious.

Thomas J. J. Altizer, author of *Mircea Eliade and the Dialectics of the Sacred*, the first book-length study of Eliade as a historian of religion, went on to become a leading voice for the 1960's "Death of God" theology, declaring in books like *The Gospel of Christian Atheism* that "the message the Christian is now called to proclaim is the gospel, the good news or the glad tidings, of the death of God," a—or rather *the*—supreme redemptive event of our times (Altizer, *Gospel*, 15). In the former work, Altizer proposed that the ultimate fulfillment of Eliade's "dialectic" of the sacred and the profane would be a *coincidentia oppositorum* in which the twain became one in a world after the death of God, for it is the deity's existence that separates holy and unholy. But Eliade, who knew Altizer and was somewhat bemused by his attention, also thought the "in our time" aspect of the death of God was a bit overdone. The primordial *deus otiosus*, God resting after making the world, could be called "the first example of the 'death of God,' that Nietzsche so frenziedly proclaimed" (Eliade, *Myth and Reality*, 95).

The idleness of one God, albeit the Creator, hardly meant the end of religion or even of gods, for his place was inevitably taken by a brood of lesser deities and ancestral spirits. In the same light, Nietzsche declared that after the divine death, "the invention of the domain of the divine . . . will once again proliferate," to become "the religion of religion," a faith focused on affirming all life and every moment (cited Lukacher, 119). We might also add that, if combined with the German philosopher's famous doctrine of eternal recurrence, the death of God itself must be an event that has happened, and will happen, an infinite number of times as worlds come and go: in Shelley's line, "like the bubbles on a river, sparkling, bursting, borne away." So also the rise and fall of religion.

Modernism and Postmodernism

Perhaps religion after the, or a, death of God is like postmodernism after modernism. For modernism we may allude to the dual "metanarratives" Jean-François Lyotard has proposed as its essence: the metanarrative of the emancipation of humanity by progress, and the metanarrative of the unity of knowledge (Preface, ix). The first means, briefly, that through the advance of democracy, education, and scientific knowledge humankind is emancipating itself from the ignorance and oppression of the past; the second informs us that this liberating knowledge is made universal through the generalized, abstract, and rational ways of knowing, and of organizing what is known, characteristic of science and social science. Thereby the particular is generally subordinated to the abstract category; the old gives place to the new and improved; the

3

local is subsumed to the universal. Gods, being typically particular, at least in name and form, being old and being local in their cults, are not exempt from this subordination. The lively, highly personal divinities of old are replaced by such abstractions as "the Absolute," their ancient and concrete worship considered premodern superstition often standing in the way of progress.

What about postmodernism? It was, first of all, said to mean a loss of that sense of unity embodied in the two metanarratives, under the influence of deconstructionists like Jacques Derrida and Michel Foucault, who criticized the notion of a single self, and therefrom of a single message in a work of art or literature, a single religious meaning, or of the unity of truth or a straight-line march of progress in the supposed modernist sense. In psychology this means no doubt the psychic neo-polytheism of James Hillman, with its disparagement of the "imperial ego" and allowance for many diverse gods within the self.

In philosophy and religious studies, the new way of thinking has led the philosopher Richard Rorty to challenge the idea that religious reality has a definite independent nature, calling such a presumption "essentialism." Instead, we should look at the pragmatic meaning the symbol of a supposedly transcendent, supernatural or sacred reality actually has in a particular situation. Perhaps it is only a social convention or a relic whose former meaning is practically forgotten, like that of a long-empty ancient temple. In any case, Rorty claimed that many people are, in Max Weber's words, "religiously unmusical," just don't get it; their experience deserves as much regard as that of the pious (Rorty 30–32).

A perspective in religious studies has emerged that is deeply influenced by the deconstructionists and antiessentialists. Jonathan Z. Smith, a progenitor of this school, has said that religion as we study it in the classroom is an artificial construct: "It is the study of religion that invented religion" (Smith, "Religion," 234. See also Smith, *Imagining Religion*). Russell McCutcheon has therefore insisted that religion is simply social formations labeled religion by a particular culture, and different cultures may have different ways of using the label. For this reason, "the study of religion has no special methodology," but rather is, or should be, "a nonessentialist, multidisciplinary field" (208).

Mircea Eliade has not seldom been the *bête noire* of such scholars. He has been charged with the academic sin of essentialism with regard to religion by claiming that religion is *sui generis*, of believing that there is either an ontological reality beyond the reach of scholarly investigation behind religious phenomena, or at least that the phenomena can be probed only down to an irreducible essence (McCutcheon, 208; Allen, 141).

Sui Generis

To these critiques, a protagonist of Eliade could make three responses. First, Eliade's claim that religion is *sui generis* need not mean "essentialism" in any ontological or even methodological sense; second, that the notion of the sacred and of *homo religiosus* as "ideal types" is not inconsistent with recognizing that, in practice, not all worshipers are on the same page in their understanding of the temple or rite, or equally "religiously musical"; and finally, that in view of the obvious fact that any modern or postmodern disappearance of religion, or of the sacred and its dialectic, has not yet taken place, Eliade's structures as ideal types can still help us in understanding its current as well as its past forms.

As for *sui generis* and essentialism, Eliade knew well enough that the sacred was not "out there" of itself but was "an element in the structure of consciousness" ("New Humanism," *Quest*, 3). Despite its central role in the arguments of his critics, Eliade actually seldom used the term *sui generis*. One place where he does is in assessing the primal monotheism ("*urmonotheismus*") of the learned priest Wilhelm Schmidt, who held that primal man developed the idea of God through a rational quest for causation. Eliade's response: "He neglects the obvious fact that religion is a very complex phenomenon—that it is, first of all, an experience sui generis, incited by man's encounter with the sacred" (*Quest*, 25).

The idea of the sacred, influenced by Rudolf Otto and "the Holy," a numinous, transrational experience lifting one out of the ordinary, was, to be sure, viewed by Eliade as a common category of perception, "indissolubly linked to the effort made by man to construct a meaningful world" (*No Souvenirs*, 313). But the sacred was really a phenomenological entity. To call a temple or mountain sacred was simply shorthand for saying that *these people* regard it as sacred or the object itself "speaks" a cultural language that denotes it as sacred.

Of course, the same person can experience religion both as insider and outsider, and perhaps such a dual stance affords deepest understanding. Eliade once remarked to Fr. Alexander Schmemann, late Dean of St. Vladimir's Orthodox Theological Seminary, that [in the Orthodox church] his faith was that of a Romanian peasant, not that of a theologian or a historian of religion (Schmemann, 268).

> So it is that the sacred, like religion, is not an abstraction outside of time or place. This does not mean, of course, that a religious phenomenon can be understood outside of its "history," that is, outside of its cultural and socioeconomic contexts. There is no such thing as a "pure" religious datum, outside of history, for there is no such thing as a human datum that is not at the same time a historical datum. Every religious experience is expressed and transmitted in a particular historical context. But admitting the historicity of religious experiences does not imply that they are reducible to non-religious forms of behavior. (*Quest*, 25)

Does *sui generis* then mean that, though it may not be "out there," the sacred or religion is in a class of its own in human society, irreducible to anything else? *Sui generis* does not mean, as some critics seem to presuppose, of its own essence, but rather of its own kind or type. Religion does not necessarily, in other words, have some *esse* as object—though of course theologians may argue that it does—but is only a unique configuration of cultural entities, each explicable in its own terms but unique in their collective organization, putatively centered around something like James's "unseen order." It is this *configuration* that is *sui generis*, not the individual parts or the object as essence.

Such a special collection could be compared to words in a conversation, as it were between sacred and profane. Nicolae Babuts has pointed out that

> a word has its own icon, that is to say, it is itself an auditory or visual image or both. . . . But words themselves are very seldom meaningful in isolation. . . . The strength of these associations comes from the frequency with which they were encountered in reading and conversation and also from the affective value attached to them. After one or several fixations, as soon as there is enough sensory, conceptual, and syntactic information given, the incoming sequences contact and activate the relevant mnemonic sequences. (*Dynamics*, 72)

In the same way, presumably the "sentences" of meaningful words, gestures, and symbols that make up a composition culturally recognized as sacred may, in those who are "religiously musical," activate remembered responses to generate actions and feelings regarded as religious, until time to leave.

Likewise, a "conversation" using words, images, and symbols to constitute a recognized "sacred" (as Babuts adds in a later work after specific reference to Eliade and sacred time) has a correlate in

> the relation between the child who obeys the mother's call for story-time, or the reader who succumbs to the allure of the written story, novel or poem. Although this time does not necessarily prevent us from entering and leaving, it is strong enough to isolate us and allow us to exist in a privileged realm that has different intensity and different rhythm. (*Mimesis*, 175)

Other configurations—symbols or stories—may be centered around the political or economic "orders" in a society. But at some point each "order" needs to be interpreted in terms unique to that order if the complete significance of the particular configuration is to be grasped in the fullness of its working. Economics, for example, is another *sui generis* collection of cultural entities. Certainly an ideologue of one camp or another could claim that economic life is "really" reducible to political, psychological, or even religious forces, and no doubt these drives do have their significant roles in world economics. But economics would hardly be fully understood unless one unraveled the myth of money—its reality certainly belonging to an "unseen order" if anything does, only manifesting as symbolic scraps of paper or zipping around the world in vast amounts at the speed of light yet having little tangible existence except as glyphs on a computer screen. A point is reached where some things about how economies work can only be explained in language unique to economic science. So with religious phenomena.

Eliade knew that the construction and symbolization of "the sacred" (i.e., considered as such in the language of a certain culture) might, part by part—the music, the architecture, the nomenclature—be explicable in other terms. But the particular assemblage of those parts to make up a temple or rite was not entirely reducible to the sum of those parts, but acquired its own meaning in the eyes of its beholders. It seems to me this is all that *sui generis* has to mean in Eliade's work. One may feel nostalgia for the sacralities of the past, as Eliade certainly did, and he thought all religion in turn felt nostalgia for paradise. But nostalgia itself indicates a certain distance between oneself and the object of nostalgia, a yearning, *sehnsucht*, for that which is no longer attainable—if indeed it ever was, for a constant in all religion seems to be a nostalgia for a supposedly more pious past, or perhaps a lost childhood. Eliadean nostalgia really counters the essentialism charge; nostalgia for essence tells of its absence; only the yearning lingers.

Structure and Anti-Structure

We must likewise consider the role of Eliade's structuralism and use of ideal types like *homo religiosus*. Do they presuppose too much? I think not, if we understand that while not everyone in a culture feels, or thinks, exactly the same about an alleged manifestation of the sacred, a particular dialectic of the sacred tells what the manifestation *itself* "says," in its own way.

The historian of religion's critics are generally of the camp termed anti-structuralist. As we have seen, for the anti party the sacred and the profane, cosmos and history, and the rest of Eliadeanism is essentialism in so far as it says there is something specific called the sacred. Configuring sacred and profane, these critics say, is far too much the imposition of modernity's abstract unities on immensely diverse phenomena. Eliadean *homo religiosus* likewise goes much too far in implying that all observers see the same thing in the same way.

Many visitors may enter one of the great cathedrals of Europe or temples of Asia; some may feel nothing, others only a vague sense that this is a different atmosphere from the bustling street outside, others deep religious devotion. But our suggestion is that the cathedral or temple, by its tokens of demarcation from the street, its walls and heavy doors and perhaps stained-glass windows, its inscriptions and symbols, its altars and religious images, at times its incense and sacred music in the air, itself declares that this is a special structure. Heard or not, the place calls for special thoughts and feelings and is clearly linked to an unseen order because little in it makes sense only in terms of the street.

Whether or not we so feel or think, Eliade's position was that at least being able to discern those symbols of the sacred coming to us out of the past, being able so to speak to read the score if not to hear the music, is a great gift. That talent enables us to empathize inwardly with our fellow humans over the long past of manifestations of the sacred, and so enriches our lives by theirs. Such sensitivity helps assuage our nostalgia. This was the theme of Eliade's essay "The History of Religions and a New Humanism," which inaugurated the journal *History of Religion*. It also enables us to see for what they are self-bespoken manifestations of the sacred today, whether in enduring traditional religions, new religions, or in what he called, in the fascinating final pages of *The Sacred and the Profane*, "camouflages of the sacred"—from the heroes of Hollywood films to "ideologies in which we can discern traces of the 'nostalgia for Eden,' the desire to re-establish the paradisal state before the Fall, when sin did not yet exist and there was no conflict between the pleasures of the flesh and conscience" (207).

Traditionalist or Post-Traditionalist?

Eliade was himself no mere traditionalist. He was radically modern in many respects, as he fully recognized. He worked in that *sanctum sanctorum* of modernity, the great modern university, where Lyotard's two metanarratives spin at full speed. In those academic halls, myth becomes mythology; religion becomes comparative religion, suggesting the existence of abstract categories for comparison across all faiths; or it becomes history of religion, no less implying common developmental themes; and both disciplines subtly undermine any ideas of significant particularity or uniqueness. Eliade's phenomenology and structuralism fully employed intellectual tools presupposing modern progress and unification of knowledge. It goes without saying this kind of approach is anathema to premodern dogmatists and post-modern deconstructionists alike who, in their own way, eschew comparativist and historical relativism for the sake of lifting up particular or disassembled cases, some perhaps packed with essences and some not.

At the same time, Eliade helped open the door for postmodernism. As his prolific research brought forth treasures new and old out of library stacks, it became clear how much had been left behind in the onrush of modernity, including the inner meanings of shamanism, yoga, myth, rite, and innumerable forgotten gods. In the 1960s and after, many of the plethora of new or revived spiritualities characteristic of that fertile era claimed inspiration from the aging scholar's work, though he seemed uncomfortable in having such an impact.[1] Yet emerging postmodernity's level playing field found new and old sacred games in the scholar's voluminous work.

Moreover, Eliade once wrote, "I feel myself wholly contemporary with all the great political and social reforms or revolutions" (*Ordeal*, 136). But his understanding of those tumultuous contemporary events was deepened by his understanding of the history of religion for, whether modernists like it or not, religion remains a very important force in the contemporary world.

Possibly religion today is even more an important force than in Eliade's times, for he was contemporary with those great pseudo-religions claiming to be post-religion, communism and fascism, and with talk of the Death of God—all undoubtedly quasi-religious causes in Eliade's sense, each touting its own "nostalgia for Eden"—whereas after their fading it can seem that traditional religion alone remains standing as ideology capable of moving masses. Second, the history of religion enabled him, and us, to see those reforms and revolutions as replays of religion in other media, as new yearnings for paradise or as the latest apocalyptic drama.

Religion is, needless to say, prolific in the contemporary world. Its forms range from the Muslim *hajj*, or pilgrimage to Mecca, to Christmas midnight mass at St. Peter's in Rome, from the New Year's rite of a Shinto shrine in Japan to the Pentecostal Christianity that is spreading vigorously in some parts of the world. All these are easily understood through categories made familiar by the work of Mircea Eliade, centering on sacred space and time, and cosmos and history. The *hajj* clearly turns on the idea of a sacred place, an *axis mundi* or pillar of the world and way of access to heaven, best approached during the sacred time of the Dhu al-Hijjah, or month of pilgrimage.

Both the *hajj* and the midnight mass, though certainly perpetuating much cosmic religion symbolism, ostensibly commemorate a datable divine event within the stream of historical time: the career of the Seal of the Prophets, a birth in a Judean town of which was said, in the words of the familiar hymn by Phillips Brooks, "The hopes and fears of all the years are met in thee tonight." Shinto, on the other hand, remains cosmic religion, in which temporal orientation is to the ongoing cycle of the seasons, new years, springtime, and harvest rather than an Axial Age intrusion into the stream of time. Pentecostalism displays yet another dialectic of the sacred, an internal exchange between ordinary profane life and life in the Spirit, when its sacred power seizes one with ecstasy and the gift of "tongues." All these phenomena, like popular religion generally, depend on clear distinction between sacred and profane, in no wise going over to their blurring for the sake of modernity or after the death of God. Here are some examples.

Sacred Space and Pre's Rock

Sometimes along American highways one sees crosses or plaques covered with flowers, ribbons, and flags, set about with teddy bears, offerings of food, drink, and clothing, and many other poignant objects. Local inquiry will usually reveal that they mark the spot of a traffic fatality or a crime and were erected by ordinary mourners, often anonymously. After the slaying of Trayvon Martin, an unarmed black teenager by a neighborhood watch officer in Sanford, Florida, in March 2012, a memorial of balloons, stuffed animals, and signs appeared at the site (Susman, 1, 15). These tributes, together with the spontaneous displays at places like the Vietnam War Memorial ("the Wall") in Washington, at the grave of Elvis Presley at Graceland in Memphis, Tennessee, where fresh flowers appear almost daily and vast crowds gather on his anniversary, or after the death of Princess Diana in London, have received increasing attention by students of popular culture (Doss, Belshaw, Everett). These are clearly folk compositions likely to end up looking like contemporary signs of the sacred.

A particularly significant example is a site called Pre's Rock, east of Eugene, Oregon. Here the long distance runner Steve Prefontaine was killed in a tragic automobile accident on May 30, 1975, at the age of twenty-four. At the time of his death, he was the most famous runner in the United States and thought likely to dominate the next Olympics.

Fans and friends from all over the world continually visit this memorial, which is always rich in offerings related to running, such as shoes, jerseys, ribbons, trophies, and spikes, as well as food and drink (characteristically energy bars and sports drinks), together with photos and handwritten letters, poems, and prayers, and of course flowers and candles. Daniel Wojcik, in his fine study of this memorial, notes that most visitors go to Pre's Rock rather the athlete's grave in Coos Bay, Oregon. Many told Wojcik that the Rock was inevitably thought to house his "spirit," however that is defined. One said that memorial "is a testament to the 'idea' of Steve, that he's somehow part of the 'spirit' of Eugene and runners worldwide. His grave site, however, simply marks the place of his dead body" (211).

In words that recall the idea of a pilgrimage site as an "energized" location where communication between humans and deities, miraculous forces, and the departed is powerfully facilitated, another writer comments:

> Pre had a tremendous strength and will-power in his life, and great determination, and this is the last place where he was in this world. I think there is some kind of a power here, I don't know what exactly, it is like the last part of him, his life, the last place he was alive, and he still lives on here, somehow . . . some kind of energy. (Wojcik 220–221)

11

Still others have spoken of Pre's intercession in helping them in their own running; some have not only left offerings, but have taken objects such as stones or handfuls of dirt from the site as though they were relics.

Undoubtedly Pre's Rock is a spontaneous contemporary example of Eliade's sacred space and the sacred's "conversation" with visitors. Its pilgrims, however inarticulate, share Eliade's first characteristic of *homo religiosus*—they do not think of the world as totally homogeneous, but experience it as layered at least to the extent that this memorial possesses a unique quality.

Like Mecca, Pre's Rock is, as it were, closer to the other side; like Lourdes, it is the site, if not of miracles of healing, at least of infusions of energy. Many other athletes believed they ran better after a visit to Pre. Like Eliade's sacred space, it was established by the equivalent of a hierophany, though in this case it is, like the shrine of many a martyr or saint, the site of a death then confirmed in its power by signs.

> Every sacred space implies a hierophany, an irruption of the sacred that results in detaching a territory from the surrounding cosmic milieu and making it qualitatively different.... Often there is no need for a theophany or hierophany properly speaking; some sign suffices to indicate the sacredness of a place. (Eliade, *Sacred and Profane*, 26–27)

The difference between Pre's Rock and the Eliadean sacred space ascribed to established shrines and temples, so far as I can see, is only that in a spontaneous contemporary site like this and many others we see sacred space "in the raw," so to speak, in process of formation within living memory of the hierophanic person and event. Familiar sites like Mecca or Lourdes have been thoroughly institutionalized with priesthoods and with routinized as well as spontaneous rituals, and incorporated into a major religious system, sooner or later acquiring the patina of venerable tradition that only adds to the "feel" of the sacred.

Nonetheless, sites like Pre's Rock remind us of the relevance of Eliadean thought for understanding the inspiration and phenomenology of such places, so long as one is focused chiefly on understanding those phenomena—what the site, as it were, says in its own way—rather than naively expecting all visitors to have similar subjective responses. But for those who do, who become at the place and for the time *homo religiosus*, Eliade has been there before.

Dark Initiation

A significant part of Eliade's work involved initiation: of shamans, of yogins, and in *Rites and Symbols of Initiation,* the initiation of young men and women in primal cultures and in secret societies. Eliade began *Rites and Symbols of Initiation* with the line, "It has often been said that one of the characteristics of the modern world is the disappearance of any meaningful rites of initiation" (Preface, ix). But in fact one can find numerous initiations, many of them powerful and transformative indeed, in contemporary settings: in sororities and fraternities, in army boot camp, in medical residency, in various religious orders and groups, and in a real sense in the ordeal of adolescence in one of our vast, clique-ridden high schools. In all these one can pass through a process of pain—mental, emotional, physical—that makes one into another person, who feels and thinks differently than before about the self and others. Eliade writes, "In philosophical terms, initiation is equivalent to a basic change in existential condition; the novice emerges from his ordeal endowed with a totally different being from that which he possessed before his initiation; he has become *another"* (*Rites and Symbols,* Preface, x). "The initiate is not only one newborn or resuscitated; he is a man who *knows,* who has learned the mysteries" (*Sacred and Profane,* 188).

Above all, this "other" is one who has gone from the profane to the sacred world, and in the process has died and been reborn. "Passing from the profane to the sacred world in some sort implies the experience of death; he who makes the passage dies to one life in order to gain access to another" *(Rites and Symbols,* 9). Initiation is, in other words, another kind of collection of entities making up a *sui generis* sacred, entities now not primarily in space but subjective, composed of special feelings, pains, thoughts, and stories, all seeming as real as death and life.

The initiate knows, as well as he or she knows her own name (which may well be a new name given as token of a new identity in the initiation) that he is now a person different from who he was before or from those who have not shared this self-changing process. Initiation is not just word teaching, of course, but a *total* experience—physical, emotional, mental—imparted in isolation from any contrasting images or conversations. Pain like that of circumcision may well have burned into the self a deep wound now emotional, from the intrusion, as well as physical. So has the inner turmoil wrought by apparently crazy-making commands, gross humiliations, and isolation from all except fellow initiates and seemingly sadistic initiators. Sometimes the initiate, being reborn and now like a newborn infant, is even supposed to have forgotten his previous life (see *Sacred and Profane*, 190–191).

In any case, having passed through torture and the birth pangs of a new life, the novice knows she is now a person sharing something profoundly important in common with those fellow initiates and initiators, something often deeper even than family. Some things only other initiates can understand. Only they can be counted on to act in the same way in some settings. All who have been through that death and rebirth know something, and value something, others might never understand. They may even dream the same dreams, dreams undreamed by others. These persons are, as they often say, brothers or sisters for life, in a real sense more so than natural siblings. As we will see, all this is not unknown in sophisticated modern initiatory settings.

Their differences from Eliade's ideal initiation in primal societies are twofold. First, that *"initiation represents above all the revelation of the sacred—and for the primitive world, the sacred means not only everything that we now understand by religion, but also the whole body of the tribe's mythological and cultural traditions"* (*Rites and Symbols*, 3; italics in the original). Modern initiations may certainly involve encountering glimpses of the sacred, or more likely particular equivalents to the sacred in the lore of some unit, group, or institution, but it will not be the whole of what is sacred in the whole of the society.

That is because of the second difference, that now, instead of one initiatory scenario for all, at least all of one gender, there are many initiations, bringing different people into roles often at odds with one another. Modern initiations, therefore, often contribute to divisiveness within society, setting one highly conditioned phalanx against another.

Nonetheless, Eliade's work on initiation can help us understand contemporary initiations and initiatory groups. He writes:

> The historian of religion will always make use—and most profitable use—of the results attained by the ethnologist and the sociologists; but he has to complement these results and give them their due place in a different and broader perspective. The ethnologist is concerned only with the societies that we call primitive, whereas the historian of religion includes the entire religious history of humanity in his field of investigation, from the earliest cults in paleolithic times of which we have records down to modern religious movements. (*Rites and Symbols*, 1)

In his sweeping survey, Eliade gave some attention to *männerbunde* initiates like the Germanic Berserkers, initiated warrior bands under the patronage of Odin who fought in a kind of ecstatic fury (*wut*) and with animal ferocity. These fervent fighters surely remind us that, while some initiations may bring one to a loftier spiritual and moral plane than before, others may have an opposite effect. The transformation may cause one to lose all inhibition, or sense of right and wrong, save for the attitudes shared by the group, so that band becomes one's identity and one's conscience. While Eliade does not deal with the dark side of initiation as much as one might wish, his analysis of the nature of the process helps us to comprehend it. (In comprehending the dark side of initiation, Eliade might have referred to his own unfortunate youthful involvement with the fascist, ritualistic, and brutally anti-Semitic Legion of the Archangel Michael in Romania; he even spent some time in prison because of his alleged membership—and prison can surely be an initiation, light or dark).[2]

A recent example is reported in a study by Peggy Sanday, *Fraternity Gang Rape.* An American college fraternity was in very serious trouble because of an incident of "gang rape" at a party.[3] The brethren's fraternity initiation had clearly induced them into a state of consciousness that made acceptable what would be morally unacceptable on an individual basis. Initiation can lead one to do with bonded fellow initiates what one otherwise would not do, and if that thing is evil, then initiation is a source of evil. One's only conscience is the group conscience.

The initiations of this brotherhood were traumatic. An insider, identified as Sean, said, "We felt that salvation is achieved through brotherhood, and nothing else (certainly not our individuality) mattered at all." He confided that after the initiation the new initiates all shared accounts of how they had "fallen apart," cried, and acted "foolishly," but that no longer mattered. They could now joke about the ordeal: "We were laughing together at our common weakness as individuals, because we were building bonds that were transforming us into something larger and, hopefully, stronger." The laughter was, he perceived, to put their separate selves at a distance. "We were collectively celebrating the death of our individuality." According to Sean, one symbol used in the initiation, the sun rising over a coffin, indicated one's rebirth as a perfect spiritual self after the former mortal self had "died" as the young man joined the society—a very Eliadean symbol and result. Brethren in the fraternity, having survived their ordeal, even to the point of having undergone death to their past individualistic kind of being, were now each living as another, more powerful brotherhood self.

The consequence was that now, according to Sean, they had no moral code except the brotherhood's. The fraternity was able to create a private society in which the initiated could see those outside its parameters as small and terrified and, in a real sense, subhuman. As Sean again put it:

> Everyone and everything [outside the fraternity] was open to ridicule, all people and all standards became vulnerable, because we had powerfully felt our own vulnerability [in the initiation]. That was our deepest kept secret, the thing that really separated us from the world outside: we knew how insignificant people can feel when they are really up against the wall—how insignificant we felt during initiation. . . . Our initiation experience and new knowledge constituted the deepest insight and a sacred revelation. . . . Now we could be masters of life. . . . We could toy with it and watch with amusement as everyone else staggered blindly through it. (Sanday, 152–53)

Ironically, in view of the fraternity's customary attitude toward women, as among those with whose lives they could "toy" and whose vulnerabilities they could exploit, the central figure in the myth behind their draconian initiation was an "astral goddess." The initiates claimed that the secrets of the brotherhood were first given them by a Greek goddess, and that it is to her astral plane that they ascend in initiation. But it is not uncommon for males who vaunt superiority over "real" women here on earth to profess devotion to a divine female figure.

Clearly what happened in this initiation was to enable men who, alone, felt powerless, as youths, as students, subject to the authority of parents, teachers, and many others, to pass through the ultimate vulnerability of symbolic death, in order to rise again bonded with a group that collectively felt all-powerful. But with this power they, like the Berserkers, could work evil as well as good, for with the loss of their former selves they felt themselves beyond good and evil as the outside world understood it, and could toy with lives at their pleasure.

The End Is the Beginning

Finally, let us consider modern manifestations of Eliade's views of eschatology. Interestingly, when Eliade discusses eschatology he talks far less about the end of time than its beginning, for he insists always that we *really* want not to reach the end but to go back to the beginning. Even more fervently, in so doing we want to abolish history and historical time, to fulfill our "longing to destroy profane time and live in sacred time" (*Patterns*, 407). In this we wish for "total regeneration of time," by which we may live humanly yet also in eternity:

> Let me point out that this desire is no "spiritual" attitude, which deprecates life on earth and all that goes with it in favor of a "spirituality" of detachment from the world. On the contrary, what may be called the "nostalgia for eternity" proves that man longs for a concrete paradise, and believes that such a paradise can be won *here*, on earth, and *now*, in the present moment. (*Patterns*, 408)

History is profane, tangential, temporary; what we truly desire is the restoration of mythical time, the time of the end and the beginning, for according to Eliade what the eschatologies of religion truly desire is not a wholly new heaven and earth, but a return to the old, *illud tempus*, when it was perfect before the fall, to the original paradise.

Where is yearning for such a paradise to be found today? Where is a millennialism that wants to abolish history and profane time to recover the strong mythic time of the beginning? In some of its most creative and provocative expressions, it is appearing not in traditional religions but in extrapolations from the cybernetic revolution, leading up to what might be called cyber apocalyptic, or in Eliadean terms nostalgia for an earthly, or cosmic, Eden that has harnessed the powers of creation.

Writers like David Noble in *The Religion of Technology* and Erik Davis in *TechGnosis* have pointed out that human invention and technological developments have long been accompanied by millennialist hopes. A new tech is always a means to transform the world and open the doors to utopia. Steam power, electricity, atomic energy, even exploration of space, it was said in their day, would finally free humankind from slavery to toil or from the limitations of one obscure world, bringing in a brave new world of peace, leisure, and high thinking. All irksome tasks would now be done by machines, including computerized robots. Though never fully realized, the dream has not died.

Indeed, as writers like these and others have proclaimed, speculative doctrine accompanying the latest and perhaps most provocative innovation of all, the Internet, have only compounded the mix of myth, magic, and millennialism informing past ages of faith and technological breakthrough alike. Might not the coming cybernetic city be a new spiritual age, inhabited by immortal beings who through cyber-links with and immediate downloads from all other minds and databases virtually share the mind of God? Eliade makes much of the medieval eschatologist Joachim of Flora, whose futuristic vision was not cyclic, like those of the ancients and the East, but whose prospect ended in the absolute freedom of the Age of the Spirit (*Cosmos and History*, 145). Now, as often before, there are those who believe they have sighted its dawning; that early light illumines objects that, collectively, are again like a *sui generis* sacred, now neither spatial nor subjective, but temporal.

Take Ray Kurzweil's best-selling books *The Singularity Is Near* and *The Age of Spiritual Machines*, which prophesy that within the twenty-first century artificial intelligence will first exceed human intelligence and then develop the ability to reproduce and enhance itself at an accelerating rate. While this might seem to be an ominous circumstance for mere human beings, Kurzweil reassures us that at around the same time, nanotechnology will be able to put minicomputers into the bloodstream, enabling us to download computerized information and intelligence directly into our brains and linking us wirelessly with the entire Internet—by then sovereign of the world if not the universe.

We will in fact be cyborgs, deathless inseparable hybrids of human and ultra high-tech machine. Another pundit, the distinguished physicist Freeman Dyson, in *Imagined Worlds*, declared of such compound beings, "In the end, physical and biological components will be so intimately entangled that we will be unable to say where one begins and the other ends" (121). At that hour—the Singularity moment—the race will forever transcend its present biological limits, and enter a wondrous though now nearly unimaginable future as immortal cosmic beings. Humanity would soon evolve into a single super-mind, a World Wide Web of consciousness directly linked to supercomputers—no more need for books, screens, perhaps not even words, in its infinite knowing.

A convergence of sources suggest an emerging quasi-secular, quasi-spiritual mentality embracing this kind of millennialism. The transhumanism movement promotes this new Jerusalem through conferences and a magazine, *H+*. Needless to say, there are critics convinced that these developments, if they really happen at all, would create diminished rather than ennobled humans, shorn of all those experiences that make us profoundly human in, say, a Shakespearean sense (Hansell and Grassie; Young). Yet the dream is there. Films like the *Star Trek* series have, in my mind, evoked a passionate following because they portray a future that, if not perfect, has overcome many of the ordinary ills of poverty and disease that still plague us today and paint a coming sacred era as full of wonder as one can well imagine. Kirk, Spock, Picard, and Janeway suggest an adventurous new age of exploration, as heroes visit strange new worlds at many times the speed of light.

As Eliade was aware, such yearning is for the primordial as much as for the future. For if, as Plato taught, knowing is really remembering, our future vision must be colored by some sort of past—perhaps the best days of childhood, perhaps Adam in the Garden naming the animals, perhaps a moment just before the Big Bang, when our embryo universe was all homogeneous, potential consciousness and matter united.

Final Note

Past or future, the ancient nostalgia for paradise remains even as it returns in new, high-tech form, showing the relevance of Mircea Eliade for understanding some of the deep motives behind longing for the Singularity, and much else. Clearly postmodern people have the same dread of the terror of history as ancients in the Axial Age. Indeed, it may be that the postmodern mood itself wants to be in denial of modernity's metanarratives of history as vehicles of progress and the unification of knowledge, now fearing more their terror, and that is why it deconstructs such statements to bits and pieces. Yet they do not stay disassembled. Postmodernism not only deconstructs, it also levels the playing field for past and future. The latest thing is no longer necessarily better than the oldest; what we learn from the history of religion can take its stand alongside everything else in the marketplace of ideas. We have tried to show how that storehouse, however badly sorted, can help us understand the return of the sacred along our roadsides, in our initiations, and our sightings of the transhuman future.

No doubt contemporary cases hinting at application of Eliade's concepts like these three examples could as well be interpreted by means of other historical or social scientific categories. Yet what makes Eliade's dialectic of the sacred and profane interesting is its relevance to three quite different contexts: territory, in the demarcation of a sacred site; inward, as initiation changes consciousness from profane to sacred, though sometimes into the dark sacred; and temporal, as a profane present anticipates a sacred eschatological future, and past. Irregular, often jagged or barely seen, sometimes loud and clear, the sacred remains an experience and a tool for understanding.

Notes

1. I once wrote an article on such a group, whose founder claimed influence from Eliade as well as his own theophany. Robert Ellwood, "Notes on a Neo-Pagan Religious Group in America," *History of Religions*, vol. 11, no. 1 (August 1971):125–139.
2. The Legion was often referred to as the Iron Guard, after its militant wing. Eliade claimed not to have been a member, but to have had sympathy with some of its goals. For discussion, see Robert Ellwood, *The Politics of Myth*. Albany: State University of New York Press, 1999, 82–96.
3. The incident occurred in 1983 at the University of Pennsylvania. The victim, seriously impaired by drugs and alcohol, was sexually used by five or six men after a fraternity party. The acts were undoubtedly not consensual, although the fraternity brethren claimed otherwise. After the offense was reported to faculty, including Professor Sanday, as well as to the administration, negative publicity ensued. The university conducted an investigation and convened a hearing. The fraternity was suspended for a year. That body responded with a suit against Penn, alleging that the hearing did not follow due process, admitting hearsay evidence and conjecture. The judge, though sympathetic to the woman, felt compelled to concur on legal grounds; the suspension was revoked. The district attorney declined to prosecute on the grounds that such a crime is almost impossible to prove beyond a reasonable doubt. In the end, neither the house nor any individual was penalized; the victim reportedly was paid a substantial sum by the university. In a second edition of her book, Professor Sanday adds an extensive new foreword and afterword, reviewing what changes in law, university policies, and public attitudes toward such cases have occurred between 1985 and 2006. Peggy Reeves Sanday, *Fraternity Gang Rape*, second edition. New York: New York University Press, 2007.

Works Cited

Allen, Douglas. *Myth and Religion in Mircea Eliade*. New York: Garland, 1998.

Altizer, Thomas J. J. *The Gospel of Christian Atheism*. Philadelphia: Westminster Press, 1966.

———. *Mircea Eliade and the Dialectics of the Sacred*. Philadelphia: Westminster Press, 1963.

Babuts, Nicolae. *The Dynamics of the Metaphoric Field*. Newark: University of Delaware Press, 1992.

———. *Mimesis in a Cognitive Perspective*. New Brunswick, NJ: Transaction Publishers, 2011.

Belshaw, John. *Private Grief, Public Mourning: The Rise of the Roadside Shrine in B.C.* Vancouver, BC: Anvil Press, 2004.

Davis, Erik. *TechGnosis: Myth, Magic and Mysticism in the Age of Information*. New York: Harmony Books, 1998.

Doss, Erika. *The Emotional Life of Contemporary Public Memorials: Towards a Theory of Temporary Memorials*. Amsterdam: Amsterdam University Press, 2008.

Dyson, Freeman. *Imagined Worlds*. Cambridge, MA: Harvard University Press, 1997.

Eliade, Mircea. *Cosmos and History*. New York: Harper Torchbooks, 1959. First published as *The Myth of the Eternal Return*. New York: Pantheon, 1954.

———. "History of Religions and a New Humanism." *History of Religions*, 1 (1961). Revised and expanded as "A New Humanism" in *The Quest*, q. v.

———. *Myth and Reality*. New York: Harper and Row, 1963.

———. "A New Humanism." In *The Quest*. Chicago: University of Chicago Press, 1969.

———. *Ordeal by Labyrinth*. Translated by Derek Coleman. Chicago: University of Chicago Press, 1982.

———. *No Souvenirs: Journal, 1957–1969*. New York: Harper & Row, 1977.

———. *Patterns in Comparative Religion*. New York: Sheed and Ward, 1958.

———. *The Quest: History and Meaning in Religion*. Chicago: University of Chicago Press, 1969.

———. *The Sacred and the Profane*. Translated by Willard Trask. New York: Harcourt Brace Jovanovich, 1959.

———. *Rites and Symbols of Initiation*. New York: Harper Torchbooks, 1965.

Everett, Holly. *Roadside Crosses in Contemporary Memorial Culture*. Denton, TX: University of North Texas Press, 2002.

Hansell, Gregory R., and William Grassie, eds. *H+/-: Transhumanism and Its Critics*. New York: Metanexus Institute, 2011.

James, William. *The Varieties of Religion Experience*. New York: Modern Library, n.d. Originally published in London, 1902.

Kurzweil, Ray. *The Age of Spiritual Machines: When Computers Exceed Human Intelligence*. New York: Viking, 1999.

———. *The Singularity Is Near: When Humans Transcend Biology*. New York: Penguin, 2006.

Lukacher, Ned. *Time-Fetishes: The Secret History of Eternal Recurrence*. Durham, NC: Duke University Press, 1998.

Lyotard, Jean-François. *The Postmodern-Condition: A Report on Knowledge*. Translated by Geoff Bennington and Brian Massumi. Minneapolis: University of Minnesota Press, 1984.

McCutcheon, Russell. *Manufacturing Religion: The Discourse on Sui Generis and the Politics of Nostalgia*. New York: Oxford University Press, 1997.

Nietzsche, Friedrich. *The Gay Science*. Translated by Walter Kaufman. New York: Vintage, 1974.

Noble, David. *The Religion of Technology: The Divinity of Man and the Spirit of Invention*. New York: Penguin, 1999.

Rorty, Richard. "Anticlericalism and Atheism." In *The Future of Religion*. New York: Columbia University Press, 2005.

Sanday, Peggy. *Fraternity Gang Rape: Sex, Brotherhood, and Privilege on Campus*. New York: New York University Press, 1990.

Schmemann, Alexander. *The Journals of Father Alexander Schmemann, 1973–1983*. Translated by Juliana Schmemann. Crestwood, NY: St. Vladimir's Seminary Press, 2000.

Smith, Jonathan Z. *Imagining Religion*. Chicago: University of Chicago Press, 1982.

———. "'Religion' and 'Religious Studies': No Difference at All." *Soundings* 71, 1988.

Susman, Tina. "Killing Strains a Tense Florida City." *Los Angeles Times* (March 23, 2012).

Wojcik, Daniel. "Pre's Rock: Pilgrimage, Ritual, and Runners' Traditions at the Roadside Shrine for Steve Prefontaine." In *Shrines and Pilgrimages in the Modern World: New Itineraries into the Sacred*, edited by Peter Jan Margry, pp. 201–237. Amsterdam: University of Amsterdam Press, 2008.

Young, Simon. *Designer Evolution: A Transhumanist Manifesto*. Amherst, NY: Prometheus Books, 2005.

2

The Place of Literature in Eliade's "Rediscovery" of the Archaic World

Eric Ziolkowski

Closing an entry of January 4, 1945, in his journal, "transcribed from pages written in the night," Mircea Eliade declares: "My mission in the culture of the twentieth century is to rediscover and make alive the pre-Socratic world" (*Portugal*, 150). If there were a *punctum Archimedis* in Eliade's vast output of writings, this sentence could be it, at least in those that comprise or pertain to his "scientific" scholarship in the history of religions. Written in Cascaes, a Portuguese seaside village near Lisbon, shortly after he had moved there from Lisbon following the death of his first wife, Nina (November 20, 1944), the sentence has as its context a period of Eliade's life filled by clinical depression, grief, and near-despair—stemming from his tragic spousal loss and his terror that an Allied victory in the war would result in the subjugation of his native Romania by the Soviet Union (see Ricketts, Preface to *Portugal*, x–xi).

The same entry opens with his suggestion that, no matter what, he will never "become resigned"; to do so would not bring Nina back and would prevent him from achieving the one goal that could satisfy him, namely,

> the conquest of the finite. But, please, don't confuse me with Kierkegaard! There is in both of us the same passion for and obsession with the real, properly speaking, in our surroundings, for the concrete and the evanescence of the fragments, of finite things. But for me the fragment can coincide with the Whole; while remaining in finitude, man can nevertheless grasp the infinite. (150)

The self-comparison with Kierkegaard is hardly surprising. Eliade, who claimed that his 1928 article "Sören Kierkegaard—Logodnic,

23

pamfletar și eremit" ("Søren Kierkegaard: Fiancé, Pamphleteer, and Hermit") was "probably the first article on Kierkegaard to appear in the Romanian language" (*Autobiography I*, 129; cf. *Ordeal*, 17), read Kierkegaard voraciously (in German, Italian, and, later, French translations), and his journals, particularly the one kept during his years in Portugal, are peppered with references to, and quotations from, the Dane's writings. Ricketts's observation that the young Eliade "was strongly impressed by Kierkegaard" (*Mircea* 2:1212) seems an understatement; as others observe, the *Portugal Journal* attests to Eliade's feeling of "a special connection" (Dobre, 261) and "psycho-intellectual affinity" (Stan, 65) with Kierkegaard. Intellectually, Eliade's instinct to identify his own "mission" seems demonstrably inspired by Kierkegaard,[1] and the two men have in common—among other kinships—their "existential exemplariness" (Dobre, 261), "stress on subjectivity (Stan, 66), and "insist[ence] that the religious experience gestures towards an utterly heterogeneous reality that cannot be understood solely in terms of science, interpersonal or virtue ethics, sociology, and psychology" (76). Personally, while sharing Kierkegaard's melancholic disposition, Eliade also interprets aspects of one if not two of his unhappy erotic involvements, including his first marriage, in the light of Kierkegaard's tragic ill-fated relationship with Regine Olsen (see, e.g., *Autobiography I*, 129; *Portugal*, 167, 177; Dobre, 260; Stan, 67–68). Moreover, Eliade recognizes in Kierkegaard a fellow oeuvre-obsessed graphomaniac who wrote in multiple genres but who, like Eliade (especially in his younger years), thought of himself primarily as a literary artist[2]—although still today, Kierkegaard is regarded mainly as a philosopher or theologian, and Eliade, as a historian of religions, particularly outside their respective homelands. In the passage from his *Portugal Journal* quoted above, Eliade continues:

> Through his rites and myths, archaic man knew how to remain in and enjoy the concrete world, yet without "falling" into the world. This conviction that I've acquired in the past eight or nine years of ethnographic research—Kierkegaard did not have. Hence his terrible despair—and my mere melancholy. He repeated and discussed . . . the examples of Abraham and Job, casting himself (but only with his mind) into an Absurd, which would allow him to recover Regina [*sic*] Olsen. But I observe that Abraham and Job have a vast prehistory back of them, that man obtained "repetition" through a whole series of rituals (cf. *Cosmos și Istorie*, where I mean to take it up), that therefore, the "repetition," the abolition of "history," the suspension

and regeneration of "time," was possible not only for a few chosen and tried by God, but for the whole of archaic humanity. (150)

It is after this that Eliade declares his cultural "mission" to be to recover and vivify of "the pre-Socratic world."

This whole passage, whose gist Eliade will often reiterate, crystallizes one of the major developments already evident in his work, while also anticipating the main course of his future scholarship. Recounting this period in his life much later, he reflects that "the whole world was . . . being transformed, and at least one of the important transformations could only make me glad, because I had foreseen it and announced it in many writings between 1933 and 1940. . . . Soon there would become possible a new confrontation—on a footing of equality—between Oriental and Occidental spirituality" (*Autobiography II*, 107). For entering this dialogue, that is, for knowing correctly and understanding "the *true* Oriental spirituality—that is, its religious matrix" (107), Eliade considered the phenomenology and history of religions to offer the best preparation because "the archaic world—that of the 'primitives' whom anthropologists had studied for a century—could not remain very long under its colonial guise. But for Occidentals, the understanding of archaic spirituality was even more difficult, because it presupposed a minimum comprehension of mythical thought" (107).

While capturing his excitement at having anticipated the imminent East/West "dialogue" and the Western decipherment of "archaic spirituality" and "mythical thought," the journal entry of January 4, 1945, also points forward to the defining subjects of repetition, abolition of history, and recovery of the "archaic" (designated here the "pre-Socratic") that not only underlie *The Myth of the Eternal Return* (*Le mythe de l'éternel retour*, 1949), to which Eliade alludes by its later variant title *Cosmos and History*, but also inform what Jonathan Z. Smith (79n47) suggests are the "four foundational works" on which any worthy "treatment of Eliade's project" in the history of religions must be "centered": *Patterns in Comparative Religion*, first published in French as *Traité d'histoire des religions* (1949); *Shamanism: Archaic Techniques of Ecstasy* (*Le chamanisme et les techniques archaïques de l'extase*, 1951, whose years of drafting, 1946–51, coincided with those of the completion of *Traité*, as noted by Smith [73]); *Yoga: Immortality and Freedom* (*Le yoga: Immortalité et liberté*, 1954); and *The Forge and the Crucible* (*Forgerons et alchimistes*, 1956). To regard these four works as so crucial is easily defensible, though there is a fifth work that should be added to this list, as Smith appears to have overlooked or forgotten Eliade's own insistence in 1958 that *The Myth of the Eternal Return* remained "the most significant of [his] books" (*Eternal Return*, xv).

Still, "Eliade's project," as Eliade conceived it, was more expansive than even the astonishingly broad interests represented by these *five* foundational works. Like his other works, these, beyond the focused attention they pay to their main subjects, occasionally hint at further directions toward which Eliade believed his ever-growing corpus of writings was aimed. The one of these directions to be considered in this article is the demonstration of genetic connections between literature, in the sense of "written work valued for superior or lasting artistic merit,"[3] particularly though not exclusively modern Western literature, and the mythic, ritual, and religious traditions of archaic peoples. In a past article comparing Eliade with the literary critic and theorist Northrop Frye, I emphasized the two men's "shared notion of the continuity of myth and literary fiction and of the capacity of both myth and literature to make possible an escape from time" (Ziolkowski, "Between," 516). The writings of Eliade I mainly dealt with were from the late 1950s onward,[4] the period that followed his writing and publication of his five foundational works mentioned above. In contrast, this present article, a kind of prequel ex post facto to that other article, will focus mainly upon *Traité*.

Because the literary dimension of Eliade's enterprise as a historian of religions remains generally ignored, it is worth noting that Eliade did not regard the perceived archaic "survivals" in literature as odd curios or mere footnotes to his central scholarly task. On the contrary, if he never produced a major, let alone monographic study of such "survivals," it was not because he did not want to do so. Rather, it was for lack of time, a matter about which some words are in order.

Eliade's Oeuvre and the Competition with Time

Before we turn to his ideas about archaic "survivals" in literature, we should note two points regarding what Eliade spoke of as his "oeuvre." The first is that he construed his oeuvre as encompassing *all* his writings, including both his scholarly and his literary writings, or, in his terminology, both those works written in the scientific, "diurnal" mode, and those, in the imaginative, "nocturnal" mode: his novels, short stories, plays, and so forth. He traced back to his thirteenth year his attraction to writing both "scientifically" and "imaginatively" (*Ordeal*, 13), and while these two "operations of the mind"—the "diurnal" and "nocturnal"—might seem opposed, they represented for Eliade an instance of *coincidentia oppositorum*, "the great whole, Yin and Yang" (13), "interdependent and express[ing] a profound unity" (*Symbolism*, 173).[5] Accordingly, reflecting on his oeuvre as he approached his thirty-fifth birthday, grasping for "a point of support that will explain it, organize it, deepen it," he concludes that it actually "need[s] several points of support," and he then enumerates eight different categories, spanning imaginative and scholarly genres alike, into which his completed and planned writings theretofore might be placed: "the art of the novel," "drama," "morals," "history and philosophy of religions," "philosophy of culture," "folklore," "Indian studies," and "essay" (January 12, 1942, *Portugal*, 17–18). By 1962, with all his most important scholarly works in the history of religions already written and long in print (with the arguable exception of the *Histoire des croyances et des idées religieuses*, 1976–83, known in English as *A History of Religious Ideas*), he compares himself to Kierkegaard once again (in an entry of April 13), this time as an author who, as Kierkegaard did in his posthumously published *The Point of View for My Work as an Author*, "could show: (a) that there exists a fundamental unity through all my works; (b) that the body of scientific work illustrates my philosophical conception . . . [of] a profound and significant meaning in everything called 'natural religion' and that this meaning directly concerns modern man" (*Journal II*, 164).

Second, it may be instructive to expand our envisagement of Eliade's oeuvre beyond the works the extant oeuvre actually comprises, taking into account some of the innumerable works that he planned and projected but never wrote, or that he began but left unfinished. This point requires some background and explanation.

From a very young age, Eliade struggled with the realization that the sheer, ever-increasing number of his ideas for writing projects far surpassed the amount of time he had to write them, a realization undoubtedly connected with the bouts of depression that plagued him from his teenage years to the end of his life. During his years at the lycée, he sought to combat his melancholy by putting into practice ideas of systematic, self-imposed sleep deprivation from Jules Payot's *Education of the Will* (*Éducation de la volonté*, 1895), waging "what I later called my 'war against sleep.' That was because *I wanted to make more time*" (*Ordeal*, 14, emphasis mine):

> I had a great need for "time"—not only to be able to cope with the reading of all the books that had piled up on my desk and shelves, but

because, besides the journal and the many other notebooks in which I had come to write daily . . . , I had begun a fantasy novel projected with gigantic dimensions. (*Autobiography I,* 64)

Effectually inverting the "terror of history" from which he would later construe the "mythic" mode of thought as having afforded archaic, "traditional" peoples the means of escape (see *Eternal Return,* 141–162), this "great need for time" and concomitant yearning "to make more time" were naturally doomed to constant frustration by mortal constraints. Indeed, only in fiction, as in Eliade's novella *Youth without Youth (Tinerețe fără tinerețe,* 1976), might a person be granted a renewal of life, and a temporary stay of time, as the result of a miraculous, kratophanic occurrence. Thus, for example, in his *Portugal Journal* from the period of April 21, 1941, to September 5, 1945, Eliade mentions or discusses no fewer than thirty-one different works that he conceptualized or planned but either left unfinished or never started.[6] Likewise, in his published scholarship, he frequently reminds us that he is providing but a partial, tip-of-the-iceberg view of the superabundance of data he has amassed on the given subject, on which he would presumably be happy to elaborate further, if only time and page space allowed.[7]

In his life as a writer, competition with time and finitude was so intense a factor that Eliade evidently resisted ever really regarding even his published works as finished and complete—as exemplified by his desire, recorded on November 4, 1941, "to make a second, more courageous edition of *Yoga,*" presumably alluding to his *Yoga: Essai sur les origins de la mystique indienne* (1936), which later was superseded by his *Yoga: Immortality and Freedom.* As Wendy Doniger points out, in Eliade's journal covering from 1979 to 1985, the year before he died, "the primary focus is books; people come second," betraying "the priority of paper over flesh" ("Epilogue" to Eliade, *Journal IV,* 151). So, in the aftermath of the fire that destroyed his office library in the Meadville Lombard School of Religion on December 19, 1985, what saddened Eliade the most, he told Doniger, was the loss of copies of his own published books in which he had continued making notes, "keeping the books alive, up to date, changing them to fix them and to correct their errors, to add new thoughts . . . and to expand the bibliographies" (152). In effect he "was keeping the books in history, . . . keeping them alive and changing," and when they were burned,

> he felt that all the years of continued growth had been erased. . . .
> The immortality that he had sought on the printed page was subject
> to material destruction, just like the immortality that he had once,
> long ago, sought in his experiments with yoga. The fire put an end to
> the history of the books, prevented their history from progressing,
> stopped them at the moment of their publication. In neither life nor
> literature could time be conquered. (Doniger "Epilogue" to Eliade,
> *Journal* IV, 152)

True. Neither life nor literature allows for the conquest of time or
for the completion of the kind of ever-expanding oeuvre that Eliade
aspired to amass. Indeed, Eliade closes *Traité* by characterizing the history of religions itself as a "drama provoked by the loss and rediscovery
of [all religious] values, a loss and rediscovery that are never, *nor could
ever be, final [définitives]*" ("Conclusions," *Traité*, 397, italics in text).[8]
Yet we might be given pause by Doniger's allusion to Eliade's quest for
immortality "long ago, . . . in his experiments with yoga," when Eliade
practiced yoga in an ashram at Rishikesh from October 1930 to April
the next year (see Eliade, *Autobiography I*, 187–200; *Ordeal*, 40–46).
For the *Bhagavad-Gītā*, which he studied and translated piecemeal into
Romanian during those six months at Rishikesh, proffers a yogic solution that could, with slight adjustment, apply to the literary-authorial
problem he struggled with all his life: the insufficiency of time to write
all he envisioned writing. As Eliade explains in his 1956 *Yoga*, the *Gītā*,
epitomizing an Indian—and, especially, Buddhist—mystical leitmotiv,
confers its highest praise not upon the yogi (yogin) utterly liberated
from worldly pain and illusions, but rather upon the one "who regards
another's pain and joy as his own" (*Yoga*, 161; see *Bhagavad-Gītā*
6.32). The practitioner of this brand of yoga is the one with whom the
Gītā sympathizes: "If he fails in this life, he will be reborn in a family
of talented yogins, and, *in another life, will succeed in accomplish-
ing what he could not achieve in this*" (*Yoga*, 161, emphasis mine; see
Bhagavad-Gītā 6.41). Were the word "yogins" replaced with "writers,"
this response to the problem of finite mortality might seem transferable to resolve Eliade's writerly frustration, as the prospect would open
up of a utopian, next-life condition in which any oeuvre that was left
incomplete in the previous life could now be completed.

Eliade makes no reference to any such notion in his journal entry of
February 19, 1945, less than two months following the entry with which
we began this article: "Now, when I look back, or when I look ahead,
I can see no meaning to my life other than the completion of my *oeuvre*"

(*Portugal*, 186). Nor, strangely, does he mention it two days later, when he explicitly connects his agony over his lack of sufficient time as an author with the question of life after death: "Among the many brief treatises I'd like to write—brief, even laconic, because I won't have time to write them all—will be one devoted to the postmortem problem" (186). Nor, for that matter, does he mention the similar solution—albeit one hinging not on the Indian notion of reincarnation, but rather on a Western notion of an eternal afterlife—distillable from Kant's postulate of the "endless progress" (*ins Unendliche gehend*, "a progress to infinity") in which rational beings can look forward to engaging toward moral perfection in the afterlife (*Critique of Practical Reason*, 102 [pt. 1, chap. 2, sec. 4]). Instead, Eliade goes on to ruminate about the notion that the deceased individual will meet whatever postmortem world he or she has accepted through religion, whether as a Buddhist, a Muslim, a Jew, a Christian, or whatever, or conceptualized through personal thought.

In evoking the Indian and Kantian theories of a postmortem condition in which beings can achieve the moral perfection toward which they strived but failed to achieve in this life, I mean to suggest that Eliade's oeuvre, as it stands, might be comparably understood—minus, of course, the moral implications of those theories. That is, we may view the oeuvre as consisting of but the imperfect fragments (meaning his published works, none of which he ever considered finally "finished") of an imagined, idealized whole, which Eliade realized all too well was unrealizable in this life, but whose countless remaining pieces (meaning his planned, projected, but never-begun or never-completed works) he was constantly envisioning (futilely, but as if they might be written), as reflected in his incessant, intermittent allusions to them in his journals and published works.

Of the multiple dimensions of his envisioned oeuvre that remained unfulfilled at his death, among the most salient was his ambition to demonstrate fully the rootedness of significant aspects of literary art, including poetry, drama, and narrative fiction, in archaic myths, rituals, and religious traditions. Let us consider the evidence of that ambition in *Traité*.

The Place of Literature in *Traité*

"What a magnificent book remains to be written," writes Eliade in closing his "Epilogue" to *Shamanism*,[9] "on the ecstatic 'sources' of epic and lyric poetry, on the prehistory of dramatic spectacles, and, in general, on the fabulous worlds discovered, explored, and described by the ancient shamans. . . ." (511, ellipses in text). How would such a book, if Eliade had written it, fit in his oeuvre? If Smith were correct, as he almost surely is not, in his hypothesis that the monographs *Shamanism* and *Yoga* and the briefer work *The Forge and the Crucible* are "three chapters" of what would have comprised the "complementary volume [*volume complementaire*]" that Eliade promised at the end of *Traité*,[10] the likewise never-written "magnificent book" described at the close of *Shamanism*'s "Epilogue" would have constituted, if it had been written, a companion to a companion, or a sequel to a sequel.

Concentric Circles of Interests

Be that as it may, the envisioned contents of that imagined "magnificent book"—"the ecstatic 'sources' of . . . poetry, . . . the prehistory of dramatic spectacles, and . . . the fabulous worlds discovered, explored, and described by the ancient shamans"—were no passing fancy for Eliade. Such phenomena were an ongoing preoccupation, intimations of which are manifest not only in *Traité* and *Shamanism*, but also in the other three of his aforementioned five foundational works: *Yoga*, *The Myth of the Eternal Return*, and *The Forge and the Crucible*. If it may be agreed that *Traité* stands at or *as* the axial "center" of Eliade's scholarly corpus, or the *axis corporis* (to play on one of Eliade's most famous Latinisms), it makes sense to construe those other works as revolving around it, concentrically, in this manner, with their focal subjects each noted in parentheses:

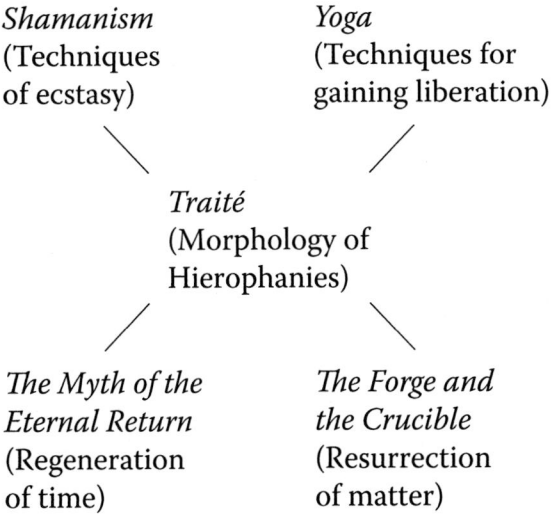

Shamanism
(Techniques
of ecstasy)

Yoga
(Techniques for
gaining liberation)

Traité
(Morphology of
Hierophanies)

*The Myth of the
Eternal Return*
(Regeneration
of time)

*The Forge and
the Crucible*
(Resurrection
of matter)

Were this schema expanded to accommodate other works from Eliade's oeuvre on religion, the first concentric circle comprised of those four core works around *Traité* would feed outwardly to a second, larger circle around it, comprised of *Images and Symbols* and other later works that likewise elaborate upon the subjects and themes of the five foundational works. These would include *The Sacred and the Profane* and various subsequent collections of essays, lectures, and interviews: most notably, *The Two and the One*; *The Quest*; *Myths, Dreams, and Mysteries*; *Myth and Reality*; *Ordeal by Labyrinth*; and *Symbolism, the Sacred, and the Arts*. And, like *Traité* and all the other works that comprise the first two inner concentric circles, this last work, with its titular nod to *the Arts*, and its devotion of three of its four parts to "Arts and the Sacred" (53–101), "[Architectural] Sites of the Sacred" (103–48), and "Literature and the Sacred" (149–79), anticipates and is ultimately confluent with a hypothetical third, and still larger, outer circle composed of works on primarily literary subjects. These works, which would yet be ineluctably linked with Eliade's concerns as a historian of religions, are ones either that Eliade began writing but never finished (most notably, a biographical study of Balzac, while in Paris in 1948 [see *Journal I*, 69, 71, 73, 75; *Journal II*, 49]), or that he envisioned but never began (for example, a biography of Luís de Camões, while in Lisbon in the early 1940s [see *Portugal*, 11–13, 17, 20; *Autobiography II*, 90–91],[11] or the abovementioned "magnificent book" described in *Traité*). In this regard we might again recall the Indian and Kantian speculations on the postmortem progress of the self or soul, for what we are trying to do here, analogously, is to get a better sense of the whole oeuvre of Eliade as he imagined it, including one of its significantly unwritten portions as though he had further time to write it.

The literary interests that account for this outer, hypothetical circle of Eliade's oeuvre become apparent through two literary analogies drawn early in *Traité*. The first occurs in the opening paragraph of Eliade's "Author's Foreword," to illustrate the irreducibility of the sacred: to try to explain religion away as a function of language, society, or economics "would be as futile as thinking you could explain *Madame Bovary* by a list of social, economic and political facts; however true, they do not affect it as a work of literature" (xiii).[12] This analogy, whose conceptual roots are retraceable to a critical article he wrote two and a half decades earlier on the French author Remy de Gourmont (Eliade, "Metodele gourmontine"; cited by Ricketts, *Mircea* 1:179; 2:1254n72), is followed in chapter 1 of *Traité* by another allusion to the discipline of literary history, this time to illustrate one of the practical methodological difficulties that historians of religions must confront when faced with the extreme diversity of material in their field, including "hundreds of thousands of scraps of evidence" (4): "It is exactly as if a critic had to write a history of French literature with no other evidence than some fragments of Racine, a Spanish translation of La Bruyère, a few texts quoted by a foreign critic, [etc.] . . . and a few more hints of the same sort" (5). These analogies anticipate Eliade's appeals elsewhere to literary history and criticism as disciplines methodologically comparable to the history of religions (*Images*, 37; *Quest*, 4–5), and his expressed conviction "of the literary value of the materials available to the historian of religion" (*Journal II*, 119; see also Ziolkowski, "Between," 507–508).

Omitted from the construal just offered of Eliade's oeuvre is his *History of Religious Ideas*. Admittedly, this "awkward, multivolume, unfinished production of Eliade's last years" (Smith, 73) would be difficult to locate in our schema. However, if we were to try to place it therein, it would best fit right next to *Traité*, at the schema's center (albeit not considered as a "foundational" text), because the *History of Religious Ideas* constitutes the closest approximation of *Traité*'s projected "complementary volume."[13] Yet the *History of Religious Ideas*, in accord with its historical rather than morphological thrust, should also be somehow imagined as coiling outwardly from that center spot, successively winding its way through all three of the schema's concentric circles, including the outer circle focused on literature. For the *History of Religious Ideas* encompasses within its scope, wherever pertinent, such inherently literary topics as "The Hindu Synthesis: The *Mahābhārata* and the *Bhagavad Gītā*" (2:2:32–46 [chap. 24, §§191–195]), "Esotericism and literary creations: Troubadours, *Fedeli d'Amore*, and the Grail cycle" (3:101–112 [chap. 34, §270]), and "Jalāl al-Dīn Rūmi: Sacred music, poetry, and dance" [chap. 35, §282]).

Gilgamesh, the Odyssey, and other Greek and Roman Sources

In *Traité*'s "Foreword," Eliade's ahistorical "morphology" of hierophanies, or manifestations of the sacred, is set forth on three sets of levels that "integrate with one another in a coherent system" (16): *cosmic* (sky, waters, earth, stones), *biological* (rhythms of the moon, sun, vegetation/agriculture, sex, etc.), and *local* (consecrated spaces, temples, etc.). Of the relatively few *literary* sources that inform this morphology, those that predominate are ancient nonsacred texts in which earlier oral traditions of legend and myth are captured and inscribed: the Mesopotamian *Epic of Gilgamesh*, the two Homeric epics, and a number of other Classical Greek and Roman works.

Although Eliade will esteem it elsewhere as "the first masterpiece of universal literature" and "the dramatized account of a failed initiation [to transcending the human condition]" (*History of Rel. Ideas*, 1:80), *Gilgamesh* is discussed in *Traité* exclusively on the biological level of hierophanies, in connection with the themes of vegetation and Great Goddesses (§105), and the tree of life and its guardians. His treatment of *Gilgamesh* with regard to the first theme typifies the highly associative manner by which, with the assistance of secondary authorities, he may weave a literary work at any moment into his morphology of archaic religion and myth. Homing in on Gilgamesh's encounter with the divinity Siduri (the "maiden") near "a miraculous tree" in a garden, Eliade cites Charles Autran's explanation of her description as *sabitu*, "the wine-woman," as suggesting that Gilgamesh "meets her beside a vine-stock; the vine was identified by the ancient inhabitants of the East [*paléo-orientaux*] with the 'herb of life,' and the Sumerian sign for 'life' was originally a vine leaf. This marvelous plant was consecrated to the Great Goddesses. The Mother Goddess was at first called 'the Mother vine-stock,' or the 'Goddess vine-stock'" (*Traité*, 247). Having thus linked Siduri implicitly with the Great Goddess or Mother figure, which he regards as a "survival" of or substitute for the supreme Sky God (see 57 [§15]), which in turn reflects "the quasi-universality of beliefs in a celestial divine being, creator of the universe and guarantor of the fecundity of the earth" (47 [§11]), Eliade next mentions W. F. Albright's "proof" that the "archaic recensions" of the Gilgamesh legend assigned her a "very important [role]" (*Traité*, 248 [§105]), that is, as the character of whom Gilgamesh requests immortality. This leads Eliade to mention Adolf Ellegard Jensen's identification of Siduri with Calypso of the *Odyssey*, the nymph who could confer immortality upon heroes such as Odysseus (*Od.* 5.135–136):

> Calypso was one of the innumerable theophanies of the Great Goddess, who revealed herself at the "center of the world" [i.e., her isle being the *omphalos thalassēs*, "the navel of the sea"; *Od.* 1.50], beside the *omphalos*, the Tree of Life and the four springs. Now, the vine was the vegetal expression of the immortality.... The Book of Enoch [24.2] places this vine/tree of the knowledge of good and evil between

seven mountains, as does also, moreover, the Epic of Gilgamesh. The serpent-goddess Hannat could taste of the fruit of the tree, as Siduri and Calypso were also permitted. (*Traité*, 248)

This passage yields a most basic example of the process of "survival," "substitution," and, as we shall later see, "degradation" that Eliade tends to assume when tracing developments of archaic hierophanies beyond their protohistorical religious origins, up into nonreligious literary texts, in this case two texts that hover on the boundary of myth and literature (*Gilgamesh, Odyssey*):

Degradation process

Protohistorical   →   Mythic/literary
substitute: survivals:

Sky God → *Great Goddess*   →   *Siduri*
                                    Calypso

Archetypal associations:
Cosmic center}
Axis mundi}
Vine} →
Cosmic tree}
Tree of knowledge}

Because, for Eliade, the concealment of the herb of immortality that Gilgamesh sought at the bottom of the sea parallels the alleged "hiddenness" of the Tree of Life in the Bible's second account of creation (Gen. 2:9; *Traité*, 249–50 [§106]), the further fact that a serpent devours that herb immediately after Gilgamesh retrieved it provides Eliade a reason to offer a concise recapitulation of Gilgamesh's failed quest for immortality (251–252 [§107]), so as to liken the Mesopotamian hero now with the fallen primal biblical man: "Gilgamesh, like Adam, lost immortality on account of the serpent's ruse and his own stupidity" (252). Yet it is neither Gilgamesh nor Adam, but rather Ulysses—Odysseus's Latinized name, used by Eliade—whom Eliade will personally identify with,[14] and come to regard as "the prototype of man, not only modern man but the man of the future too, because he typifies the hunted traveler" (*Ordeal*, 95), and because "Every exile is a Ulysses traveling toward Ithaca. Every real existence reproduces the *Odyssey*" (*Journal II*, 84).

If this sort of universalizing—"the prototype of man," "Every exile is a Ulysses"—is one of the irrepressible tendencies of Eliade that most exasperates his legions of detractors and critics, there is no mythic or literary figure about whose story he more grandiosely generalizes than Ulysses. In *Traité*, as in subsequent works, Eliade also invokes him in conjunction with the motif of the labyrinth, rooted in (what he presents as) the mythic, symbolic, ritual notion of "the difficulty . . . of penetrating into a 'center' without harm. . . . To penetrate into a labyrinth and return from it, this is the preeminent initiatory rite, and yet every existence, even [*même*]"—a term whose special usage in Eliade's vocabulary to mark paradoxes will be discussed below— "the least eventful, can be likened to trudging along in a labyrinth. The sufferings and 'trials' gone through by Ulysses are fabulous, and yet any *return to the hearth* 'is equal to' Ulysses' return to Ithaca" (*Traité*, 327, italics in text [§145]).[15] In this respect, Eliade presents *Traité* as an initiatory microcosm, and each of its readers as a Ulysses, stating in his "Foreword" his intent to "introduce the reader to the labyrinthine complexity [*complexité labyrinthique*] of religious data, [to] familiarize him with their basic structures and with the diversity of cultural circles they set in relief" (14).

It is an unappreciated fact that the first authority to whom Eliade appeals in explicating his own understanding of taboo and the "ambivalence of the sacred," still in the opening chapter of *Traité*, is neither the ancient Greek scholar and bishop Eustatius, nor Jane Harrison, Robertson Smith, James G. Frazer, Arnold van Gennep, or any of the other modern scholars subsequently cited, but rather, the prototypical Western poet, Virgil—or, more precisely, the ancient commentator Servius, remarking (in *Ad. Aen.* 3.75) that the term *sacer* in Virgil's phrase *auri sacra fames* "can mean at the same time 'cursed' and 'holy'" (*Traité* [§6], which miscites *Servius ad Vergili Aen.* 3.57 [as 3.75]). Likewise, in his discussion of sacred time, to illustrate the inversion of the restoration of mythical time, it is to Virgil's Fourth Eclogue (v. 22), together with the Bible's Isaiah (9:6), that Eliade turns for a paradigmatic example of how, at the end of history, "the whole world begins to live in sacred time, in eternity": *nec magnos metuent armenta leones*, "cattle will not fear great lions" (*Traité* [§150]; Ecl. 4:22). Shortly thereafter, the same Eclogue's prophecy *magnus ab integro saeclorum nascitur ordo* (v. 5) yields a formula that Eliade finds applicable "to any sovereign. In effect, with every new sovereign, even if he be insignificant, a 'new era' has begun" (*Traité*, 346 [§154]).

36

We lack the space to examine in detail Eliade's other appeals to Greek and Roman poets and dramatists in *Traité*: his juxtaposition of Sophocles's *Oedipus Rex* (22–30) with the *Odyssey* (19.109–114) and Hesiod's *Works and Days* (225–237) to illustrate the timeless principle of "cosmo-biological solidarity," the connection between earth and the vegetable, animal, and human forms (*Traité*, 224 [§90]); his assemblage of passages from Aeschylus and Sophocles, and a reference to Albrecht Dieterich's citations of analogous passages in other classical texts illustrating the identification of the fertility of the land with that of women (*Traité*, 224–225 [§91]); or any number of Eliade's other references to Homer (163 [§58], 174 [§64], 179–180 [§68], 211 [§83]), Hesiod (76–77 [§23], 78 [§24], 179 [§68], 180 [§69], 211 [§83], 212 [§84], 217 [§86]), Aeschylus (77 [§23], 211 [§83], 217 [§86], 228 [§94]), Euripides (132 [§44], 173 [§64], 228 [§94]), Virgil (173 [§64]), and Ovid (264 [§115], 320 [§142]). However, let us consider the places in *Traité* where Eliade makes reference to literary sources that reflect for him the persistence of archaic myths and other themes in ancient, medieval, Renaissance, and, finally, modern forms.

There is reason to suspect that Eliade believes that to trace the occurrences of archaic religious themes or motifs up into, let alone through, a tradition of *literature* may strike some if not most readers as exceeding the proper boundaries of a morphology of religion. The first such reference occurs in his discussion of Jupiter, Odin, Taranis, and several other celestial deities whose reverence, like that of Zeus, he views as substitutes for the worship of primordial sky gods such as Ouranos. The titles that had captured Jupiter's supreme divineness and absolute sovereignty, such as *Jupiter Omnipotens, Jupiter Optimus Maximus*, "survive even in literary texts [*survivent même dans les textes littéraires*]," as exemplified by examples Eliade then cites from the Roman poets and playwrights Naevius, Plautus, and Accius (*Traité*, 79 [§25]). Here, the verb "survive" and the phrasing "even in" are suggestive of a sense that it may seem unexpected or paradoxical for such notions as those of the omnipotence and total sovereignty of a sky god to endure to the point of being inscribed "in [nonreligious] literary texts." This same sense of unexpectedness seems conveyed where, after explaining how the prehistoric identification of woman with the ploughed earth implies an association of phallus with shovel, and of tilling with the generative act, Eliade observes that a period as early as that of the Kassites of sixteenth–twelfth century BCE Mesopotamia yields a pictorial

37

representation of a plough linked with symbols of the generative act: "archaic intuitions of this sort do not easily disappear, not only from the current popular language, but even from the vocabulary of noted writers [*mais même du vocabulaire des écrivains de marques*]" (*Traité*, 227 [§95]). Immediately following this statement, having again suggested the surprise of a literary connection through his use of the telltale word "even," Eliade (227) cites Rabelais's use of the expression "*membre qu'on nomme le laboureur de la nature*" in *Gargantua*, book 2, chapter 1.

Aside from the reference to Flaubert's *Madame Bovary* in the "Foreword" and a section on "The Degradation of Myth" to be considered later, this allusion to Rabelais is *Traité*'s only reference to a post-medieval Western literary artist. Moreover, the only literary artist, unless Kierkegaard is considered as such, to be mentioned more than once in *Traité* is Dante. His glimpse, in Saturn's heaven, of the golden ladder on which contemplative souls ascend (*Paradiso* 21–22), is cited as an example of ascension symbolism anticipated by the biblical Jacob's dream of the heavenly ladder (Gen. 28:12) and a Muslim tradition that ascribes a similar vision to Muḥammad, and in turn anticipating St. John of the Cross's representation of the steps of mystical perfection as an ascent of Mount Carmel (Eliade, *Traité*, 100 [§34]). Dante's description of "*l'albero che vive de la cima*" (the tree which lives from the top), viewed in heaven (*Paradiso* 18.29), is later cited as exemplifying the ideogram of the inverted tree or plant with which the cosmos has been identified, from (reportedly) Plato, through Jewish mysticism (in the *Zohar*), a particular Muslim tradition, and Dante's fellow Florentine poet and imitator, Federigo Frezzi (in his *Il Quadriregio*, bk. 4, ch. 2), as well as Finnish and Icelandic folklore, and various Lapp and Australian Aboriginal rituals (*Traité*, 240–41 [§100]).

As should be clear from our examples, Eliade's general phenomenological tendency in *Traité* is to survey instances of a given hierophany cross-culturally or, when tarrying momentarily upon one particular culture, by moving forward in time. When he does the latter, he typically starts with the hierophany's primordial "model," "prototypical," or "archetypal" form and then examines a succession of its perceived recurrences chronologically. In the rare instances where he follows these through to any literary manifestations, he stops with the mention of one or several of them—and offers no elaboration. In one exceptional case, the movement is counter-chronological. This occurs when he considers ritual contests between summer and winter to illustrate his own thesis that every ritual repeats a primal action involving divine beings *in illo tempore*. Summarizing Swedish folklorist Waldemar Liungman's (1883–1978) compilation of numerous variants of songs in which representatives of each "season" take turns reciting a stanza, he starts with Liungman's consideration of "the popular-literary form," which Liungman deemed to be "not earlier than the fifteenth century [CE]," and then follows Liungman's retracing of the theme of this contest backwards through "numerous medieval and ancient literary traditions (*Des Poppe Hofton*, a fifteenth-century manuscript, Hans Sachs' poem *Gesprech zwischen dem Sommer und Winter*, 1538, the Latin poem *Conflictus Veris et Hiemis* of the eighth–ninth centuries, Virgil's third Eclogue, the fifth Idyll of Theocritus, etc.)," eventually "identifying the mythic archetype with the [annual] contest between Tiamat and Marduk" (*Traité*, 275 [§122]).

"The Degradation of Myths"

The last, and by far the most elaborated and suggestive, discussion of literature in *Traité* is the entire section titled "The Degradation of Myths" (§165), which closes the book's twelfth and penultimate chapter. The title is unfortunate. To be sure, theories of the "degeneration" and "decay" of religions, easily transferable to myths, were posited by renowned scholars from the seventeenth century on.[16] Yet, when applied, as it is by Eliade so soon after the fall of Germany's Third Reich, with modern literature largely in mind as the forum in which the mythic "degradation" has occurred, the word may be easily confused with Nazi theories of and rhetoric about "degenerate art" (*Entartete Kunst*). Be this as it may, the positive flipside of the negative-sounding term "degradation" for Eliade is "survivals," in Edward B. Tylor's quasi-evolutionist sense of it as denoting "processes, customs, opinions, and so forth, which have been carried on by force of habit into a new state of society different from that in which they had their original home, and they thus remain as proofs and examples of an older condition of culture out of which a newer has been evolved" (*Primitive*, 1:16). In opening his section on "degraded" myths in *Traité*, Eliade adapts this term (with no mention of Tylor) to connote specifically literary "survivals," among others:

> The myth may become degraded [*peut se dégrader*] into an epic legend, a ballad, or a novel, or still survive [*survivre*] in the diminished form of "supersititions," customs, nostalgias, etc.; for this, it loses neither its structure not its import. . . . The "trials," sufferings,

peregrinations of the candidate for initiation survive [*survivent*] in the narrative of sufferings and obstacles that the epic or dramatic hero goes through before arriving at his goal (Ulysses, Aeneas, Parsifal, similar characters of Shakespeare, Faust, etc.). All these "trials," these "sufferings," from which the epic, drama, or novel form their material are easily linked with the ritual sufferings and obstacles of "the way to the center" (§146). Without doubt, the "way" does not unfold on the same initiatory plane but, to speak typologically, the wanderings of Ulysses or the quest of the Holy Grail are found again in the great novels of the nineteenth century, not to mention chapbooks [*la littérature de colportage*], whose archaic origins are well known. (*Traité*, 367–368)

Few if any sections of *Traité* epitomize more vividly Eliade's aforementioned habit of offering but a suggestive, tip-of-the-iceberg view of the given subject he is dealing with. In this case, to illustrate further "the degradation of myths," he first points out that the criminal versus detective conflict in police novels recalls the good genie versus bad genie or dragon versus Prince Charming of earlier tales, and various other comparable examples from earlier generations, revealing that the "faint differences of plot are explained by the coloration, orientation, variances of popular sensibility, but the theme has not changed" (368). Regarding this idea that the "theme" remains unchanged beneath its countless varying literary guises whose "faint differences" reflect their shifting times and places, we cannot help its consistency with Eliade's caution elsewhere against the Western inclination to try to reconstruct the history of Indian documents and techniques based upon their apparent innovations, development, and modifications over time. From the Indian perspective, "the historical context of a 'revelation' has only a limited importance; the 'appearance' or 'disappearance' of a soteriological formula on the plane of history can tell us nothing about its 'origin,'" because "the various 'historical moments'—which are at the same time moments of the cosmic becoming—do not *create* doctrines, but only produce *appropriate formulas* for the timeless message" (*Yoga*, 154, italics in text).

Back in *Traité*, whether consciously or not, Eliade appears to adapt this principle of Indian metaphysics to his explanation of mythic degradation in literature—and, in Kierkegaard's case, in life itself. For Eliade, every "new slipping [*nouveau glissement*]" of the theme entails a "thickening [*épaississement*] of the dramatic conflict and personages, a darkening of the original transparency, at the same time as a multiplication of touches of 'local color,'" and yet, like those Indian revelations referred to in *Yoga*, "the models transmitted from the distant past do not disappear; they do not lose their power of reactualization. They remain valuable for the 'modern' consciousness" (*Traité*, 368). To drive home this point, the first example Eliade offers—from "among thousands [*entre mille*]"—is an example almost humorous in its extraordinariness: Achilles and Kierkegaard! Earlier in *Patterns*, in the section on "Periodicity—the Eternal Present" (§149), Kierkegaard's construal of the Christian condition through the formula of "being contemporary with Jesus" was cited, likewise paradoxically, as being "less revolutionary than it first seems," as it resembles the efforts of all "primitives" to place themselves in "mythic time": "Kierkegaard has done nothing but formulate in new terms a general and normal attitude of archaic man" (*Traité*, 336–337). Here, however, the focus is on Kierkegaard's lifelong bachelorhood, a trait he shares with Achilles. Achilles, Eliade points out, resisted the happy, fecund life that had been predicted for him, had he married, because in that case he would have given up his becoming a hero, and his uniqueness and immortality that came concomitantly with that status.

> Kierkegaard passes through exactly the same existential drama with regard to Regina (*sic*) Olsen; he refuses marriage in order to remain himself, "the unique," to be able to hope for the eternal, by rejecting the modality of a happy existence in the "general." He discloses himself clearly in a fragment of his intimate Journal. . . . "I would be happier, in a finite sense, if I could remove this thorn that I sense in my flesh; but in an infinite sense, I would be lost." And behold how a mythic structure continues to be realizable, in effect realizes itself, on the plane of existential experience, and, in this particular case, assuredly, with neither consciousness of nor influence by the mythic model. (*Traité*, 368)

This passage is remarkable for two reasons, the first of which is its implication that the process of "degradation of myths" not only persists on the literary plane, but pushes through to the "the plane of existential experience" itself. But second, and even more extraordinarily, in recalling for us Eliade's self-comparison and sense of "psycho-intellectual affinity" with Kierkegaard, with which we began this article, the Kierkegaard-Achilles comparison, and particularly the inclusion of the famous, cryptic "thorn in the flesh" allusion from Kierkegaard's journal (which Eliade was reading obsessively in the period of *Traité*'s composition, as we know from his *Portugal Journal*), represent an unmistakable point of contact between *Traité*'s morphology and

Eliade's own life.[17] Inasmuch as he both identifies with Kierkegaard existentially while remaining alien to the "mythic structure" under discussion, Eliade appears here, whether intentionally or not, to have *lived out* his methodological conviction, articulated in *Forge*, that the "only one way of understanding a cultural phenomenon which is alien to one's own ideological pattern . . . is to place oneself at its very centre and from there to track down all the values that radiate from it" (11).

Eliade does not end his discussion of "degradation of myths" without elaborating a second and last example of his rule that "the archetype continues to be creative even though it has 'degraded' to lower and lower levels" (*Traité*, 369): the myth of the Fortunate Isles or of the Terrestrial Paradise, which, he explains, developed from the Phoenicians to the Portuguese, inspiring all the great geographical discoveries, and "retain[ing] their mythic character long after geography became scientific" (369). Having passed through the Age of Reason and the Romantic era, the "Isles of the Blessed" survive to the present day, though "the mythic island no longer signifies the Terrestrial Paradise": it is the "Isle of Love" in Camões' epic *Os Lusíadas*, the Island of the "good savage" in Daniel Defoe's *Robinson Crusoe*, the Isle of Euthanasius in Mihai Eminescu's *Cezara*, a novel on which Eliade had written a study published in 1943 (see *Insula*; and also *Portugal*, 76; *Images*,12n3). These examples, and more, occasion a final reiteration of Eliade's theory that "at all levels of human experience, as lowly as one may consider them, the archetype continues to valorize life, and to create 'cultural values': the Isle of modern novels or the Isle of Camões is no less a value of culture than the so many islands of medieval literature" (369). In these literary works, as in even the most banal actions of modern humans expressing "the nostalgia for Paradise," "archaic spirituality survives . . . as a *nostalgia* that creates autonomous values: art, sciences, social doctrine, etc." (370, italics and ellipses in text).

Conclusion

This sign-off to *Traité*'s section on "degradation of myths," far from actually concluding anything, seems bursting with open-ended suggestiveness, as is punctuated by the use of "etc." in place of a definitively final period. As with the "magnificent book" envisioned at the end of *Shamanism* (likewise with closing ellipses), but never written, on the ecstatic sources of epic, lyric poetry, and drama, we may safely suspect that Eliade here is again contemplating a whole other book, likewise never to be written, on "degraded" myths in modern literature. (This latter book would be quite distinct from the also-never-to-be-written "complementary volume" to *Traité*, projected in his "Conclusions.") We know this from a footnote in his *Images et symboles*, published in 1952, three years after *Traité*: "What an inspiring study it would be, to bring to light the real spiritual function of the nineteenth century novel which, despite all scientific, realistic or social 'formulas,' remained the great repository of degraded myths!" (*Images* 11n2).

Such works as these that Eliade dreamed of, but never wrote, including also the planned books on Balzac and Camões, would have followed through on his perception of symbol, myth, and image as "the very substance of the spiritual life," which have been "disguised, mutilated or degraded" as well as "humbled, minimised, condemned to incessant change of form, and yet survived that hibernation, *thanks chiefly to literature*" (*Images*, 11, emphasis mine). Beyond *Traité*, glimpses of the directions this vision would have led Eliade can be caught here and there throughout his other writings—most explicitly, albeit tersely, in the little piece "Literary Imagination and Religious Structure" (1978; in *Symbolism*, 171–77), as well as in his various accounts of the modern "camouflaging" of the sacred and of myths (see, e.g., *Symbolism*, 32–52).

Consider some of the glimpses afforded by his other four foundational works. In *Yoga*, there is his substantial treatment of that centerpiece of the Indian literary—or, more precisely, *smṛti*, "what is remembered"—tradition, the *Mahābhārata*, as amounting to an "encyclopedia" (150) of the Yogic tradition. This includes of course the epic's "jewel," the *Bhagavad Gītā*, the "highest point" (153) or "apogee of Indian spirituality," in which "by far the greater part of the modern yogic literature . . . finds its theoretical justification" (161). In *Shamanism*, there is not only the effort to trace epic, lyric, and drama back to shamanic origins (213–214, 395, 510–511), but Eliade also detects survivals of shamanic spirituality in Nordic sagas and Eddic literature (*Shamanism*, 161–162, 379–387), and elaborates further upon the tradition of visions of a heavenly ladder, including Dante's, summarized in *Traité*, now linking that tradition to the "countless examples of shamanic ascent to the sky by means of a ladder" (487–494; here 487). In *The Myth of the Eternal Return*, Eliade identifies Dostoevsky as a questioner of Hegelian and Marxist dialectic as antidotes to the terror of history (*Eternal Return*, 149), and recognizes works of T. S. Eliot and James Joyce as being "saturated with nostalgia for the myth of eternal repetition and . . . for the abolition of time" (153). And in *Forge*, aside from finding what he takes to be the central idea of alchemy, the elimination of time, expressed (predictably) in Ben Jonson's play *The Alchemist* (*Forge*, 53, 171) but also (perhaps unexpectedly) in the "literary ideologies of Balzac and Victor Hugo" (173), Eliade submits that "the smith, in virtue of the sacred character of his craft, the mythologies and genealogies of which he is the keeper, and his association with the shaman and the warrior, has come to play a significant part in the creation and diffusion of epic poetry" (88; see also 111).

To any of these hints would apply Eliade's comment regarding the last: "We cannot dwell . . . on this complex and fascinating problem, which would indeed require quite a lengthy exposition" (*Forge*, 88). Yet one thing is certain. Had he indeed pursued "a lengthy exposition" on any of these or innumerable other points he broached in bringing the history of religions and literature to bear upon one another, he would have done so with a cross-cultural, comparative, "universalist" orientation—as when, in *The Myth of the Eternal Return*, he points to the *Mahābhārata* and the Homeric epics, where "at least one of [a hero's] parents is divine" (42), to show how the metamorphosis of historical figures into mythic or epic heroes typically conforms to a mythic paradigm. Such sweeping generalizations would be sure only to exasperate his critics, intent on the virtue of emphasizing "difference" over "sameness." Eliade was of a different camp, as he states in, of all places, his preface of 1975 to his *History of Religious Ideas*:

> I also share the conviction of those who think that the study of Dante or Shakespeare, and even of Dostoevski or Proust, is illuminated by a knowledge of Kalidasa, the Noh plays, or the *Pilgrim Monkey* [i.e., the Chinese epic novel *Xiyouji* or *The Journey to the West*]. This is . . . simply a matter of not losing sight of the profound and indivisible unity of the history of the human mind. (*History*, 1:xvi)

Notes

1. Three weeks after making the claim quoted at the opening of our present article, Eliade writes: "I've known for a long time, and have liked, Kierkegaard's obsession with finding 'the idea for which I would live and die'" (January 25, 1945, *Portugal*, 167).

2. On Kierkegaard's self-conception as a literary artist, see Ziolkowski, *Literary Kierkegaard*, 3, 26–32. Likewise, in his journal from the early 1940s, Eliade acknowledges his own "literary genius" (May 6, 1942, *Portugal*, 21), having already sensed "that I am a great writer and that my novels will be the only things read . . . a hundred years from now" (June 13, 1941, ibid., 6). Eliade has much to say about Kierkegaard's graphomania and prolixity;

see Eliade, *Portugal*, 154–55, 158, 175, 184; *Ordeal*, 17. For my own comparison of Eliade and Kierkegaard as graphomaniacs and writers, see Ziolkowski, "Kierkegaard, Fire, and the Prolixity of Filling Time."

3. *OED*, 2nd ed., s.v. "literature," def. 3.b; cf. Ziolkowski [forthcoming]).

4. That is, Eliade, *Journal II* and *III*, covering together 1957–1978; *Autobiography I* and *II*, which he began writing in 1960; *Sacred and the Profane*; *Quest*; *Ordeal*; etc.

5. Claude-Henri Rocquet correctly observes that to label Eliade simply a historian of religions "entails the risk of misunderstanding," for the sacred, as Eliade construes it, "is the lodestone of art as well as of religion." Like Malraux, Eliade "sees art as the coinage of the absolute" (Rocquet, "Preface" to Eliade *Labyrinth*, ix).

6. These works are listed in the index to Eliade, *Portugal*, 278. As Eliade notes in an entry of November 4, 1941, "I make a great many books in my head, but I don't even take the trouble to start writing them" (13).

7. Aside from other examples quoted later in the present article, consider, e.g., "Such an exhaustive comparative study [of shamanic vs. magical elements] is impossible here" (*Shamanism*, 416); "Such a [cultural] history [of metallurgy and the myths accompanying it], even if it were possible, would run into some thousands of pages. But it is extremely doubtful whether it could in fact be written" (*Forge*, 7).

8. Scholars have often complained about Sheed's translation of *Traité*. Throughout this article, I offer my own translations in place of hers, citing the section number (§) where pertinent to assist any reader wanting to consult the same passage in *Patterns*.

9. The "Epilogue" was added to the English translation (1964).

10. See Eliade, *Traité*, 393–394, 395 (cf. his reference in his "Foreword" to "a future work" [xiii]); and Smith, "Acknowledgments," 73. The journals of Eliade, particularly the *Portugal Journal* whose composition coincided with the writing of *Traité*, offer no support to Smith's hypothesis, which Smith set forth a decade before the publication of the English translation of *Portugal*, of whose contents he almost certainly had no knowledge by that time. In any event, in an "additional note" appended to the 2004 reprint of his "Acknowledgments" (79n48), Smith concedes that Ricketts's article "Tangled Tale," which examines the compositional history of *Traité*, "supersedes" Smith's "Acknowledgments," as it "also offers evidence from Eliade's journals that Eliade considered, at least in retrospect, the *Histoire des croyances et des idées religieuses* to be the promised sequel to *Traité*." Most telling is Eliade's claim in the "Preface" to *History of Religious Ideas*: "For years I have had in mind a short, concise work, which could be read in a few days. For continuous reading reveals above all the fundamental unity of religious phenomena and at the same time the inexhaustible newness of the expressions. . . . Alas, that short, concise book has not yet been written. For the moment, I have resigned myself to presenting a work in three volumes, in the hope of eventually reducing it to one volume of some 400 pages" (xiv–xv). Clearly that envisioned but never-written "short, concise [one-volume] work," whose "some 400 pages" would roughly match the length of *Traité*, would have been the "complementary volume" Eliade had originally projected for *Traité*. For, while *Traité* accounted *morphologically*

(or phenomenologically) for "the fundamental unity of religious phenomena," *A History of Religious Ideas*—presumably the extended version of that never-written "concise work"—accounts *historically* for "the inexhaustible newness of the expressions [of the sacred]."

11. Although Eliade never wrote the book he envisioned on Camões, an entry of September 3, 1942, in his journal states: "The second major article of mine, 'Camões e Eminescu,' appears today in *Acção*. A whole page" (*Portugal*, 33).

12. Cf. Eliade's analogy citing Dante's *Divina commedia* and Balzac's *Comédie humaine* in *Quest*, 4–5.

13. See note 10 above.

14. Consider the subtitle of *Autobiography II*, viz. "Exile's Odyssey."

15. Eliade likewise links the Ulysses myth with the labyrinth motif in his *Ordeal by Labyrinth* (see 95), whose title he conceived as "a quite accurate expression, I feel, of the whole human condition" (27).

16. Thus, for example, the Dutch classicist and theologian Gerardus Johannes Vossius (Gerrit Janszoon Vos, 1577–1649), in his *De theologia gentili et physiologia christiana, sive de origine ac progressu idoloatriae . . .* (Amsterdam, 1642), submitted that the earliest humans had a perfect understanding of God, but that heathen religions had led that primordial monotheism to degenerate and disappear (Ström, 234). Four centuries later, Wilhelm Schmidt, in his *Ursprung der Gottesidee*, developed a similar theory, well known to Eliade (e.g., *Quest*, 24–25, 46–47), of an *Urmonotheismus* that gradually later "degraded" and "degenerated." Meanwhile, F. Max Müller spoke more generally of "the inevitable decay to which every religion is exposed" (*Chips* 1:xxii–xxiii), and of every religion's "dialectic growth and decay" (*Introduction*, 201 [lect. 4]).

17. On Kierkegaard's "thorn in the flesh" see Ziolkowski, *Literary*, 229. Stan, for whom Eliade's "interaction" with Kierkegaard reaches "its apex" in the *Portugal Journal* (Stan, 63), conjectures: "Eliade equates the 'thorn in the flesh' with an 'actual,' though indirect and unpremeditated, murder of the beloved" (68), i.e., his feelings of guilt over the death of his first wife from an affliction that may have resulted from an abortion she had once had, at his encouragement—whereas scholars have variously hypothesized that Kierkegaard's own "thorn in the flesh" is an allusion to a Kierkegaard family curse brought on by a sin committed by Søren's father, or to an alleged visit Søren made to a brothel as a youth, or to syphilis contracted as a result. On these hypotheses, see, e.g., Stan 68n100; and Ziolkowski, *Literary*, 29, 116, 350n27. In any event, just as Kierkegaard's "biographical relevance [for Eliade] disappears when Eliade leaves Lisbon for Paris [September 1945], where he would launch his imposing scholarly career" (Stan, 75), it makes sense in view of his long and happy second marriage (from 1950 to his death) that Eliade would henceforth identify neither with Achilles nor Kierkegaard but, as we have seen, with that other Homeric hero, the contentedly married Ulysses.

Works Cited

Dobre, Catalina Elena. "Kierkegaard and the Romanian Culture (After Kierkegaard's Example)." *Acta Kierkegaardiana* 2 (2007):257–269.

Eliade, Mircea. *Autobiography, Volume I: 1907–1937: Journey East, Journey West.* Translated by Mac Linscott Ricketts. San Francisco: Harper and Row, 1981.

———. *Autobiography, Volume II: 1937–1960: Exile's Odyssey.* Translated by Mac Linscott Ricketts. Chicago: University of Chicago Press, 1988.

———. *The Forge and the Crucible: The Origins and Structures of Alchemy.* 2nd edition. Translated by Stephen Corrin. Chicago: University of Chicago Press, 1978.

———. *A History of Religious Ideas.* 3 vols. Translated by Willard R. Trask et al. Chicago: University of Chicago Press, 1979–85.

———. *Images and Symbols: Studies in Religious Symbolism.* Translated by Philip Mairet. Princeton: Princeton University Press, 1991.

———. *Insula lui Euthanasius.* Bucharest: Fundatia Regala pentru Literatura si Arta, 1943.

———. *Journal II: 1957–1969.* Translated Fred H. Johnson Jr. Chicago: University of Chicago Press, 1989.

———. *Journal III: 1970–1978.* Translated by Teresa Lavender Fagan. Chicago: University of Chicago Press, 1989.

———. *Journal IV: 1979–1985.* Translated by Mac Linscott Ricketts. Epilogue by Wendy Doniger. Chicago: University of Chicago Press, 1990.

———. "Metodele gourmontine." *Cuvântul* (August 6, 1927):1–2.

———. *Myth and Reality.* Translated by Willard R. Trask. New York: Harper and Row, 1963.

———. *Myths, Dreams, and Mysteries: The Encounter between Contemporary Faiths and Archaic Realities.* Translated by Philip Mairet. New York: Harper and Row, 1960.

———. *The Myth of the Eternal Return or, Cosmos and History.* [1954] Translated by Willard R. Trask. [Reprint with corrections] Princeton: Princeton University Press, 1965.

———. *Ordeal by Labyrinth: Conversations with Claude-Henri Rocquet.* Translated by Derek Coltman. Chicago: University of Chicago Press, 1982.

———. *Patterns in Comparative Religion.* [1958] Translated by Rosemary Sheed. New York: New American Library, 1974.

———. *The Portugal Journal.* Translated by Mac Linscott Ricketts. Albany: State University of New York Press, 2010.

———. *The Quest: History and Meaning in Religion.* Chicago: University of Chicago Press, 1969.

———. *The Sacred and the Profane: The Nature of Religion.* Translated by Willard R. Trask. New York: Harcourt Brace Jovanovich, 1959.

———. *Shamanism: Archaic Techniques of Ecstasy.* Translated by Willard R. Trask. Princeton: Princeton University Press, 1964.

———. "Sören Kierkegaard—Logodnic, pamfletar și eremit" ["Søren Kierkegaard: Fiancé, Pamphleteer, and Hermit"]. *Cuvântul* 4, no.1035 (1928): 1.

———. *Symbolism, the Sacred, and the Arts.* Edited by Diane Apostolos-Cappadona. New York: Crossroad, 1988.

———. *The Two and the One.* [1965] Translated by J. M. Cohen. Chicago: University of Chicago Press, 1979. [= *Méphistophélès et l'Androgyne.* Paris: Gallimard, 1962.]

———. *Traité d'histoire des religions*. [1949] Paris: Payot, 1953.

———. *Yoga: Immortality and Freedom*. 2nd ed. Translated by Willard R. Trask. Princeton: Princeton University Press, 1969.

Kant, Immanuel. *Critique of Practical Reason*. Translated and edited by Mary Gregor. Cambridge: Cambridge University Press, 1997.

Liungman, Waldemar. *Der Kampf zwischen Sommer und Winter*. Folklore Fellowship Communications, no. 130. Helsinki: Suomalainen Tiedeakatemia, Academia Scientiarum Fennica, 1941.

Müller, Friedrich Max. *Chips from a German Worship*. 4 vols. New York: C. Scribner, Armstrong, 1871–1876.

———. *Introduction to the Science of Religion* [1873]. London: Longmans, Green, 1899.

Ricketts, Mac Rinscott. *Mircea Eliade: The Romanian Roots, 1907–1945*. 2 vols. New York: Columbia University Press, 1988.

———. "The Tangled Tale of Eliade's Writing of *Traité d'histoire des religions*." *Archaeus: Études d'histoire des religions* 4 (2000):51–77.

Schmidt, Wilhelm. *Der Ursprung der Gottesidee, eine historisch-kritische und positive Studie*. Münster, Aschendorff, 1912–1955.

Smith, Jonathan Z. "Acknowledgments: Morphology and History in Mircea Eliade's *Patterns in Comparative Religion* (1949–1999), Part I: The Work and Its Contexts" [2000]. In *Relating Religion: Essays in the Study of Religion*, 61–79. Chicago: University of Chicago Press, 2004.

Stan, Leo. "Mircea Eliade: On Religion, Cosmos, and Agony." In *Kierkegaard's Influence on the Social Sciences*, edited by Jon Stewart, 55–77. Vol. 13 of *Kierkegaard Research: Sources, Reception and Resources*. Burlington,VT: Ashgate, 2011.

Ström, Åke V. "Monotheismus." In *Theologische Realenzyklopaedie*. 36 vols. (Berlin: De Gruyter, 1977–2004), 23:233–237.

Tylor, Edward B. *Primitive Culture: Researches into the Development of Mythology, Philosophy, Religion, Art, and Custom* [1971]. 2 vols. 6th ed. London: John Murray, 1920.

Ziolkowski, Eric. "Between Religion and Literature: Mircea Eliade and Northrop Frye." *The Journal of Religion* 71.4 (October 1991): 498–522.

———. "Kierkegaard, Fire, and the Prolixity of Filling Time," *Toronto Journal of Theology* 21/1 (spring 2013): 19–36.

———. *The Literary Kierkegaard*. Evanston, IL: Northwestern University Press, 2011.

———. "Literature." In *Vocabulary for the Study of Religion*, edited by Kocku von Stuckrad and Robert Segal. Leiden: Brill, [forthcoming].

3

Eliade and Girard on Myth

John D. Dadosky

Introduction

Mircea Eliade (1907–1986) has fallen out of favor in the mainstream study of religion. The reasons are compound: (1) the increasingly specialized emphasis in religious studies as evidenced by the particular topics in the journal *History of Religions*, a journal that, ironically, Eliade founded, and (2) the postmodern/post-structuralist resistance to the kind of theories he espoused, which often claims them to be ahistorical and unable to account for the particularism of various groups. To make matters worse, there are questions surrounding Eliade's affiliation with fascist groups in Romania during the Second World War. Still, time will tell whether this neglect of his thought is permanent or just a passing fad, and whether the criticisms are well-founded or not. Personally, I believe there is a lot of value to his work. For example, I discovered in my research with the Diné (Navajo) of the Southwestern United States that Eliade's notion of *sacred time, sacred space* and *cosmogenesis* seem to be corroborated by the Diné creation story and in their religious architecture, especially the *hooghan*.

While Eliade may have receded in popularity, the literary critic turned religious thinker, René Girard (b. 1923) is winning fans for his theories of mimetic rivalry and religious violence, theories that are inextricably linked with his interpretation of myths. A peculiar aspect of Girard's method is that his insights are gleaned directly from literary criticism rather than from other scientific approaches. However, at least one aspect of this theory, mimetic envy and rivalry, can often be adequately corroborated by a direct concrete self-reflection and scrutiny of one's own interpersonal relations, rather than by some scientific measure.

Both Eliade and Girard have made contributions to the study of ancient myths and both have a particular view of traditional aboriginal myths. However, Eliade takes a much more favorable view toward aboriginal and indigenous myths than Girard does. Indeed, Girard has what seems to be a pejorative view. For him, all extra-Christian myths contain the themes that embody and perpetuate the cycle of violence. I should state that this is a controversial and untested aspect of Girard's theory that requires a critique and more nuanced reflection. Certainly many myths contain themes of ritual sacrifice, but whether they all do is another question. Hence, Girard makes provocative claims that remain subject to scrutiny by anthropologists and other disciplines.

The purpose of this paper is to present an overview of Eliade's and Girard's respective theories on religious/sacred myths with a view toward clarifying and contrasting the different aspects of sacred myths.

Different Approaches to Myth

It is relevant to this analysis to situate the comparison of Eliade's and Girard's approaches in context of Robert Segal's distinction between the nineteenth- and twentieth-century Western approaches to myth. In the nineteenth century, myth was seen as the "primitive counterpart to science" (*Myth*, 3). Accordingly, myth is inferior to the rational method of science, which is now viewed as replacing previous mythic explanations. "Science rendered myth not merely redundant but outright incompatible, so that moderns, who by definition are scientific, had to reject myth" (3). In contrast to nineteenth-century views of myth, Segal states, "twentieth century theories have tended to see myth as almost anything but an outdated counterpart to science" (3).

Accompanying the nineteenth-century pejorative view of myth were the colonial presuppositions, which dismissed any value to traditional aboriginal views in the so-called New World. Moreover, we can make some further points about the potentially negative aspects of myth.

First, the nineteenth-century approach to myth by science had some legitimate historical context for its suspicion against myth. This is to say there is a distorted approach to myth that refuses the legitimate advances of human knowledge due to an unwillingness to engage mistaken assumptions about the universe or nature. Such mythic consciousness,[1] for example, was behind the condemnation of Galileo. His advances in science challenged the reigning assumptions about the origins of the universe in the Genesis accounts. The Roman Catholic Church pardoned him 500 years later.

Related as well to the context of the nineteenth-century approach to myth is the scientific rejection of myth as superstition—the belief that fortune or misfortune are linked to certain nonrational acts, and by nonrational, I mean that there is no apparent logic or intelligible reason behind a certain behavior. For example, there is a superstition that bad things are more likely to happen on Friday the Thirteenth. While this may indeed have religious rationale in some ancient folk tradition, there is no apparent logical reason to assume that bad luck may befall a person on that day as opposed to any other day or that there is any such thing as bad luck at all. It is a superstition, a perhaps mild example of mythic consciousness. Closely related to this aspect of myth is the belief that the external elements can be controlled. Historically, for example, the practice of alchemy with its belief that base metals can be turned into gold occupied the minds of many, including the early proponents of modern science such as Isaac Newton.

Furthermore, one can ask to what extent did Newton's fascination with alchemy influence his own mythic consciousness regarding the explanatory power of science? If Newton's example teaches us anything, it should be noted that mythic consciousness can be so pervasive that even those who are deeply involved in science can succumb to mythic consciousness. This is especially prevalent in those adherents of classical science whose theories strain for a comprehensive explanation and lead to a scientific reductionism. In such cases, the idea that the scientific classical laws can completely explain natural processes becomes itself a "myth." The legacy of Newton's mechanist determinism, although eclipsed by modern physics, remains an all too seductive ideal for many social scientists.

Finally, there is a pejorative notion of myth that is in many ways less a product of the nineteenth century and a more a product of a less critical approach to myth characteristic of the twentieth century. I refer to the myths that are present in political and religious ideologies. Robert Johnson refers to the ancient Nordic myths that were part of the fabric of the German psyche and provided a propellant for the Third Reich (Johnson, 61). Ideologues can co-opt myths and with rhetorical skill incite mass movements and bloodshed. It is perhaps this aspect of myth that most worries Girard. Myths can function as psychological fuel for the cycle of mimetic rivalry and scapegoating of innocent people.

In addition to the pejorative, negative, and even dangerous aspects of myth, Segal also identifies a positive approach to myth. Such views are more reflective of the twentieth-century approaches in which myth is taken more seriously in its ability to communicate meaning. The rise of anthropology, psychology, and religious studies, to name a few of the principal disciplines, have brought a more positive attitude toward the content and function of myths. Myths can offer data for insight either into a particular group or perhaps more universally into humanity as a whole. Anthropological theories focus on the role of myth in providing a communal frame of reference and meaning for particular societies. Psychological theories, particularly those of Carl Jung, presuppose a universal significance to myth and their function in psychological development. Religious scholars, such as Mircea Eliade, highlight the ability of myths, and non-Western traditional understanding of myths, to communicate something about the deep structures of human societies in their natural expression of religiosity. It is to this expression that Eliade refers in his phrase *homo religiosus*. The myths, like a sacred text, mediate the mysteries of the originating time and place of the creation of a people. In reenacting those myths in ritual contexts, societies can recreate themselves and their worlds. The meaning of such myths provide explanations for the seasons, cycles, and geography by which people live.

In terms of this study, Eliade and Girard reflect positive and pejorative aspects of myth respectively. For Eliade, myth mediates the sacred meanings surrounding the foundations of the cosmos particularized to specific cultural groups. For Girard, myths are about the origin of a culture, but it is a violent origin. Although they may be seen as sacred, the myths conceal extratextual events of violence and a founding murder.

In the following sections, I will look at the respective approaches of Eliade and Girard more closely and offer some concluding thoughts on their different approaches to the understanding of myth.

Eliade: Myth as Sacred, Exemplary, and Cosmogenic[2]

Given the plurality of meanings ascribed to the word "myth," Eliade's definition is very specific. Myth refers to "a 'true story' and, beyond that, a story that is a most precious possession because it is sacred, exemplary, significant." This view of myth is in contrast with the legacy of Enlightenment presuppositions that dismiss myth as fantastic fiction (*Myth and Reality*, 1). In this way, Eliade is in agreement with Segal's comment above, although Eliade places the dismissal in the broader context of the Enlightenment's privileging of logical reason, whereas Segal associates it with the epistemic privilege that accompanied the rise of modern science.

For Eliade, myths of traditional societies are *cosmogenic* in that they recount the original act of creation of the universe or the origin of some created reality that the followers consider to be sacred. He explains:

> Myth narrates a sacred history; it relates an event that took place in primordial Time, the fabled time of the "beginnings." In other words, myth tells how, through the deeds of Supernatural Beings, a reality came into existence, be it the whole of reality, the Cosmos, or only a fragment of reality—an island, a species of plant, a particular kind of human behavior, an institution. Myth, then, is always an account of a "creation"; it relates how something was produced, began to *be*. Myth tells only of that which *really* happened, which manifested itself completely. The actors in myths are Supernatural Beings. They are known primarily by what they did in the transcendent times of the "beginnings." Hence, myths disclose their creative activity and reveal the sacredness (or simply the "supernaturalness") of their works. In short, myths describe the various and sometimes dramatic breakthroughs of the sacred (or the "supernatural") into the World. It is this sudden breakthrough of the sacred that really *establishes* the World and makes it what it is today. (*Myth and Reality*, 5–6)

Since myths of traditional societies recount the origin of existing realities, they are considered sacred and likewise *true* or *real*:

> [M]yth is thought to express the *absolute truth*, because it narrates a *sacred history*; that is, a transhuman revelation which took place at the dawn of the Great Time, in the holy time of the beginnings (*in illo tempore*). Being *real* and *sacred*, the myth becomes exemplary, and consequently *repeatable*, for it serves as a model, and by the same token as justification, for all human actions. In other words, a myth is a *true history* of what came to pass at the beginning of Time, and one which provides the pattern for human behavior. In *imitating* the exemplary acts of a god or of a mythic hero, or simply by recounting their adventures, the man of an archaic society detaches himself from profane time and magically re-enters the Great Time, the sacred time. (*Myths, Dreams*, 23)

Myth is "regarded as a sacred story, and hence a 'true history,' because it always deals with *realities*." Accordingly, Eliade contrasts sacred or mythic time with profane, historical time. "[B]y 'living' the myths one emerges from profane, chronological time and enters a time that is of a different quality, a 'sacred' Time at once primordial and indefinitely recoverable" (*Myth and Reality*, 6, 18). Douglas Allen explains:

> In Eliade's interpretation, the mythic person views homogeneous, irreversible, ordinary profane time and history as without significant

meaning. By contrast, the sacred time and history of myth and religion are significant and meaningful. What is ordinarily part of profane time and history can become part of a coherent, significant world of meaning only when it is experienced through superhuman, exemplary, transcendent, mythic and other sacred structures. (206)

For Eliade, myth, as a recounting of the "true" history of a particular group, serves as an exemplary model for human behavior. Consequently, the origin of much of the cultural and religious norms of traditional societies are traceable to the paradigmatic patterns established by the characters in these sacred myths. As a sacred story, the myth recounts the actions of the gods or divinities in the primordial time of creation. The principal resource for the behavioral and ethical code of the community lies in the sacred myths. These contain the significant meanings of a group or culture that they hold to be sacred, ultimately true, real, and valuable (*Myth and Reality*, 6–7). Moreover, the themes of these myths carry over into the symbolic life of a group in the symbols of the (1) sacred center, the place representing where the sacred is most readily accessible, (2) sacred space that symbolizes the sacred geography and reenacts its creation, and (3) sacred time that depicts the original moment of creation. In the case of the Diné, or Navajo, for example, the traditional dwelling or *hooghan* is at once a center, in that it is the primary setting for religious ceremonies; a symbol of sacred space, in that it symbolically represents the sacred geography; and a symbol of sacred time in its representation of the originating time of creation and the emergence of the people from between the four sacred mountains.[3]

Sacred myths are the perennial resource for the religious and cultural behavior of the community and so serve as the foundation for religious life and rituals. The primary means of contact with the sacred for the religious person is through a ritual life that repeats or ritually imitates the original acts and original time of the gods or mythical ancestors depicted in the sacred myths (*Eternal Return*, 22). Eliade claims that "for the traditional societies, all the important acts of life were revealed *aborigine* by gods or heroes. [Human beings] only repeat these exemplary and paradigmatic gestures *ad infinitum*" (*Eternal Return*, 32).

This ritual performance of sacred myths is inextricably linked to his anthropology of *homo religiosus*. Psychologically, the latter represents the self-transcending person who yearns for perennial contact with the sacred beyond the ephemeral. The sacred is a reality often symbolized in a powerful regenerative center where one can more easily accesses it.

More precisely, myths reveal reality through *archetypes*, although Eliade does not mean what Jung means by archetypes. Eliade means that myths contain the source for ritually repeated "exemplary and paradigmatic gestures." He explains:

> I have used the terms "exemplary models," "paradigms," and "arche-
> types" in order to emphasize a particular fact—namely that for the
> man of traditional and archaic societies, the models for his institutions
> and the norms for his various categories of behavior are believed
> to have been "revealed" at the beginning of time, [and] that, conse-
> quently, they are regarded as having a superhuman and "transcen-
> dental" origin. In using the term "archetype," I neglected to specify
> that I was not referring to the archetypes described by Professor
> C. G. Jung. This was a regrettable error. For to use, in an entirely
> different meaning, a term that plays a role of primary importance in
> Jung's psychology could lead to confusion. I need scarcely say that, for
> Professor Jung, the archetypes are structures of the collective uncon-
> scious. But in my book I nowhere touch upon the problems of depth
> psychology nor do I use the concept of the collective unconscious. As
> I have said, I use the term "archetype," just as Eugenio d'Ors does, as
> a synonym for "exemplary model" or "paradigm," that is, in the last
> analysis, in the Augustinian sense. But in our day the word has been
> rehabilitated by Professor Jung, who has given it new meaning; and
> it is certainly desirable that the term "archetype" should no longer
> be used in its pre-Jungian sense unless the fact is distinctly stated.
> (*Eternal Return*, xiv–xv)

For Eliade, the archetypes operate as paradigms or exemplary models that are revealed in the creation myths of traditional societies. We have indicated that they are considered sacred and real, relative to profane time history. Specifically with respect to myth, the archetypes are *real* and have the power to confer reality insofar as one imitates them. In turn, the extent to which reality is conferred on the profane time is the extent to which the profane becomes sacred. Imitation involves repeat-ing the archetypes or exemplary models established by the "gods" or mythical ancestors. Accordingly, Eliade states: "an object or act becomes real only insofar as it imitates or repeats an archetype. Thus, reality is acquired solely through repetition or participation; everything which lacks an exemplary model is 'meaningless,' i.e., it lacks reality" (*Eternal Return*, 34). Hence, the repetition of archetypes as acted out in the ritual life of traditional aboriginal cultures enables the actors to stay in close contact with the sacred while simultaneously enabling them to confer reality and meaning (i.e., constitute reality and meaning) upon every aspect of their lives. "[T]his repetition has a meaning. . . . [I]t alone confers reality upon events; events repeat themselves because they imitate an archetype—the exemplary event" (*Eternal Return*, 90). He explains further:

> What does living mean for a man who belongs to a traditional culture? Above all, it means living in accordance with extrahuman models, in conformity with archetypes. Hence it means living at the heart of the *real* since . . . there is nothing truly real except the archetypes. Living in conformity with the archetypes amounted to respecting the "law," since the law was only a primordial hierophany, the revelation *in illo tempore* of the norms of existence, a disclosure by a divinity or a mystical being. And if, through the repetition of paradigmatic gestures and by means of periodic ceremonies, archaic man succeeded, as we have seen, in annulling time, he none the less lived in harmony with the cosmic rhythms. (*Eternal Return*, 95)

To sum up, for Eliade, sacred myths are the "revelations" to particular traditional societies that tell the story of the sacred origins of a people, their land or geography, and their customs and rituals. They are imbued with archetypes that serve as models to guide ethical and religious behavior and rituals. As stories acted out in rituals, myths can be restorative: during the ritual, one returns to the sacred time and place of the foundation of the world, and one is regenerated, symbolically reborn in the renewed creation represented by the ceremony or ritual. Closely related to the cycles and cosmic rhythms, the sacred myth reflects the continuing of the sacred story in the memory and performance of a people.

Girard: Myth and Violence

In order to summarize Girard's view of myth, one must first be acquainted with some basic features of his theory of religious violence. Girard's background is not religious studies but literary criticism. From his genetic engagement with classical literary texts, he developed a theory of religious violence that also has implications for psychology, particularly for what he would come to call "interdividual psychology" (Girard, *Hidden*, 368 ff). In contradistinction to Emmanuel Levinas's emphasis on the spontaneous deference to the other that flows from a sense of responsibility, interdividual relations imply an obsession with another person, that is, either a "model" who has something one covets, or with the mimetic rival or double with whom one is in competition for the coveted "object."

The root of Girard's theory is mimetic or triangular desire (Golsan, 1–2). It begins when a desire is aroused in a person for something a mediator or model possesses. In order to obtain it, one emulates the model. Individuals inevitably find themselves in competition with others for the same thing. We envy what the model possesses, and this sets off a mimetic rivalry with others who want the same thing we do. The triangular nature of this desire is comprised by the model and the two parties who are competing for what the model possesses. There is a frustration that the competitors encounter as they pursue the object of their mutual desiring. The obstacles to one's attainment or scandals (from the Greek *skandalon*) increase the volatility and frustration of the rivalry. Within a community, the rivalry becomes contagious and leads to the desire to vent the frustration on someone who is innocent (Girard, *Satan*, xi–xii). The scapegoating of an innocent person restores equilibrium and gives the community a temporary reprieve from the mimetic tensions (*Satan*, 43).

For Girard, this scapegoating or single-victim mechanism is inextricably bound up with the origin of a culture or civilization. Such a mechanism is coded into the founding myths of the cultures, but as the myths are handed down generationally and dispersed through various versions, they also disguise the founding murder, the original scapegoating event upon which the culture is founded. Girard calls this *mythic crystallization* (*Scapegoat*, 88–94).[4] Myths "originate in real or historical events and are in fact distorted representations of these events" (Golson, 61). Over time, this mythic crystallization distorts, waters down, or disguises the extra-textual events of the founding murder. Prima facie it may not appear that a particular myth contains the founding murder. However, upon closer inspection, Girard is able to detect its traces. Those traces, he believes, inevitably lead back to the founding murder of a scapegoat, which subsequent retellings have disguised.

One of the examples Girard cites is the myth of Romulus and Remus, the founders of Rome. First, there are varying accounts of the death of Romulus: in one of them he ascends to heaven on a cloud. However, in three of the accounts, according to Plutarch, Romulus is also a victim of collective violence (*Scapegoat*, 88). For Girard, these latter versions are probably more accurate than the one of his celestial ascension. This is because, Girard claims, as myths are handed down from generation to generation, there is a tendency to sanitize them of any evidence of a collective murder. "Mythological transformation moves in only one direction, toward the elimination of any traces of violence" (*Scapegoat*, 94).

Similarly, there are conflicting accounts of the death of Remus. In one account, Remus is killed spontaneously by mocking and thus provoking Romulus. In other accounts, Remus is killed out of envy as the culmination of a rivalry between the two. The collective component of Remus's death is literally lost in the translation from the Latin (Girard, *Scapegoat*, 6).[5] Again, for Girard, the second story is probably the older and more authentic account. In the words of Golson, "It has been 'doctored' by subsequent transmitters of myth so that the unpalatable taste of unanimous violence is removed" (80).

At this point, Girard's argumentation may sound impossible to refute. One is reminded of the tautological arguments made by Freud, where resistance to his theory is indicative of a person in denial. While it may be that Girard is too exhaustive in the application of his theory, perhaps out of the enthusiasm of his important discoveries, it is still interesting that a similar presupposition in his analysis of Job corroborates the historical critical analysis (Golson, 97). For example, it is commonly held that the prologue of Job (i.e., Job 1:6–8), where God makes an agreement with the accuser, was probably added later and is historically separate from the dialogues of the text. "The Job of the Dialogues is not the Job of the prologue" (Girard, *Job* 11). In the dialogues, Job's anguish is linked to his being taunted and blamed by the community for his own misfortune (*Job* 19:13–19). Job has been scapegoated by his community, and the prologue covers up this event.

The redaction of adding the prologue after the fact is evidence, at least for Girard, of the crystallization of the story. In his view, this reveals the de-emphasis or covering over of the mob's scapegoating and blaming of Job that is evidenced by their accusations that he is somehow responsible for his own misfortune. The addition of the prologue not only glosses over the community's scapegoating of Job, but it does this by emphasizing that his misfortunes are justified by the divine sanction, i.e., God's desire to test his faithful servant by sanctioning the devil to do so.

Because Eliade focuses on archaic and traditional indigenous traditions, let's look at how Girard analyzes a Nanda myth of South Africa (Girard, "Nanda," 152–53). As we will see, there is not much difference in his analysis from the Western notions of myth. Girard focuses on the story of the god Python. He has two wives. The second wife does not realize that her husband is a god. The first wife conspires to keep Python's divine identity hidden from the second wife. However, the second wife remains curious and eventually discovers his true identity.

In response to her discovering his secret, Python takes flight and hides in the bottom of a distant lake. However, following upon his withdrawal, all of the water from his home area also disappears and a drought ensues. Upon discerning the "true" nature of the problem, the village seeks to appease the god by returning his second wife to him. They send her into the lake with a beer offering. She submerges and disappears. The drought abruptly ends, and the crisis is resolved. According to Girard, this myth conceals an "extratextual" event of a real death to a real victim at the hands of a crowd. The second wife is a scapegoated victim of collective violence. Generations of mythic crystallization conceal this fact.

Girard spends a considerable amount of time arguing for his distinctive hermeneutics. While a more extensive critical engagement of this approach lies outside the scope of this paper, his creative hermeneutics is worth probing deeper, if for no other reason than to raise the issue of the cause of religious violence, or what he sometimes refers to as "deviated transcendence."

To sum up Girard's thinking about myths: he does not distinguish between ancient classical Western myths and the myths of traditional aboriginal societies. Therefore, his approach to the latter is equally pejorative and even echoes previous colonial approaches. Myths are often communal stories that refer to extratextual events of collective murder against the innocent. This scapegoating functions as the founding of a society. Subsequent versions of the myth, as they are handed on through generations, conceal the fact of these violent origins in an attempt to sanitize them. The emerging historical revelation in the ancient Hebrew and Christian scriptures reveal that God intervenes in history to take the side of the victim and propel humanity beyond these violent mechanisms. While Girard's arguments concerning the extratextual events are all but impossible to verify, still, the provocative nature of his approach demands further reflection. As stated at the outset, on several accounts Girard's approach to myth is controversial.

Observations and Concluding Comments

The first thing to observe when comparing Eliade and Girard's respective approaches to myth is that they both have philosophically anthropological starting points. For Eliade, human beings are naturally religious, and he calls this universal orientation of the human spirit *homo religiosus*. It is this religious component of human beings that moves them to imbue their world with religious symbols of transcendence. In this way, communities inevitably express the religious symbols of their lives consciously or unconsciously. This is true even in a secular age where explicit religious belief has been eclipsed in many ways. The religious imagination does not fail to find its expression in elaborate architecture, whether it be in the towers of finance or, as the elaborate cathedral-style Eaton Centre in downtown Toronto demonstrates, in shopping malls. In developing his theory of *homo religiosus*, after scouring the data on the various world religions, Eliade's anthropology opens up to a universal religiousness beyond the specificity of a particular tradition. It is an anthropology that matches, at least to some extent, his own movement away from the Eastern Orthodox Christianity of his upbringing in Romania and toward a more generic interest in the sacred as contradistinguished from the profane.

Girard's anthropological presuppositions, on the other hand, are not as generous as Eliade's toward the nature of the human spirit. Rather than being naturally religious in the positive sense of the word, human beings are naturally prone to mimetic rivalry and violence, a drive perhaps rooted in their lower animal instincts for survival. They are far too easily caught up in the contagion that leads to the scapegoating mechanism—the death of the innocent victim. Moreover, Girard's generic encounter with myth leads to his belief that the evidence emerging in the Hebrew scriptures and coming to fullness in the Christian New Testament is the historical insight that God is not violent, does not want sacrifices, and that Jesus Christ is the ultimate scapegoat whose sacrifice began the end of scapegoating once and for all. He is the scapegoat who sets history on an eschatological trajectory toward the ultimate overcoming of the murder of innocent people.

In contrast to Eliade, who moved away from the religious traditions of his youth, Girard's discoveries lead to his conversion, or perhaps more accurately, to a profound reappropriation of the nominal Christianity of his childhood. It is perhaps paradoxical that, as a postmodern theorist, the priority Girard gives the Christian narrative over and above other myths, including aboriginal myths, invites a postcolonial critique.

Next, the two thinkers have differing presuppositions about the foundations of culture in relation to myth. For Eliade, cultural codes, customs, moral behavior, and the like have their origin within traditional societies in the stories contained in the sacred myths. The myths provide the etiological explanations for the codes and conduct of a people, despite the fact that the specific knowledge of those explanations varies among individuals in a society.

For Girard, on the other hand, the sacred myths often cover over, through mythic crystallization, the fact that many societies are founded on the basis of the murder of an innocent person as the resultant climax of a mimetic scandal. We noted above the founding murder upon which Rome was established, but in addition Girard notes that following Cain's murder of Abel and the former's exile, Cain founds a community (Gen. 4:16–17). Girard emphasizes the violent origins of a society and the role that myth plays in covering over that "real" history (*Things Hidden*, 39, 146, 159).

Closely related to these contrasting views of the foundation of culture are the scholars' differing views about religion. For Eliade, religion is a primary vehicle through which *homo religious* may encounter, and perennially return to, the sacred. Religious beliefs, practices, and rituals provide an ongoing access to the sacred, and with it, a resource for personal and social transformation. For Girard, on the other hand, the criteria for authentic religious practice is proportionate to the extent to which the religious tradition overcomes the scapegoat mechanism and becomes an advocate for the poor and the marginalized. For Girard, the Judeo-Christian tradition exemplifies this view in the unfolding of the historical revelation where God incarnate, crucified and resurrected, sets humanity on a new course of nonviolence by testifying, reversing and ameliorating this mimetic cycle of violence. This is not to say that there are no authentic manifestations of nonviolence in other religious traditions, nor is it to hide the fact that throughout history Christians have participated in the scapegoating process. Rather, for Girard, it is to say that that religion can be a vehicle for violence, and it is only true religion, that is, religion that transcends sacrifice, that overcomes such violence.

Closely related to their contrasting views of religion are their views on history relative to myth. For Eliade, myth is distinguished from temporal history. As distinguished from temporal history, the sacred myth provides an escape from profane time to that originating moment of cosmogenesis. It represents the eternal moment to which one returns in order to reencounter the sacred and rejuvenate and restore oneself and one's community. Religious rituals repeat archetypal gestures to relive the time of creation. And Eliade writes: "any repetition of an archetypal gesture, suspends duration, abolishes profane time, and participates in mythical time" (*The Myth of the Eternal Return*, 36). Clearly, "there is an implicit abolition of profane time, of duration, of 'history'" (*The Myth of the Eternal Return*, 35).

By contrast, given his reappropriated Christian faith, Girard's theory entails a history that is linear and eschatological. It is one that implies a salvation history wherein centuries of revelation unfold in order to communicate and implement the insight that God takes the side of the victim, detests violence, and seeks to overcome it in the eschatological proleptic reverberations of the Christ event. History is linear, but it also has a term, a goal, and a potential culmination.

Also, something should be said about the contrasting use of the term *model* in the two thinkers' respective approaches to myth. For Eliade, the myth provides what Girard would describe as *external mediators* in that the sacred myths provide the accounts of actions of the divinities and gods from the time of creation to be emulated. In order to regenerate and recreate oneself and one's community, one imitates the models or characters of the sacred stories. This certainly corroborates my own work with the Dine-Navajo in the Southwestern United States. At a certain point in their ceremonies, the *hatathli*, or chanter, performing the rites becomes one with the divinity being invoked. So for Eliade, the model is used in a positive sense because it is the model that provides a pathway to the potency of the sacred.

For Girard, on the other hand, the model as an internal mediator can be the occasion for mimetic rivalry, as we said above, insofar as two people are in a rivalry for what the model possesses. The model is a modeler for what is to be desired. Girard has perhaps primarily focused on the negative aspects of modeling, although more recently he has turned his attention to the positive aspects. Still, the provocative implications of his theory lend themselves to focusing on the negative connotations of modeling.

Finally, this brief overview of these towering interpreters of myth does not do justice to the subtle nuances of their thought nor have we been able to explore, for example, Girard's profound respect for Eliade's work. Still, I hope I have illustrated in these representations the two dimensions of myth articulated by Segal, a positive one, where myth authentically mediates mystery, and a more pejorative one, where myth conceals the violent acts on which a society is founded.

Notes

1. The term "mythic consciousness" comes from Lonergan, *Insight*, 560–566.
2. I have addressed the topic of sacred myths in Eliade's thought in the larger context of the ontological status of the sacred in chapter 7 of my book on Eliade. I have adapted and reworked some of the exposition from that chapter into this section. See Dadosky, *The Structure of Religious Knowing*, 102–105.

3. For an account of the Diné (Navajo) creations story, see Zolbrod, *Diné bahané: The Navajo Creation Story*.
4. Girard does not use this explicit phrase very often, but Golson's (74) highlighting of this phrase appropriately speaks to Girard's distinctive hermeneutics of myth.
5. Girard points out that Livy's account of the myth where Remus is killed "in the scuffle" should be translated from the Latin "in the crowd," *in turba*, thus suggesting the collective murder. Girard, *Scapegoat*, 92–93.

Works Cited

Allen, Douglas. *Myth and Religion in Mircea Eliade*. Theorists of Myth Series. New York/London: Garland Publishing, Inc., 1998.

Dadosky, John. *The Structure of Religious Knowing*. Albany, NY: SUNY Press, 2004.

Eliade, Mircea. *Myth and Reality*. Translated by Willard R. Trask. New York: Harper & Row, 1963.

———. *Myths, Dreams, and Mysteries*. New York: Harper Torchbooks, 1967.

———. *The Myth of the Eternal Return, or Cosmos and History*. Translated by Willard R. Trask. Bollingen Series 46. New York: Harper Torchbooks, 1959.

Girard, René. *I See Satan Fall Like Lightning*. Maryknoll, NY: Orbis Books, 2001.

———. *Job: Victim of His People*. Stanford, CA: Stanford University Press, 1987.

———. "A Venda Myth Analyzed." In *René Girard and Myth: An Introduction*. Edited by Richard J. Golson, 151–179. New York: Routledge, 2003.

———. *The Scapegoat*. Translated by Yvonne Freccero. Baltimore, MD: John Hopkins University Press, 1986.

———. *Things Hidden since the Foundation of the Word*. Edited by Stephen Bann and Michael Metteer. Stanford, CA: Stanford University Press, 1987.

Golson, Richard J. *René Girard and Myth: An Introduction*. New York: Routledge, 2003.

Johnson, Robert A. *Inner Gold: Understanding Psychological Projection*. Hawaii: Koa Books, 2008.

Lonergan, Bernard. *Insight: A Study of Human Understanding*. Collected Works, vol. 3. Edited by F. E. Crowe and R. M. Doran. Toronto: University of Toronto Press, 1992.

Segal, Robert A. *Myth: A Very Short Introduction*. Oxford University Press, 2004.

Zolbrod, Paul. *Diné bahané: The Navajo Creation Story*. Albuquerque, NM: University of New Mexico Press, 1984.

4

Eliade on Myth and Science

Robert A. Segal

I see Mircea Eliade as a typical, if also would-be atypical, twentieth-century theorist of myth. In contrast to nineteenth-century theorists, who set myth against science, Eliade, like other twentieth-century theorists, sought to reconcile myth with science. He maintained that moderns can consistently have both. After summarizing the nineteenth-century approach to myth, I will turn to the twentieth-century one. I will compare Bronislaw Malinowski's position with Eliade's, on which I will then concentrate. Whether Eliade succeeds in reconciling myth with science is the main issue I will consider.

Myth and Science

The challenge to myth may be almost as old as myth itself. In ancient Greece, the main challenge was on moral grounds. Plato rejected the myths of Homeric gods because those gods, rather than models for humans, behaved shamefully, immorally. In the *Timaeus* and other works, Plato created his own myths. Alternatively, the Stoics reinterpreted popular myths as moral and metaphysical allegories.

In modern times, the main modern challenge to myth has been on intellectual grounds. Myth, it has been asserted, is incompatible with natural science as an explanation of the physical world. Because modernity is taken to be almost identical with science, the question is whether myth is compatible with science. The question is not whether science, which is the given, is compatible with myth.

Science is assumed to do so well what myth, taken to have existed from hoary times, does: explain the origin and operation of the physical world. Where myth attributes events in the world to the decisions of gods, science ascribes events to impersonal, mechanical processes. To accept the scientific explanation of the world is automatically to reject the mythic one. The two explanations are assumed to be incompatible.

The most facile response to the gauntlet thrown down by science has been to ignore science. An only slightly less facile response has been to pronounce science itself mythic. A more credible response has accepted science as the reigning explanation of the world and has then either "surrendered" or "regrouped." Surrendering means simply replacing myth with science. Regrouping means re-characterizing myth to make it compatible with science.

The nineteenth-century approach to myth, exemplified by the pioneering anthropologists E. B. Tylor and J. G. Frazer, was that of surrendering. The twentieth-century approach, with a wider array of exemplars, was that of regrouping, which itself took various forms. One form was to recharacterize the subject matter of myth. Now myth was no longer about the physical world. It was instead about the social world, about human nature, or about the experience of living in the physical world, which was different from being about the physical world itself. The exemplars of this approach were above all existentialists—Rudolf Bultmann, Hans Jonas, and Albert Camus—and psychologists—Sigmund Freud and C. G. Jung.

A second form of regrouping was to recharacterize the function of myth. No longer serving to explain—or, for Frazer, also to control—the physical world, myth now served to do almost anything else. Myth could comfort, could command, could evaluate, or could justify. The function now served reflected the subject matter. The subject matter could now be the social world, though it could also remain the physical world—the physical world itself and not merely the experience of the physical world. For example, a myth about mortality could serve to justify it. A myth about the hierarchy in society could serve to command acceptance of that hierarchy. The exemplars of this approach were the anthropologist Bronislaw Malinowski and the historian of religions Mircea Eliade, with Freud and Jung also altering the function, not just the subject matter, of myth.

The recharacterization of the subject matter of myth often involved the translation of myth from a literal reading—the reading assumed by both Tylor and, with some qualification, Frazer—into a symbolic one. A myth about Zeus was now taken to be a myth about a king, a father, the father archetype, or thunder itself. The recharacterization of the function of myth did not always require any translation, so that myth was often still read literally.

Nineteenth-Century Theories of Myth: Tylor and Frazer

The leading exponents of the nineteenth-century view of myth were Tylor, whose main work, *Primitive Culture*, was published in 1871, and Frazer, whose key work, *The Golden Bough*, was first published in 1890. For Tylor, myth provides knowledge of the world as an end in itself. For Frazer, the knowledge that myth provides is a means to controlling the world, above all to secure food. For both Tylor and Frazer, the events explained or effected by myth are physical—either ones in the external world, such as rainfall and death, or ones in humans, such as reproduction and death. Myth is not about social events, such as marriage and war. Myth is the primitive counterpart to natural, not social, science. It is the counterpart to biology, chemistry, and physics rather than to sociology, anthropology, psychology, and economics. For Tylor, myth is the exact counterpart to scientific theory. For Frazer, myth is the exact counterpart to applied science.

Myth, which is part of religion, attributes rain to either a decision by a god (Tylor) or the physical state of a god (Frazer). For Tylor, rain falls because a god decides to send it, and the reason can be anything. For Frazer, rain falls because a god either urinates or is incontinent. In science, rain falls because of impersonal, meteorological processes.

For Tylor and Frazer, mythic and scientific explanations are incompatible because both are direct. In myth, gods operate not behind or through impersonal forces but in place of them. God does not set meteorological processes in motion but instead likely dumps accumulated buckets of water on a designated spot below (so Tylor). For Tylor and Frazer alike, one therefore cannot stack the mythic explanation atop the scientific explanation, crediting science with the direct explanation and crediting myth with the indirect explanation. Rather, one must choose between competing direct explanations. Because moderns by definition have science, the choice has already been made. They must give up myth, which is not merely outdated but outright false. Moderns who still cling to myth have failed either to recognize or to concede the incompatibility of it with science.

Twentieth-Century Theories of Myth: Malinowski and Eliade

In the twentieth century, myth was reconciled with science. Moderns, while still defined as scientific, could now retain myth. Tylor's and Frazer's theories were spurned on many grounds: for ignoring myths about other than the physical world, for precluding modern myths, for subsuming myth under religion and thereby precluding secular myths, for deeming the function of myth scientific-like, and for deeming myth false. Even a myth in which a god sends rain was seen as about other than rain.

Yet twentieth-century theorists did not try to reconcile myth with science by challenging science. They did not take any of the easy steps: "relativizing" science, "sociologizing" science, making science "masculine," or making science "mythic." No less than their nineteenth-century predecessors did they accept science as the prevailing explanation of the physical world. Rather, they recharacterized *myth* as other than a literal explanation of the physical world. Myth was, then, made compatible with science, but only by removing myth from competition with science.

For both Malinowski (see his "Magic, Science and Religion" and "Myth in Primitive Psychology") and Eliade (see his *The Sacred and the Profane* and *Myth and Reality*) myth is, to be sure, an explanation in part, but the explanation is only a means to a nonscientific end rather than the end itself. For Malinowski, that end is to reconcile humans to disease, death, and other brute aspects of the physical world. For Eliade, the end is to carry humans back to the time of the myth, which is always the past, in order to encounter god. Myth is like a magic carpet, but a carpet that goes in only one direction.

For both Malinowski and Eliade, myth is as much about social phenomena—customs, laws, and institutions—as about physical ones. The subject matter of myth is thus more than the physical world. For Malinowski, myths about social phenomena serve to reconcile members to impositions that they might otherwise reject, such as class division. The beneficiary is society, not the individual. For Eliade, myths about social phenomena serve the same magic carpet-like function as myths about physical ones. The beneficiary is the individual.

Insofar as myth for Malinowski deals with the social world, it turns its back on the physical world. But even when myth deals with the physical world, its connection to that world is limited and so still evinces the twentieth-century approach to myth. Myth may explain how flooding arose—a god or a human brought it about—but science, not myth, explains why flooding occurs whenever it does. And science, not myth, says what, if anything, to do about it. Myth assumes that nothing can be done about it and espouses resigned acceptance of a largely uncontrollable world.

Unlike Tylor and Frazer, Malinowski maintains that primitive peoples, not just moderns, have science as well as myth, however rudimentary their science is. Myth and science are compatible because their functions are distinct. But Malinowski never tries to reconcile the mythic explanation of the origin of physical phenomena like flooding with the scientific explanation of the recurrence of the phenomena. He never ventures beyond function to content. He simply assumes that because the functions of myth and science for primitive peoples are distinct, the contents must be compatible. (He also distinguishes religion from both myth and science on the same grounds: function.) Whether for him moderns even have myth he never makes clear. It may be that they have ideology in place of social myths.

By contrast to Malinowski, Eliade, like Tylor and Frazer, assumes that primitive peoples have just myth and not also science, so that the issue of the compatibility of myth with primitive science does not arise. But unlike Malinowski, Tylor, and Frazer alike, Eliade argues that moderns have myth as well as science. Whether he, unlike Malinowski, actually tries to reconcile myths of the physical world with science, we will see. At the least, he appeals to the fact of the coexistence of myth and science for moderns to argue that the two must be compatible, just as Malinowski does for "primitives." At the same time he concentrates on distinctively modern myths, which are of social rather than physical phenomena. Modern myths attribute events not to gods but to merely exceptional human beings—to culture heroes. For Malinowski, even the creation of physical events, such as mortality, can be the work of humans, and those humans need hardly be heroic. Eliade ventures far beyond Malinowski, not to say Tylor and Frazer, in making myth universal and, as presumably is the case for Malinowski, not merely primitive.

Neither Malinowski nor Eliade challenges Frazer's and especially Tylor's literal reading of myth. Whatever their break with Tylor and Frazer on the function and subject matter of myth, they continue to read myth literally. By contrast, fellow twentieth-century theorists Bultmann, Jonas, and Camus reject a literal reading of myth. For them, myth read literally means Tylor's and Frazer's nineteenth-century approach. They insist that the key to understanding myth is to read it symbolically, which thereby removes it from competition with science. By contrast, Malinowski and Eliade reconcile myth with science by recharacterizing the function of myth.

Eliade

Eliade does not reject the explanatory function of myth. For him, as for Tylor, myth serves to explain how gods created and control the world:

> Myth narrates a sacred history; it relates an event that took place in primordial Time, the fabled time of the "beginnings." In other words, myth tells how, through the deeds of Supernatural Beings, a reality came into existence, be it the whole of reality, the Cosmos, or only a fragment of reality—an island, a species of plant, a particular kind of human behavior, an institution. (*Myth and Reality*, 5–6)

> Myths, that is, narrate not only the origin of the World, of animals, of plants, and of man, but also all the primordial events in consequence of which man became what he is today—mortal, sexed, organized in a society, obliged to work in order to live, and working in accordance with certain rules. (*Myth and Reality*, 11)

Clearly, myth is about more than the physical world. Seemingly, it can be about anything in the world and so far exceeds the scope of myth for natural science.

Most other twentieth-century theorists—Freud, Jung, Bultmann, Jonas, and Camus—reconcile myth with science by cutting off myth from the physical world. They substitute the human mind, society, or the experience of the physical world as the subject matter of myth. Eliade does not. For him, as also for Malinowski and a few others, the physical world remains a subject matter of myth, and any other subject matter supplements, not replaces, it. Eliade is thus bolder than most of his fellow twentieth-century theorists because he refuses to concede the physical world to science exclusively. And he is bolder than Malinowski because he refuses to concede the physical world to science for moderns any more than for "primitives."

Eliade meets the challenge of science by, like Malinowski, proposing functions served by myth in addition to the explanatory one. Myth for Eliade justifies as well as explains phenomena, and does so in the same way that it does for Malinowski. Myth does not pronounce phenomena good. It pronounces them inevitable and in that restricted sense seeks to reconcile humanity to them. For example, myth justifies death less by postulating an afterlife, though Eliade notes myths that do, than by rooting death in an event in primordial time, when the world was still malleable but when any action made permanent whatever it created. In primordial, or mythic, time the cosmic clay was soft. By subsequent, historical, ordinary time it had hardened. According to myth, human beings die because "a mythical Ancestor stupidly lost immortality, or because a Supernatural Being decided to deprive him of it, or because a certain mythical event left him endowed at once with sexuality and mortality, and so on" (*Myth and Reality*, 92). Myth makes the present less arbitrary and therefore more tolerable by locating its origin in the hoary past, just as for Malinowski.

But Eliade goes beyond Malinowski to maintain that myth does more than explain and justify. It also regenerates. To hear, to read, and especially to reenact a myth is magically to return to the time when the myth took place, the time of the origin of whatever phenomenon it explains and justifies:

> But since ritual recitation of the cosmogonic myth implies re-actualization of that primordial event, it follows that he for whom it is recited is magically projected *in illo tempore*, into the "beginning of the World"; he becomes contemporary with the cosmogony. (*The Sacred and the Profane*, 82)

In returning one to primordial time, myth reunites one with the gods, who were nearest just after creation, as the biblical case of "the Lord God['s] walking in the garden in the cool of the day" typifies (Gen. 3:8). That "reunion" reverses the post-lapsarian separation from the gods, a separation that is equivalent to the fall, and renews one spiritually: "What is involved is, in short, a return to the original time, the therapeutic purpose of which is to begin life once again, a symbolic rebirth" (*The Sacred and the Profane*, 82).

The American bank robber Willie Sutton, continually caught and imprisoned, was asked why he continued to rob banks. His reply: because that's where the money is. For Eliade, humans go back in time because that's where the gods are. They enlist myth, which for Eliade is always about the origin of something in the past, to do so. The ultimate payoff is experiential: encountering divinity. The ultimate payoff of ritual is the same, but ritual involves space rather than time. Clearly, science offers no regenerative or even justificatory function. Science merely explains. Myth can do things that science cannot, in which case science does not compete with myth, at least not altogether.

But Eliade argues more. For him, myth not only serves functions that transcend the function served by science but also serves them for moderns as well as for "primitives." Moderns for Eliade fancy themselves scrupulously rational, intellectual, unsentimental, and forward-looking—in short, scientific. Nothing could veer farther from their collective self-image than adherence to myth, which they dismiss as egregiously backward and irrational. Yet even they, according to Eliade, cannot dispense with myth:

A whole volume could well be written on the myths of modern man, on the mythologies camouflaged in the plays that he enjoys, in the books that he reads. The cinema, that "dream factory," takes over and employs countless mythical motifs—the fight between hero and monster, initiatory combats and ordeals, paradigmatic figures and images (the maiden, the hero, the paradisal landscape, hell, and so on). Even reading includes a mythological function . . . because, through reading, the modern man succeeds in obtaining an "escape from time" comparable to the "emergence from time" effected by myths. Whether modern man "kills" time with a detective story or enters such a foreign temporal universe as is represented by any novel, reading projects him out of his personal duration and incorporates him into other rhythms, makes him live in another "history." (*The Sacred and the Profane*, 205)[1]

Plays, movies, and books are the genres that express modern myths because they reveal the existence of another world alongside the everyday one—a world of extraordinary figures and events akin to those found in traditional myths, which are myths about gods. The figures in modern myths are, strictly, human, but they have one or more godlike qualities. They are therefore akin to gods.[2] Eliade, zealous to maintain that all humans are religious, wants to make the humans in modern myths godlike in order to make modern myths religious.

The difference for sophisticated theologians between humans and God is one of kind. For example, God has no body. But the popular difference between humans and gods is one of degree: a god's body is bigger. Not only "pagan" gods but also the biblical God has a body. Otherwise, to cite a single instance, Moses at the burning bush (Exod. 3) would not have to look away to avoid seeing God and would not have to stop at the perimeter to avoid stepping on the ground where God has walked. Myths evince the popular, not the sophisticated, characterization of God.

Furthermore, the actions of those figures account for the present state of the everyday world. For example, in the movie *Braveheart*, William Wallace is celebrated as the founding father of Scotland, even if he did not live to see an independent nation. In the movie, as in the legend, Wallace is credited with almost superhuman charisma, military prowess, and courage. In one scene in the movie, several members of his army are discussing their leader when he passes by. When one of the soldiers says that there goes Wallace, another, who has never seen him close up, denies that that person can be he. Why? Because that person is not tall enough.

Most of all, moderns get so absorbed in plays, movies, and books that they imagine themselves to be back in the world before their eyes. Spectators and readers get "lost" in a play, a movie, or a book. They get "carried away." They travel from present, profane time back to the sacred time of the story. True, they do not identify themselves with the characters of the stories. True, they do not deify themselves. True, they retain the divide between heroes and ordinary persons—a divide more rigid than that between heroes and gods. They imagine themselves not to be William Wallace but simply to be in his presence. They do not think that they can change history. They yearn only to witness it. This is what Eliade means by an encounter with God.

It is celebrities in all walks of life who are the heroes of modern myths, though indisputably only a few of them are credited with establishing any custom, law, or institution. The most elevated of celebrities are Hollywood stars, and it is they who loom closest to gods. On screen, stars, like gods, are greater than ordinary folks in degree. To begin with, they are gargantuan in size. Merely human virtues are magnified into superhuman ones: bravery becomes fearlessness, kindliness becomes saintliness, beauty becomes incandescence, strength becomes omnipotence, wisdom becomes omniscience.

But there are also differences of kind. Like gods, film stars are rarely seen in person. When beheld on screen, film stars, like gods, can do anything and can take on disguises—their roles. And of course, stars are immortalized in their films. In all of these ways, film stars far surpass sport and rock celebrities, whose prime appearances are live and are thereby limited to what talent and special effects can concoct. Compare Michael Jackson's moonwalk with the mobility of Spider-Man.

Going to the movies is going to a sacred space. The cinema blocks out the outside world and substitutes a world of its own. The more effective the movie, the more the audience forgets where it is and finds itself in the time and place of the movie. Things are permitted in movies that never happen in the proverbial "real world." In the movies, as in heaven, anything is possible. The phrase "only in the movies" is telling. To go to the movies is to suspend disbelief. It is to agree to "play along." The ultimate payoff of moviegoing is encountering the actors themselves, even if only on the screen. Going to the movies is like going to church—to a set-off, self-contained place where God is likeliest to be found.

If, argues Eliade, even moderns, who are self-professed scientific atheists, actually have their own myths, then science does not preclude myth. Therefore myth and science are compatible. Where for Malinowski myth and primitive science are compatible, for Eliade myth and modern science are.

Questions

However appealing, Eliade's dual counterargument to Tylor and Frazer—that myth serves functions that science cannot duplicate and that even moderns cherish myth—is dubious. First, the nonexplanatory functions of myth depend on the explanatory one, as Eliade himself recognizes in always characterizing myth, as quoted, as at least an explanation: "In other words, myth tells how, through the deeds of Supernatural Beings, a reality came into existence." But then myth can serve its other functions only if it can fend off science in serving its explanatory function. How it can do so, Eliade never says.

Perhaps Eliade is assuming that the phenomena explained by modern myths are entirely social—for example, the origin of tools, marriage, government, and nationhood—and not at all natural—for example, the origin of the sun and the moon. But then his distinctiveness among fellow twentieth-century theorists dissolves. They too reconcile myth with science by removing myth from the physical world.

Furthermore, if not natural science, then social science seeks to account for social phenomena. Mythic explanations of customs, laws, and institutions attribute them to heroics rather than to economic, social, and political processes. Mythic explanations are of the "Great Man" variety, epitomized by Thomas Carlyle's *On Heroes, Hero-Worship and the Heroic in History* (1847).

It was the pioneering Victorian sociologist Herbert Spencer who offered the classic dismissal of this romantic brand of explanation. Rather than the cause of society, a great man is the product of society. In Spencer's famous summary phrase, "Before he [the great man] can re-make his society, his society must make him" (*The Study of Sociology*, 35). The changes any great man makes are marginal and are merely the direct causes of change. The underlying causes are the ones that produced the great man himself: "So that all those changes of which he is the proximate initiator have their chief causes in the generations he descended from" (*The Study of Sociology*, 35). Mocking Carlyle, Spencer declares that if you wish to understand social change, "you will not do it though you should read yourself blind over the biographies of all the great rulers on record" (*The Study of Sociology*, 37). Biographies are the myths of modern heroes.

Nothing has changed since Spencer's day. The social scientific position is still that individuals, however great, do not make history. Impersonal processes do, just as in natural science. In short, mythic explanations of even social phenomena seem at odds with science—here, social science.

Second, modern myths do not always go backward in time. They may instead go forward, as in science fiction, or go sideways, such as to other cultures around the world. Even myths that do move backward by no means always go back to the occasion on which a present-day custom, rule, or institution was created. Of course, Eliade can reply that these kinds of "myths" thereby do not qualify as myths and so do not challenge his theory. But this reply would then make the theory nonfalsifiable.

Third, moderns travel back in time only in their imaginations, not in reality. In seeing a play or movie or reading a book about George Washington, Americans may feel *as if* they are present at the Revolution, and may especially feel so during celebrations of Independence on July 4. But Americans hardly claim actually to be whisked back on a mythic time machine. Or if they do, it is only for the duration of the activity. Once the play, movie, or book is over, so is the myth. The experience of sacred time ceases abruptly. One may remember a stirring story long afterward, but as a memory or an inspiration only.

Above all, Eliade, like Malinowski, simply declares that myth is compatible with science without working out how. The natural science that for Malinowski "primitives" have is rudimentary, and there may be no primitive social science. The natural science that moderns have is far more developed, and there is also social science.

Eliade is so eager to show that moderns, despite themselves, harbor myth that he misses the burden of figuring out *how* moderns, whose culture is overwhelmingly scientific, can still have myth. For Tylor and Frazer, moderns who apparently have both have simply failed to recognize the clear-cut incompatibility of them. Surely Eliade does not want to leave the presence of myth alongside science as a contradiction. But then he must work out how a mythic explanation is consistent with a scientific one. He never does so. His overall claim that moderns have myth demands a sturdier argument.

Notes

1. On modern myths, which Eliade often mixes with rituals, see his *The Sacred and the Profane*, 201–213; *Myth and Reality*, 181–193; *Myths, Dreams,*

and Mysteries, 23–38; *Cosmos and History*, 141–162; *Rites and Symbols of Initiation*, 127–136; *Patterns in Comparative Religion*, 431–434; *Images and Symbols*, 16–21; *The Quest*, 112–126; and *Occultism, Witchcraft, and Cultural Fashions*, 1–68.

2. On the loose divide between humans and gods, see Segal, "The Blurry Line between Humans and Gods."

Works Cited

Eliade, Mircea. *Cosmos and History*. Translated by Willard R. Trask. New York: Harper Torchbooks, 1959. Also titled *The Myth of the Eternal Return*. Originally published in 1954.

———. *Images and Symbols*. Translated by Philip Mairet. London: Harvill Press, 1961.

———. *Patterns in Comparative Religion*. Translated by Rosemary Sheed. Cleveland: Meridian Books, 1963. Originally published in 1958.

———. *Rites and Symbols of Initiation*. Translated by Willard R. Trask. New York: Harper Torchbooks, 1965. Also titled *Birth and Rebirth*. Originally published in 1958.

———. *Myths, Dreams, and Mysteries*. Translated by Philip Mairet. New York: Harper Torchbooks, 1967. Originally published in 1960.

———. *Myth and Reality*. Translated by Willard R. Trask. New York: Harper Torchbooks, 1968. Originally published in 1963.

———. *The Sacred and the Profane*. Translated by Willard R. Trask. New York: Harcourt Harvest Books, 1968. Originally published in 1959.

———. *The Quest*. Chicago: University of Chicago Press, 1969.

———. *Occultism, Witchcraft, and Cultural Fashions*. Chicago: University of Chicago Press, 1976.

Frazer, J. G. *The Golden Bough*. 1st edition. 2 vols. London: Macmillan, 1890.

Malinowski, Bronislaw. "Magic, Science and Religion" (1925). In *Magic, Science and Religion and Other Essays*, edited by Robert Redfield, 17–92. Garden City, NY: Doubleday Anchor Books, 1954. Originally published in 1948.

———. "Myth in Primitive Psychology" (1926). In *Magic, Science and Religion and Other Essays*, edited by Robert Redfield, 93–148. Garden City, NY: Doubleday Anchor Books, 1954. Originally published in 1948.

Segal, Robert A. "The Blurry Line between Humans and Gods." *Numen* 60 (2013):39–53.

Spencer, Herbert. *The Study of Sociology*. New York: Appleton, 1874. Originally published in 1873.

Tylor, E. B. *Primitive Culture*. 1st edition. 2 vols. London: Murray, 1871.

5

Mircea Eliade:
Theös Éghènou . . .

Introduction
Mac Linscott Ricketts

This article was written in Eliade's second year at the University of Bucharest, at age twenty, soon after he had published his twelve-article series *Itinerariu spiritual* [The Spiritual Itinerary], that confirmed him in the position of "Chief of the young generation." It was published a year before Eliade embarked on a three-year Indian adventure and was his first contribution to the monthly magazine *Gândirea* [*Thought*].

Gândirea had been founded in 1921 by another "young generation" of intellectuals a decade older than Eliade's, as a vehicle for expressing their ideas about the "Romanian phenomenon." In 1926, one of them, Nichifor Crainic (1889–1972), became editor of the magazine and attempted to impose a "literary Orthodoxy" on those who wrote for it. At this time, Eliade was on the staff of the newspaper *Cuvântul* [*The Word*], whose editor (after 1927) was Nae Ionescu (1890–1940), his philosophy teacher, mentor, and friend. This article was his first for *Gândirea*. He would contribute seven more in 1928 and one in 1930 (from India). But Crainic was scandalized by Eliade's novel *Isabel şi apele diavolului* [*Isabel and the Devil's Waters*] (1930), and he would have nothing to do with him thereafter.

Eliade had been a prolific writer since high school, publishing in periodicals for young people and school newspapers. Not until his senior year, however, did he begin to show interest in subjects classifiable as the history of religions, a subject he would make his lifetime vocation. Early on, he became fascinated with mystery religions, about which he learned from two Italians, Raffaelle Pettazzoni and Vittorio Macchioro. He began a prolific correspondence with the latter, a specialist on Orphism, in 1926—a correspondence that would be ended by the war in 1939.[1] Eliade held this man in high regard and undoubtedly was influenced by his theories, some of which are mentioned in this article.[2] Macchioro inspired him to write, in 1926: "The religious reality [or fact: *fapt*] is not a matter [*fapt*] of knowledge, but of *experience*."[3] This concept of religion would remain basic to Eliade's thought, expressed later as the *sui generis* nature of religion. Eliade would abandon hereafter the terminology of the two planes, used often by him in the late 1920s—perhaps replacing it later with "the sacred" and "the profane."

The concept of the Christian goal as *theosis* [divinization or deification] is taught, in the view of Orthodox theologians today, by many of the Church Fathers (Irenaeus, Origen, Athanasius, Gregory of Nyssa, Basil the Great, et al.) and even in the Bible: for example, "He [God] has given us . . . his precious and very great promises, so that through them you may . . . become participants of the divine nature" (2 Pet. 1–4, NRSV).[4] Athanasius puts it succinctly: "God became man so that men might become gods." An excellent presentation of this doctrine can be found in *Eastern Orthodox Christianity: A Western Perspective*, by Daniel Clendenin.[5]

Theös Éghènou . . . [6]
Mircea Eliade

> *Theös éghènou ex anthropou . . .*[7]
> *"From a man you have been born a god . . ."*

There are men who consider life "theirs." They are charming and happy people. But life is "ours" only in our illusions. We have been born from wombs so that we can give birth to ourselves *anew*. Physiological life is a pretext. We will be ourselves, however, only by tearing loose from the humiliating psychophysical causality and by not constructing our consciousness from the bitter fragments of the spirit [*duh*] received from outside, but instead by constructing it through efforts made on spiritual [*spirituale*] planes, remelting it and crystallizing it under a certain light from a certain heat.

Spiritual planes? I distinguish two: the one complex and polyvalent, the other irrational, transcendent, and divine. There is that spiritual plane at which one arrives through aesthetic contemplation, logic, ethical experience, and vitalistic exaltation. And there is the other spiritual plane about which we know nothing, that transcends us wholly, at which one arrives through religious experience.

Therefore, thus two spiritual realities of a very different essence exist. A whole world of spiritual phenomena, with varied values and

organizations, surrounds us. Some have sprung from the inner substance of this secret and terrifying universe; others are projections of
the activities of the human soul [*duh*]. The projections are aesthetic,
ethical, rational, metapsychic, and naturist (I give this word the sense
of "magical nature"). They can be attitudes of the same consciousness.
They have, however, their effective reality in the inner law of their existence, in the fact of their organized unity, of their identity. They exist
because they have an existential continuity that does not contradict
itself. But we are not doing metaphysics here. Our aim is to arrive elsewhere. We shall say that religious experience differs, in essence, from
all other spiritual experiences (aesthetic, ethical, rational, sentimental,
etc.)—and go on to something else.

Life begins from the moment in which these spiritual planes become
effective, immediate, with possibilities of having experiences within
their limits, because [*spiritual*] life is immortal. Physiological life,
with its tissues and organs ceaselessly changing, is a continuous death.
Spiritual life is the only deathless life. A spiritual gesture can be actualized at any time. But is there still need—in these pages whose aim is
something else—to prove why the spiritual life is life without death?

For me, a man starts to live at the moment when his consciousness attaches itself, through an experience, to a spiritual plane. There
are many things to be added, to be made specific. I believe everyday
consciousness, the instrument created of flesh, of the social media, by
life in general, is a bundle of sensations, sentiments, ideas, which have
no *meaning in themselves* but are borrowed from their surroundings
or imposed by necessities other than spiritual ones. This everyday
consciousness is perishable, naturally. Because its supports are physiological functions, it disappears along with those functions.

Thus, spiritual life consists of experiences on spiritual planes, while
physiological life, too, only exists as continuous experience within the
three kingdoms of nature. But do these spiritual planes exist factually,
objectively? Are they *realities* that we approach or creations of our
consciousness detached from the soul [*suflet*] and projected? On the
truth of the response hangs the affirmation or the refutation of the
meaning [*sens*] of existence.

It is impossible to prove rationally the real existence of the two
planes. It is impossible to prove mathematically the aesthetic value
of Michelangelo's *David*. Why? There are two different spiritual attitudes from which the two functions spring, being exercised on various
planes and with various valorizations: art and mathematics. To grasp

79

the impossibility of rational discussions about the real existence of organisms with varied structures and of the spiritual manifested in the mysterious and inward concretization of that which we can only call divine, I will make use of a simple observation combined with a hypothetical presupposition.

It is known that minerals lack the ability of attaching themselves ("attaching" can be a cognition, because it is an experience) to the whole realm of nature. Minerals cannot know anything except the mineral kingdom, that is, the part of reality that falls under the control of physical laws. For a mineral, reality reduces itself to surface, volume, weight, gravity, universal attraction, and derived laws. *Living* vegetal phenomena will be, therefore, for it, fantasies. [A plant] is a reality that cannot fall under its "senses": it is *life*. The creative dynamism of life is in contradiction to the mineral state of stasis. It will try, therefore, to approach vegetal phenomena in mechanical ways; vegetal growth will be, for it, an illusion explained by the growth of crystals, the osmotic function by physical permeability. Likewise, for a vegetable, functions peculiar to animals (instinct, sentiment, will, intelligence) *do not exist*. They transcend the realm of its possibility of understanding. If the vegetable were to admit their reality, it would deny itself and contradict its nature.

Man is an animal endowed with a single virtue: potential, latent consciousness. All animals have consciousness as a result of their physiological organism. Man has more: his consciousness can be transfigured, attaining—after innumerable experiences, repeated in abbreviated form in every child-become-adolescent, adolescent-become-youth, youth-become-mature—authentic spiritual planes. Consciousness with its physiological basis (in fact, the pure derivation of the soul [*suflet*] from physiology is an aberration of the last century) is only a bridge for passing to the true spiritual worlds. The human animal cannot conceive the reality of these worlds. This reality can only be known by direct attachment, through experience. Direct knowledge of all manifestations on both planes—realized through attitudes, but the attitudes are subjective dispositions of the soul [*suflet*] through which the effective material of the experiences is filtered—brings a transfiguration of the consciousness, a reconstitution around a nucleus, a *nisus formativus* [formative effort], a *meaning*. The meaning is a gift of the spiritual experiences, a prelude to the reconstruction of the consciousness with new material, new values. About this meaning of the world, of life, of man, there are discussions and disputes without number. It is the focal point around which the soul [*suflet*] is organized. It is, then, the cornerstone of a man and a people. And the meaning is the most certain proof of the inner unity of the consciousness, the most encouraging sign, announcing the realization of immortality.

From men to become gods [*zei*]. This has been the goal of man since he awoke from his sexual and alimentary torpor. Without this goal, life is empty, useless—and consciousness a burden. History—the contingent crystallization of spiritual experiences—preserves deep traces of several attempts at transfiguring man into the divine. All I have written so far has been only a preparation for understanding these attempts.

* * *

The pagan Greeks had the most excruciating nostalgia for the realization of god in man. I cannot pursue here the causes and circumstances of this fact, about which I have written several times before. There emerge, however, from the intense spiritual activity of the Greeks, two positions beyond which they could not advance. I shall call them *Plato* and *Orpheus*. After a courageous synthesis, Greek idealism deduced rationally the path of man toward divinization. For that reason, Cicero said about the doctrine of immortality in the *Phaedo* that it persuades you only so long as you are reading the perfumed Platonic dialogue. Closing the book and reentering the continuous experience of life, the certainty of immortality seems a simple illusion, the momentary acceptance of a tempting philosophic fantasy. Why? Because Platonic idealism—from which derives the consciousness of the divinity of the soul [*suflet*], therefore of immortality—is *constructed*; it is the sublimation of human nostalgias, and not the embodiment of spiritual realities made evident by experiences. The absence of the experiential concrete leaves this whole brilliant Platonic scaffolding—empty, devoid of content. The immortality of the soul in Plato does not impose itself as an immediate reality but as possibility.

An effective bridge to the transcendent, which destroys the tragic isolation of the Greek consciousness, has been thrown down by Orphism. Orpheus discovered mystical experience through which the consciousness is transfigured, taking on divine, Dionysian patterns. Plato and Greek idealism are contemplative; Orphism is dynamic. Plato imagines a spiritual world logically but virtually; Orpheus fuses the human soul to spiritual realities—which transcend it—through an effective attachment, through an identification with

Dionysus. Orphic initiation is nothing but the reconstitution of the consciousness on spiritual planes. I have proved this in my book on the "Mysteries."[8]

The ancient world, the pagan elite, suffered from an absence of a *meaning* [*sens*] to life; hence the tragic despair of the Greek consciousness ever since it began to be aware of itself, hence the success of the mystery cults that filled man with illumination, giving him a vision and a purpose. But not all could be saved through Orphism (salvation means the harmonization of all spiritual functions around a meaning, leading to self-creation and then to effective immortality). It was a renunciation in the face of which many perished. Orphism—although it spread to all social classes—always remained the religion of an elite. Nor was it practiced authentically other than by an elite, the other initiates eventually remaining outside the supreme transfiguration.

Salvation was, in Orphism, the fruit of a life of restraints, of renunciations, of religious and occult experiences. It was, therefore, accessible to a limited number of individuals.

Salvation in Christianity is near to the soul [*suflet*], and it can be picked like a fruit by the very fact of the existence of the fruit, of the desire of the man, and of the arm he extends toward it. Christ was Spirit [*Duh*], and he was made flesh. Orpheus used the myth of Dionysus. But the myth is much harder to experience, to actualize in the soul [*suflet*], than a real life. (I have shown in another place why the meaning of Christian religiosity cannot be brought down by a critical exegesis of the New Testament; belief in Christ is a spiritual *fact*, an inner reality, and not a *dogma*.) The Christian is saved by killing the sin from which springs the hybrid animal nature; by becoming a man of God [*Dumnezeu*] through the simple fact of the appearance of Christ and through the will to repeat this appearance in himself.

In my view, Jesus has inverted man's values, bringing the spirit [*Duh*] in place of the flesh. Greek idealism and the Orphics [those who practiced the cult of Dionysus] also attempted to invert it. But Jesus realized the spiritual [*spiritual*] in his flesh. Jesus has leapt over the bounds of the human. He has proved how what is human can become—*naturally*—divine. The incarnation of the divine in the human body gives meaning to the life pulsing in that body. The Christian is sure of his salvation, and, at the same time, he is conscious of the divine essence of that salvation. No longer is he forced to construct a Dionysian consciousness along with the many experiences converging in the promotion of single meaning.

The soul (*suflet*] of the Christian is enlightened; it is attached to the divine through the simple descent, through experience, of the Christ-spirit [*Cristic*]. The imitation of Christ is the mystery of salvation, which any faith or uneasiness can release.

* * *

These notes on *Theös éghènou* are far from establishing all the points of orientation of the problem. It will be understood, however, that the only life is the spiritual one, nourished on spiritual experiences through attachments to spiritual realities. The Greeks arrived at a dead end through idealist, contemplative syntheses; the reconstruction of consciousness, its birth into a new world, is fulfilled through experience, and not through reason. The Orphics discovered the soul's potentialities for actualizing the religious transcendent through the concrete and living actualization of the Dionysian myth. Christians sublimated the example of the only Man who lived and died for a *spiritual meaning* [*sens spiritual*]. Christ brought a rich religious potential. Men, for two thousand years, have found the axis of their souls, the organic and harmonic unity of their consciousness, their *salvation*, through experiential assimilation of the meaning and vision of the Universe that was Jesus's—the Spirit [*Duh*] incarnate.

Naturally, this simple attachment to the Christ-spirit represents the central problem, and it means permanent and fecund agony in Christ. Never has the agony been more acute than in our time. The continuous conflict between the consciousness of the flesh and the consciousness reborn in Christ is the very wellspring of contemporary spiritual life. And it is, at the same time, the frame within which the original syntheses—the personality of every anxious soul—will be made clear.

Translated from the Romanian by Mac Linscott Ricketts.

Notes

1. See *Eliade, Corespondenţă, I-P*, Bucharest: Humanitas, 2004, 109–183; and *Eliade şi corespondenţi săi.* 3, Bucharest: Academia Română, 2003, 82–118.
2. See three articles by Eliade from 1927 on mystery religions, reprinted in *Mircea Eliade, Scrieri de tinereţe, 1926*, Bucharest: Humanitas, 1998, 145–165, 171–175 (edited by Mircea Handoca).
3. Eliade, "Experienţa religioasă," first published in *Cuvântul*, November 24, 1926; reprinted in *Scrieri de tinereţe, 1926*, 219–221. Eliade's first "personal" article about his views on the Christian life.
4. Compare also Psalm 82:6 and John 10:34, and the Johannine literature generally.

5. Grand Rapids, MI: Baker Books, 1994, chapter 6, "The Deification of Humanity: *Theosis*, 117–137. See also Christoforos Stavropoulos, "Partakers of the Divine Nature," in Clendenin, ed., *Eastern Orthodox Theology, A Contemporary Reader*, 183–192, Grand Rapids, MI: Baker Books, 1998, 1995.

6. Appeared first in *Gândirea* [*Thought*] 7, December 12, 1927; republished in *Mircea Eliade, Itinerariu Spiritual. Scrieri de tinerețe* [*The Spiritual Itinerary: Writings of Youth*], 1927 (Bucharest: Humanitas, 2003, edited by Mircea Handoca, 392–397.)

7. The words are inscribed on a gold Orphic amulet of the second century BC discovered at Thurium, Italy. The Greek original is θεὸς ἐγένου ἐξ ἀνθρώπου, but Eliade transliterated γ into gh to be close to the Romanian pronunciation. Thanks to Liviu Bordaș for this information.

8. This book seems to have been ready for publication when the article was written. It had been planned as early as 1926. See Eliade's correspondence with Vittorio Macchioro, in Mircea Eliade, *Europa, Asia, America. Corespondență*, I-P, Bucharest: Humanitas, 2004, 136 fn.

6

Eliade's Phenomenological Approach to Religion and Myth

Douglas Allen

Mircea Eliade, while always controversial, was often described, from the 1950s through the 1960s and 1970s, as the world's leading interpreter of religion, myth, and symbolism.[1] Starting in the decade before his death in 1986 and continuing to the present, Eliade's scholarly influence greatly diminished. Part of this decline is related to historical and biographical controversies and attacks. These involve troubling incidents and sometimes distortions about Eliade's personal relations and values in India, Romania, and later. These especially involve charges about his political views and involvements, primarily in Romania in the 1930s and extending to England and Portugal during the World War II period, in which critics claim to expose his complicity with fascism and anti-Semitism.

More relevant to this essay, Eliade's decline can be related to significant changes in scholarly approaches in general and in the history of religions in particular: greater specialization and rejection of universalizing theorists; rejection of previously dominant essentialist and foundationalist approaches; insistence on more empirical, scientific, and historical approaches and more rigorous methods of verification; emphasis on respect for cultural, racial, gendered, ethnic, religious, and other differences with a critique of universalizing and generalizing approaches and theories that reveal hegemonic power relations of economic, political, cultural, and ideological domination. In short, in terms of the post-Eliade pluralist and dominant approaches to religion, myth, history, and other central concerns in Eliade's writings, Mircea Eliade became increasingly out of fashion, marginalized, and most often ignored.[2]

Nevertheless, it is my position that Eliade has much to offer contemporary scholarship on myth and religion, and his insights and interpretations are often very significant for understanding our contemporary mode of being and worldly crises. Eliade can serve as an invaluable catalyst in allowing us to rethink many of our impoverished and trivial contemporary approaches to religion, myth, and history and to reformulate our scholarship in more adequate and relevant ways.

Eliade's Approach as Unifying and Synthesizing

In his phenomenology and history of religions, Eliade has a bold and incredibly ambitious vision of his subject matter. As he repeatedly affirms, his subject matter is the entire spiritual history of humankind. The best illustration of this is Eliade's three-volume *A History of Religious Ideas*, in which he conceives of his scholarly project as his history of religions, synthesizing mythic and other religious data from the entire history of humanity, from the earliest prehistory to the present.[3] With his remarkable curiosity and openness to the most diverse religious phenomena of others, his studies include phenomena that modern scholars had ignored or dismissed as primitive, backward, aberrant, and superstitious. Quite the contrary, Eliade often emphasizes illiterate peasant and other premodern phenomena devalued or ignored as unworthy by other scholars, and he claims to uncover deep, hidden, camouflaged, mythic and religious structures, ideologies, and meanings. Critics, with their different views of scholarly subject matter, approaches, and methods of verification, often claim that Eliade is unscholarly, subjective, and reads all kinds of profound meanings into the data.

With his remarkably holistic approach, in which he analyzes meaning through the structural interrelatedness of phenomena, Eliade's phenomenology of myth and religion consists largely of bold unifying and synthesizing interpretations. Always moving beyond the self-imposed limitations of safe, narrow, empirical, and historical specialization, Eliade is willing to take risks in proposing imaginative formulations with claims about universal, essential, mythic, religious, historical, and transhistorical structures, meanings, and modes of being. That is why various anthropologists and other social scientific and historical critics sometimes charge that Eliade is simply an unscholarly new Tylor or Frazer, even if he repeatedly criticizes these nineteenth-century universalizing essentialists (Eliade, "Methodological Remarks," 88; Eliade, *Quest*, 50).

In this regard, as a unifying and a synthesizing scholar, Eliade's methodology is consistent with his theory of religion and myth and his view of reality. In most of his scholarship, such a unified view of reality expresses Eliade's description and interpretation of the meaning of the religious orientations of *homo religiosus*. However, there are dramatic controversial passages in which Eliade goes beyond any phenomenological, perspectival limitations of interpretations of reality through the framework of various traditional religious approaches, and he makes judgments based on his own view of reality or his view of reality as such (Allen, *Structure*, 208–12).

With regard to Eliade's universal theory of religion, he interprets religion as a human way of being in the world that allows religious beings to experience mythic and other sacred values, to relate to and put into practice exemplary mythic and other sacred models and ideals, in order to bring order, coherence, and meaning to their fragmented, spatial, and temporal world. While synthesizing a huge subject matter of diverse data and making claims about unifying structures and meanings, Eliade often interprets the essential function of religion as allowing traditional human beings to become integral parts of a Cosmos, a meaningful, coherent, integrated whole.

This essential synthesizing and unifying characteristic may be most evident in Eliade's theory of symbolism that is central to his methodology and his theories of myth and religion. Eliade's phenomenological hermeneutics is largely grounded in his theory of symbolism in which multivalent symbols are interpreted as particular expressions or valorizations of coherent, structurally interconnected wholes or symbolisms. As a unifying and synthesizing generalist, Eliade interprets the meaning of the particular mythic or religious phenomenon by integrating it within its essentially structured, internally coherent system of symbolic valorizations.

The emphasis on the synthesizing and unifying function in Eliade's methodology and his theories of religion and myth is also evident in his descriptions and interpretations of the "modern" mode of being. The "modern," in Eliade's essentialized categorization, refers to a universal, exemplary mode of being in the world in which human beings consciously reject the religious, the sacred, the mythic, and all appeals to transhistorical transcendent reality. In a dramatic passage, Eliade contrasts the modern mode of being in the world with the traditional religious intentional structures of transcendence:

> [The] nonreligious man refuses transcendence, accepts the relativity of "reality," and may even come to doubt the meaning of existence....

87

Modern nonreligious man assumes a new existential situation; he regards himself solely as the subject and agent of history, and he refuses all appeal to transcendence. In other words, he accepts no model for humanity outside the human condition as it can be seen in the various historical situations. Man *makes himself*, and he only makes himself completely in proportion as he desacralizes himself and the world. The sacred is the prime obstacle to his freedom. He will become himself only when he is totally demysticized. He will not be truly free until has killed the last god. (*Sacred*, 202–3; see also *Myths, Dreams*, 236)

Moderns define themselves as temporal, historical, conditioned, relative, contextualized beings. According to Eliade, in the modern mode of being, humans are "condemned" to history, cannot defend themselves against "the terror" of time and history, and live lives that are fragmented, alienated, arbitrary, full of anxiety, absurd, and nihilistic. They reject religious and mythic appeals to synthesizing and unifying forces that allow for integrated living as participants in a coherently structured and meaningful cosmos (*Eternal Return*, 141, 150, 159–62; *Myths, Dreams*, 231–45; *Ordeal*, 126–28).

Usually, when Eliade offers such interpretations and judgments about modernity, he is presenting views from the perspective of traditional religious and mythic cultures. However, in many dramatic passages, his judgments refer to his own viewpoints and claims about the human condition and the human mode of being as such. In key passages (e.g., *Shamanism*, xiv–xix; *Myths, Dreams*, 106), expressed at the most general level of synthesizing and universalizing formulation, Eliade offers dramatic controversial claims about the essential human mode of being in the world generally and about the true nature of human consciousness as such. Certain phenomena of ecstasy, freedom, celestial ascent, and other mythical and symbolic, sacred, transcendent expressions reveal experiences that are always historically and culturally contextualized, but that burst open limiting contextual conditionings and reveal structures and meanings that are essentially nonhistorical and universal. As universal spiritual expressions, the structures of the sacred are significant for understanding and renewing contemporary human beings and cultural life, continuing to shape our lives and offer possibilities for new creative revalorizations, even when moderns ignore or consciously reject these essential dimensions of their existence.

Eliade's Theory of Religion

In Eliade's phenomenological approach, religion involves the experience of the sacred. Scholars do not have direct access to the experiences of the religious other. Instead, they assemble, describe, and attempt to interpret the meaning of data that are the expressions of religious beings. The scholar attempts to interpret the nature, function, meaning, and significance of the religious experiences that give rise to those religious expressions.

Eliade claims that the sacred, an "element" in the structure of consciousness, is the essential, defining, irreducible, religious invariant, core, structure, or category revealed in all religious phenomena. Eliade uses the term *sacred*, rather than *God, gods*, or some other particular religious expression because he intends this to refer to a universal phenomenological category (*Quest*, v; *History*, I, xiii; *No Souvenirs*, 313). Based on the categorization of Roger Caillois, and often similar to Durkheim's terminology but without sociological reductionism, Eliade claims that religion always involves the relational, oppositional, sacred-profane dichotomy (*Patterns*, 1; *Sacred*, 10; "Structure and Changes," 353; Caillois, 13, 19).

The sacred and the profane express the two foundational modes of being in the world (*Sacred*, 14). In religious experience, the sacred expresses the revelatory breakthroughs of the transcendent (the supernatural, eternal, transhistorical, infinite, unconditional, absolute reality) into the profane world of ordinary, natural, temporal, historical, finite, conditioned, relative phenomena.

> [R]eligion maintains the "opening" toward a supernatural world, the world of axiological values. . . . Myths are the most general and effective means of awakening and maintaining consciousness of another world, a beyond, whether it be the divine world or the world of the Ancestors. This "other world" represents a superhuman, "transcendent" plane, the plane of *absolute realities*. It is the experience of the sacred—that is, an encounter with a transhuman reality—which gives birth to the idea that something *really exists*, that hence there are absolute values capable of guiding man and giving a meaning to human existence. It is, then, through the experience of the sacred that the ideas of *reality, truth*, and *significance* first dawn, to be later elaborated and systematized by metaphysical speculations. (*Myth and Reality*, 139)

The foundational experiences of the sacred, as revealed through *hierophanies* or manifestations of the sacred, are extended through the dynamics of sacralization through symbolic revalorization and structural integrations, mythic, ritualistic, and other expressions. This allows religious individuals and cultures to provide mythic and other explanatory accounts, coherent models for living meaningful religious lives, and religious solutions for personal existential and worldly crises. In terms of the religious orientation, the temporal and historical profane qua profane, without access and relation to the transcendent sacred, is lacking in meaningful existence, is not fully human, and separates us from the essential nature of reality.

Formulated as the dialectic of the sacred (the dialectic of the sacred and the profane, the dialectic of *hierophanies*), Eliade claims that he can distinguish religious from nonreligious phenomena primarily through his criteria for this dynamic, essential, universal, structural process of sacralization. I have formulated Eliade's phenomenological account of the dialectic of the sacred as expressing five universal structures revealed in all religion and all religious phenomena (*Myth and Religion*, 74–93).

First, in all religious experience, there is the sacred-profane dichotomy and the separation of the *hierophanic* phenomenon (object, activity, word, mythic story, scripture, rite, mountain, tree, prophet, shaman, dream, vision, etc.), through which the sacred is revealed, from other spatial, temporal, natural, and historical phenomena. Second, there is always the paradoxical coexistence of sacred and profane. From the rational, logical, conceptual perspective of ordinary profane existence, how can something transcendent and absolute become imminent and relative, supernatural become natural, transhistorical and eternal become historical and temporal, and so on? How can something ordinarily natural, historical, finite, and conditioned reveal what is supernatural, beyond history, infinite, and unconditioned?

Third, religious humans are always involved in a process of evaluation and choice with regard to sacred and profane. They experience the sacred (God, Allah, Nirvana, the eternal, the transhistorical, the supernatural, heaven, the soul, etc.) as the reality. They choose the sacred as that which provides meaning and reality to their worldly existence, reveals ways of coping with and solving their existential crises, and allows them to experience what is eternal and salvational or liberating.

Fourth, in all religious experience, there is the necessary, contrary, dialectical movement between sacred and profane. On the one hand, for religion to become humanly accessible and existentially meaningful, there is always the incarnational movement from transcendent sacred to imminent profane expressed through language, culture, localization, ethnicization, and other forms of historical and social contextualization. On the other hand, for religion to maintain its sacred foundational essence, there is always the opposite transcending movement in which religious human beings attempt to purify themselves, devalue the historical and temporal profane conditionings, and realize the sacred reality as fully as possible. If either incarnational or transcending movement becomes overemphasized and completely eclipses the other, religion loses its force as a meaningful mode of being in the world.

Fifth, the dialectic of the sacred reveals the sacralizing structure of camouflage and concealment. In the same dialectical process through which the sacred discloses itself in religious experience, it also hides itself. The transcendent sacred reveals itself as historically and culturally imminent, but such disclosure is always partial, perspectival, and incomplete, and it necessarily conceals other possibilities for experiencing and constituting religious meaning.

In sharp contrast with the most rapidly growing forms of religion in the contemporary world, usually emphasizing variations of religious fundamentalism and other exclusivist, absolutist, often militant, and intolerant religious expressions, Eliade's dialectic of the sacred is dynamic, open-ended, and resists all humanly imposed closures. It is arrogant and an expression of limited religious experience for relative, conditioned, historical, contextualized human beings to claim that they, and only they, fully comprehend the absolute, unlimited, transcendent, and sacred reality. Particular symbolic expressions express particular ways that religious beings relate to and contextualize experiences of the sacred. But religious symbolism expresses the inexhaustible possibilities for other present and future symbolic revalorizations expressing new religious experiences.

In this respect, Eliade's universal dialectic of the sacred, at its deepest levels of sacralization, emphasizes and embraces certain kinds of complexity, contradiction, paradox, enigma, and ambiguity. These are not interpreted as defects to be removed—either through clear, logical, rational analysis or through clear, absolute, exclusivist revelation—but as essential in Eliade's phenomenology of religious and mythic experience, development, and creativity.

Eliade's Theory of Myth

In Eliade's phenomenology of religion, some religious phenomena are mythic. Myths are interpreted as irreducibly religious and as irreducibly mythic ways that human beings symbolically express their experiences of the sacred through the creation of narratives. Therefore, *homo religiosus* is *homo symbolicus* and *homo mythicus*.[4] Eliade's theory of myth formulates the mythic consciousness and mode of being as illustrating and developing his theory of religion and his theory of symbolism.

Departing from past Western privileging of Greek mythology, with scholarly approaches "demythicizing" Greek myths and regarding mythic stories as "fictions," Eliade maintains that "our best chance of understanding the structure of mythical thought is to study cultures where myth is a 'living thing,' where it constitutes the very ground of the religious life; in other words, where myth, far from indicating a *fiction*, is considered to reveal the *truth par excellence*" (*Quest*, 72–73). This is why Eliade focuses on traditional "archaic" cultures in which myth is believed and lived. Mythic believers distinguish myths from their fables, tales, and other stories because myths are "true stories" that reveal directly how the world and humans became what they are today and how the mythic believers can live a meaningful mode of existence by participating in the mythic realities.

While granting that it may be impossible to formulate one generally acceptable definition of myth, Eliade presents his most developed definition in *Myth and Reality*:

> Speaking for myself, the definition that seems least inadequate because most embracing is this: Myth narrates a sacred history; it relates an event that took place in primordial Time, the fabled time of the "beginnings." In other words, myth tells how, through the deeds of Supernatural Beings, a reality came into existence, be it the whole of reality, the Cosmos, or only a fragment of reality—an island, a species of plant, a particular kind of human behavior, an institution. Myth, then, is always an account of a "creation"; it relates how something was produced, began to *be*. . . . In short, myths describe the various and sometimes dramatic breakthroughs of the sacred (or the "supernatural") into the World. It is this sudden breakthrough of the sacred that really *establishes* the World and makes it what it is today. Furthermore, it is as a result of the intervention of Supernatural Beings that man himself is what he is today, a mortal, sexed, and cultural being. (5–6)

Eliade develops this definition of myth by formulating the following five characteristics of myth:

> In general it can be said that myth, as experienced by archaic societies, (1) constitutes the History of the acts of the Supernaturals;

> (2) that this History is considered to be absolutely *true* (because it is concerned with realities) and *sacred* (because it is the work of the Supernaturals); (3) that myth is always related to a "creation," it tells how something came into existence, or how a pattern of behavior, an institution, a manner of working were established; this is why myths constitute the paradigms for all significant human acts; (4) that by knowing the myth one knows the "origin" of things and hence can control and manipulate them at will; this is not an "external," "abstract" knowledge but a knowledge that one "experiences" ritually, either by ceremonially recounting the myth or by performing the ritual for which it is the justification; (5) that in one way or another one "lives" the myth, in the sense that one is seized by the sacred, exalting power of the events recollected or re-enacted. (*Myth and Reality*, 18–19)

Therefore, living a myth involves living religiously. Mythic time is sacred time, mythic space is sacred space, and mythic history is sacred history. Structurally related myths disclose a hierarchy privileging origin myths, especially cosmogonic myths, as revealing how sacred realities came into existence and established the world and its human and other realities, and they provide believers with exemplary supernatural or sacred models for all truthful and meaningful existence. "The main function of myth is to determine the exemplar models of all ritual, and of all significant human acts" (*Patterns*, 410; *Myth and Reality*, 8).

It is through fulfilling its function of revealing sacred exemplary models, and hence giving meaning to the world and to human life, that myths reveal for mythic believers the nature and meaning of *reality*, *value*, and *transcendence*. "Through myth, the World can be apprehended as a perfectly articulated, intelligible, and significant Cosmos. In telling how things were made, myth reveals by whom and why they were made and under what circumstances. All of these 'revelations' . . . make up a Sacred History" (*Myth and Reality*, 145).

Eliade's theory of myth is informed by the following presupposition: the mythic, as an essential human mode of being in the world, is coextensive with the human and is constitutive of what it is to be human. He believes that there is recent research supporting this mythic approach and interpretation. Human beings have a universal, natural, or inherent need to tell stories. An analysis of the "organic need for narration would bring to light a dimension peculiar to the human condition": that the human being is *par excellence* "a historic being," not in the sense of modern historicistic philosophies but in the sense of mythic, sacred histories that are revealed through the function and structure of mythic narratives (*Forbidden Forest*, vii–viii). It is through the creation of such significant narratives that we construct our views of reality and give truth, meaning, and significance to our worldly existence.

For Eliade's theory, this is most evident for traditional archaic cultures in which the mythic believers live the mythic as structured by supernatural, transcendent, transhistorical mythic realities and exemplary values and models for human existence. In Eliade's theory, this is also evident in the so-called historical religions of Judaism, Christianity, and Islam, even if they introduce creative innovations that seem to give value and meaning to normal, conditioned, linear, worldly "history" as sanctified. Sometimes, with Greek and other Western influences, they also claim to demythologize other religions as presenting false stories and fictions so that only the Hebraic religions express the exclusive, nonmythic God or sacred reality. Nevertheless, Eliade interprets these "historical" religions as illustrating the definition, function, and structural characteristics of myth. As with all religion, traditional Jews, Christians, and Muslims believe in the supernatural, transhistorical, transcendent God or sacred reality, formulate significant creation and other symbolic narratives, present mythic breakthroughs of the sacred in establishing our world, and provide mythic exemplary models for living the meaningful religious life.

Most challenging for Eliade's theory is how to relate the mythic to "modern" humans and to our contemporary world. Moderns consciously deny the mythic truths and realities and certainly do not seem to "live the mythic." This includes modern religious believers, who may profess religious faith, but who usually will not recognize or embrace Eliade's interpretation of the deeper mythic meanings of their own religions. They are completely oblivious of, or uncomfortable with, seemingly premodern and antimodern mythic ways of existing in the world, and they insulate their lives, with modern nonreligious economic, political, and cultural priorities, by devaluing the mythic representations as "merely symbolic." For Eliade, if these moderns are religious, then they are necessarily mythic, although he maintains that they do not live the myths fully and hence do not experience the deep, unifying, symbolic revelations of their mythic realities in terms of creative, contextually informed, symbolic, and mythic revalorizations.

The greatest challenge is from modern humans, who consciously live in a nonreligious, nonmythic world. As we've seen, in Eliade's phenomenology of religion, his theory of religion is dependent on making the clear distinction between the traditional sacred and modern profane modes of being. Eliade interprets the modern human being as denying all appeals to supernatural, transhistorical, and sacred realities. Because Eliade interprets myth as religious, the nonreligious modern rejects the mythic. In Eliade's theory, it seems clear that the modern denies any mythic reality as has been presented in the definition, function, and structures of myth. Not only does the modern secular being fail to live the myth fully, the secular profane human rejects the religious mythic totally.

What complicates this formulation and makes religion and myth relevant and even deeply significant for the contemporary world are other claims in Eliade's theory. In his most abstracted, universalizing, and controversial interpretations, Eliade's theory of religion functions on the metaphysical plane of reference, often presenting an essentialized philosophical anthropology, with bold ontological moves and judgments, and claims about time, history, the human mode of being, and the human condition as such. He submits that the sacred is an essential structure of human consciousness and an essential structure of the human mode of being. Similarly, he submits that "modern man, like the man of archaic societies, cannot exist without myths, without exemplary stories" (*Journal*, I, 150). As religious, the mythic is an essential sacred structure of human consciousness and of the human mode of being.

What this means is that in Eliade's theory, modern human beings are necessarily mythic beings and continue to be influenced by the mythic. However, because moderns reject the sacred and the mythic and do not consciously live the mythic as part of their intentional consciousness, they live fragmented, impoverished, meaningless, undeveloped human lives without mythic exemplary models and without realizing the inexhaustible, contextually relevant, symbolic mythic possibilities for reconstituting their lives and their world. The mythic can still be uncovered and deciphered in modern, temporal, historical, secular modes of existing. But the modern mythic is repressed, hidden, and camouflaged and expressed indirectly and not fully through structures of the unconscious, dreams, fantasies, nostalgias and yearnings, modern art and literature, films, nationalisms and Marxist and other political ideologies, alternative cultural creations and ecological experimental living, and in modern expressions of alienation, meaninglessness, and banality.

Even more than this, Eliade's theory of myth, in which the sacred and mythic are essential for constituting what is significantly human, leads to his dramatic conclusions that modern human beings are incapable of solving their deepest existential crises. Eliade's *The Myth of the Eternal Return* is his best writing for many formulations of this interpretation. The modern, who defines one's self completely as a temporal, historical, natural, and conditioned being and who denies all appeals to transcendent mythic models, cannot solve her or his modern existential crises in relating to death, genocide, "the terror of history," alienation, anxiety, and the arbitrariness, hopelessness, and meaninglessness of nonmythic phenomenal existence.

Such judgments relate to the primary focus on mythic renewal in Eliade's theory. He submits that "the periodical renewal of the World has been the most frequent mythico-ritual scenario in the religious history of humanity" (*Mephistopheles*, 158; see 125–59; and *Myth and Reality*, 39–53). The intentional structure of the dialectic of the sacred reveals the yearning of mythic beings for spiritual renewal through the abolition of meaningless profane time and regeneration of sacred time (*Sacred*, 68–113; *Patterns*, 388–409). In Eliade's theory, the cosmogonic myth has ontological and structural primacy because it allows for the total renewal of the world by recovering the perfection of the sacred beginning before "the fall" into time, history, and our conditional, human, existential condition and mode of being in the world. Similarly, certain traditional end-of-the-world myths, as also illustrated by several popular formulations in the contemporary world, as central to certain eschatological mythic structures, have great influence because this total destruction is necessary for a total mythic and sacred renewal of the newly constituted cosmos, including the spiritual renewal of the mythic believers.

This theme of mythic renewal is also central to Eliade's critique of modernity. Modern human beings, who deny the mythic and sacred, are in a state of deep existential crisis. Modern secular beings are not able to solve crises involving meaninglessness, anxiety, death, "the terror of history," and other contemporary experiences. But, according to Eliade, human beings today are offered dynamic, creative, and inexhaustible symbolic and mythic possibilities for dealing more adequately with these contemporary crises and for realizing cultural regeneration and renewal if we become aware of and revalorize essential symbolic and mythic structures that allow for the reconstitution of meaningful, significant, coherent, and spiritual lifeworlds.[5]

Several Frequent Misinterpretations

Eliade's theory of religion, as informed by the dialectic of the sacred, and his theory of myth frequently lead to serious misinterpretations. Such misinterpretations often take the opposite inadequate approaches of viewing Eliade's phenomenology of religion and myth either as presenting an essentialized, nonhistorical, noncontextualized theory completely abstracted from "real," particular, worldly, religious mythic beings or as presenting interpretations focusing on what "real" religious mythic beings experience and understand about their mode of being in the world.

From his prolific writings focusing on historical and phenomenological investigations of religion, symbolism, myth, ritual, and other religious phenomena, scholars easily praise, or more often criticize, Eliade for providing highly abstract, idealized, and essentialized interpretations of the sacred. His interpretations often seem to devalue or completely ignore the historical, temporal, contextualized experiences of real, embodied, religious and nonreligious humans, including the numerous, diverse, contextualized ways of existence of contemporary religious and secular beings.

Eliade, for example, will study particular lunar symbolic expressions, mythic constructions, and ritualistic reenactments, and then arrive at the bold essential insight and dramatic conclusion that such diverse expressions reveal the essential sacred meaning of inexhaustible life repeating itself rhythmically (*Patterns*, 154–59, 169–71, 176–77, 180, 182–85). In interpreting the profound meaning, say, of a particular snake phenomenon as lunar, Eliade adopts a hermeneutical framework in which this snake expression has existential value as part of a complex, "logic of symbols," multivalent, unifying, coherent, structural system of symbolic valorizations. He claims that the particular symbolic expression contains within itself and reveals the entire lunar system of symbolic associations and meanings. The fact that few or any of the religious participants might recognize such a symbolic and mythic interpretation of their religious phenomena seems irrelevant to Eliade's theory of religion. Repeatedly, Eliade contends that the symbol communicates its meaning, even if it is not understood, and the symbolic meaning is "there," even if other scholars do not see it.

In these and most of his other historical and phenomenological studies, Eliade often seems to abstract completely from all historical and contextual variables to formulate his theoretical account of the pure phenomenological categories, the nonhistorical exemplary structures and models. It is little wonder that most empirical, historical, and scientific critics have charged that such an essentialized phenomenology of religion, regardless of its possible literary, aesthetic, or other value, is inadequate for a serious history of religions.

What complicates such an understandable view of Eliade's theory of religion is the fact that he is deeply concerned with real, lived, religious, mythic experience and not only some pure, idealized, abstract theory. For example, in his formative influences in India and his approaches to India's religious phenomena, Eliade, unlike most Westerners in India, is not drawn to otherworldly, life-renouncing texts and traditions, and he was not attracted to the abstract, pure, spiritual monism of Advaita Vedanta that devalues and dismisses the historical and temporal phenomena as *maya*, mere illusion without status in reality. What most fascinates Eliade, by way of contrast, is a usually overlooked Indian approach in which the human being, the world, and life are not illusory, but are real. As best illustrated and analyzed in his *Yoga: Immortality and Freedom*, life and the world can be mastered, controlled, and enjoyed through knowledge of certain psychophysiological techniques and methods, expressing a tendency toward the concrete in which life is transfigured, allowing for the resanctification of life and nature (*Ordeal*, 54–55).

Similarly, Eliade is not often drawn to the "lofty" essentialized interpretations of high-caste philosophical and religious texts, interpretations, and privileged ideological justifications, but instead to the way Hindu peasants and others concretize, incarnate, and live the sacred symbols, myths, and other religious phenomena as integral to a multivalent, structurally coherent, and meaningful mode of existence in the world (*Ordeal*, 54–60). In this focus, Eliade's approach is of value in greatly expanding the subject matter of the history and phenomenology of religion by including phenomena most scholars have ignored or devalued as unworthy and as not expressing the abstracted, idealized, transcendent sacred referent of authentic religion and religious phenomena.[6]

This frequent misinterpretation, that Eliade's history of religions is concerned only with some essentialized and abstracted sacred and not with historical and cultural contextualization, can be related to an opposite misinterpretation that Eliade's focus is on real human beings and their actual lived religious and mythic experiences. Eliade frequently focuses on religious beings as *homo religiosus*, including *homo mythicus*, as the proper, irreducibly religious subject of religious experience. *Homo religiosus* is an essentialized, irreducibly religious interpretation of the human being as a religious being.

In his methodological assumption of the irreducibility of the sacred, Eliade upholds the hermeneutical principle that "the scale creates the phenomenon" so that the scholar must interpret the meaning of religious and mythic phenomena "on their own plane of reference." As Eliade asserts, in a frequently cited and debated passage,

> [A] religious phenomenon will only be recognized as such if it is grasped at its own level, that is to say, if it is studied *as* something religious. To try to grasp the essence of such a [religious] phenomenon by means of physiology, psychology, sociology, economics, linguistics, art or any other study is false; it misses the one unique and irreducible element in it—the element of the sacred. (*Patterns*, xiii; see also *Myths, Dreams*, 13–14, 131; *Quest*, 4)

Therefore, as Eliade frequently asserts, when studying traditional symbols, myths, primordial images, divine figures, transformative techniques, and other spiritual creations and their significance today for a "cultural renewal" and "new humanism," we need a new hermeneutical procedure, qualitatively different from dominant reductionistic approaches with their "nonhuman" models of scholarly "detachment" and "scientific" and "naturalistic objectivity." To use a historical, anthropological, sociological, psychological, or other reductionistic approach is "false" or inadequate in that it reduces and explains away the irreducibly religious and mythic nature of phenomena for the religious person as *homo religiosus*. The proper procedure for grasping the meaning of these documents expressing the history of the human spirit "is not the naturalist's 'objectivity', but the intelligent sympathy of the hermeneut. *It was the procedure itself that had to be changed*" (*No Souvenirs*, xii). "This conviction guided my research on the meaning and function of myths, the structure of religious symbols, and in general, of the dialectics of the sacred and the profane" *(No Souvenirs*, xii).

The misinterpretation consists in the assumption that when Eliade describes and interprets meaning for *homo religiosus*, he is focusing on real, contextualized, religious persons, and that when Eliade investigates religion, myth, ritual, and other religious phenomena, he is focusing on how such religious phenomena function and what they mean for religious human beings expressing a religious mode of being in the world. Although Eliade usually presents his studies in this manner, it leaves him open to the numerous criticisms that his scholarly interpretations have little to do with serious scholarly analysis and verification.

This common misinterpretation arises from not recognizing that Eliade is primarily interested in providing a *theory* of religion, myth, and other religious phenomena. *Homo religiosus* is an essentialized and universalized phenomenological category, an exemplary type, imaginatively abstracted from the historical, cultural, and other contextualized variables of the worldly existence of religious human beings. In the same way, *homo mythicus* is an essentialized and universalized religious category, an exemplary structural formulation of how religious beings have created and reenacted sacred, foundational, symbolic narratives revealing an irreducibly mythic way of being in the world. Eliade is not primarily interested in interpreting how some flesh-and-blood traditional Tibetan or Eskimo or modern Chinese worker understands or misunderstands, lives or fails to live, in complex ways that relate to the nature, function, symbolic structures, and essential religious meanings of their myths.

In his emphasis on theory, this does not mean that Eliade is only interested in abstract theoretical formulations with no relation to lived worldly existence. We have emphasized the opposite in much of Eliade's investigations. For example, Eliade could not interpret the sacralizing dynamics of the universal dialectic of the sacred without focusing on the historical, temporal, contextualized profane, and he often emphasizes "ordinary" and rather mundane ways of being in the world ignored by most scholars of religion as not sufficiently sacred. Eliade's theoretical formulations are dependent on historical and empirical data and the entire contextualized history of how human beings have expressed their religious phenomena in their worldly experiences. However, his interpretations of the essential structures and meanings of religion and the dialectics of the sacred, myth, and symbolism are dependent upon but not found fully in any of the religious phenomena.

Consistent with some of later existential and hermeneutical phenomenology, in contrast with Husserl's earlier pure essentialized transcendental idealism, Eliade intends his imaginatively formulated, essentialized theory of religion, myth, and other religious phenomena to function in ways that inform and illuminate our religious, and even nonreligious, modes of being in the world. Thus, he repeatedly claims that his theoretical interpretations of religion, including religious myth and symbolism, shed light on the unconscious, dreams, fantasies, nostalgias, ideologies, anxieties and alienation, political and cultural constructions, and other seemingly secular phenomena of modern, Western, profane existence.

The Sacred and Reality

What is the reality of the sacred in Eliade's phenomenology of religion? As we have seen, the sacred is what is evaluated as real, as the transcendent reality, by mythic religious beings. The sacred is the essential real as the experiential foundation of an authentic, spiritual, human mode of being in the world in which the real is revealed through the dialectic of the sacred and symbolic and mythic revelations.

Does this mean that the sacred is real as a structure of human consciousness? Is the sacred real as the way religious and mythic subjects perceive, structure, and constitute their worlds? Or is the sacred real as expressing the real structures of the cosmos and as given or revealed to us as reality independent of any intentional human consciousness? In this regard, are religious and mythic symbols created by human consciousness, expressing the symbolic ways that humans experience and structure meaningful phenomena? Or are symbols "ciphers" of the real world, valorizations of coherent structural systems that provide meaningful ways to experience the world, because they express cosmic sacred structures independent of human subjectivity? In passages found throughout his history of religions, morphological studies, and phenomenology religion, as well as his journals and autobiographical writings, Eliade provides affirmative answers to all of these questions, even if the alternatives may seem mutually exclusive and represent different philosophical views of the relations of the sacred and reality.

The above questions can be answered in many ways, depending on the subject matter and the methodology of Eliade's hermeneutical studies. In his phenomenology of religion and myth, his interconnected analyses and claims about the reality of the sacred are directed at different hermeneutical levels. They extend from more descriptive, historically and culturally controlled studies to universalized interpretations and judgments about the essential structures and meanings of religion, myth, and symbolism, Occasionally his formulations reveal highly normative judgments and express the most general interpretations involving ontological moves, going beyond the perspectival limitations of the phenomenology of religion, and function on the level of metaphysics and philosophical anthropology.

Eliade is usually describing and interpreting the status of sacred reality in various cosmogonic and origin myths, specific rites of initiation, prophetic and shamanic expressions, and other religious phenomena for those religious and mythic beings. For example, it is the disclosure of the sacred mythic reality that allows a traditional tribe to understand how and why the cosmos and the tribe were created, how they are to relate to their transcendent sacred realities, and how they are to live a structured meaningful mode of existence in this world.

Often, as we've seen, Eliade abstracts, generalizes, and provides universalized interpretations and claims about the sacred reality in terms of essential structures and meanings of the dialectic of the sacred, symbolism, myth, and other phenomena on a phenomenological religious plane of reference. Finally, and most controversially, Eliade offers interpretations and judgments about the sacred reality for human consciousness in general, for the human condition as such, and for our essential human mode of being in the world.

As interpreted in my *Structure and Creativity in Religion* and other works, I've analyzed Eliade's phenomenological approach as functioning on interconnected but radically different levels of analysis and with radically different methods and criteria of verification. Arriving at and providing empirical historical evidence and justification for an interpretation of, say, a particular Australian rite of initiation as experienced by those mythic believers is very different from justifying an interpretation of some universal, nonhistorical, mythic structure and essential noncontextualized meaning. Eliade does not distinguish his interpretations as functioning on different levels of analysis and justification, sometimes extending to bold imaginative speculative formulations, and he feels little need to defend his interpretations against the many criticisms. This not only creates confusion but also opens Eliade's phenomenology of religion and myth to strong scholarly criticisms.[7]

Without providing documentation, I'll simply note that Eliade's writings present numerous assertions about the sacred and reality that point toward an interpretation of philosophical and spiritual idealism. This can be related to Eliade's endorsement of methodological and hermeneutical positions expressing formulations of both epistemological idealism and metaphysical idealism.

As an epistemological idealist, Eliade frequently writes of the sacred as a structure of human consciousness and as a way that human beings intuit, perceive, structure, and constitute their meaningful worlds. In this regard, Eliade often expresses a kind of neo-Kantian orientation in which the sacred is a universal essential category of human consciousness in terms of which humans necessarily subsume and structure the diverse spatial, temporal, empirical, and historical phenomena of their worldly experiences. This can be related to the neo-Kantian formulations in Rudolf Otto's phenomenology of religion in his *Idea of the Holy* in which the *numinous* is interpreted as an irreducibly religious, universal, a priori structure of human consciousness.

One of Eliade's major presuppositions and themes as an epistemo-logical idealist involves the irreducibility of the sacred with his frequent attacks on epistemological reductionism. Modern psychologism, naturalism, and other forms of reductionism reduce the irreducibly sacred and mythic structures of human consciousness to nonreligious and nonmythic scales of explanation. The essential sacred structure of human consciousness and active human constituting subjectivity are completely ignored or reductionistically explained away.

As integral to his epistemological idealism, Eliade strongly upholds a metaphysical idealism. The sacred reality is experienced and under-stood as supernatural not natural, transhistorical not historical, and spiritual not material. Once again, Eliade offers his strong attacks on ontological or metaphysical reductionisms that violate the prin-ciple that the scale creates the phenomenon and reduces the sacred reality to nonreligious and nonmythic explanations. Here one finds his frequent criticisms of Marx and other forms of materialism, scientism, naturalism, and historicism, and of Freud and other forms of psychologism. It is tempting for supporters to claim that Eliade, in his phenomenology of religion and myth, is attacking reductionistic scientism but not devaluing science, reductionistic historicism but not historical analysis, reductionistic psychologism but not psychological approaches, reductionistic materialism but not economic and mate-rial analysis, and reductionistic rationalism but not critical rational thought. While certainly making such scholarly claims, common to much of hermeneutical and phenomenological scholarship, Eliade is claiming much more.

Eliade makes metaphysical idealistic claims, as seen in his sympa-thetic formulations of the "archaic ontology," about the nonhistori-cal, nontemporal, nonmaterial, sacred nature of reality. It is human consciousness, as sacred consciousness, that is most authentically human, most meaningful, and most real. It is the experience of the cosmos or world symbolically and mythically as transhistorical, transhuman, spiritual, sacred reality that is most real. When modern human beings express epistemological and ontological viewpoints, expressing historical, temporal, naturalistic, and materialistic modes of being in the world, they adopt partial, undeveloped, and inadequate approaches and separate themselves from the deepest sacred levels and nature of reality.

Once again, it is less controversial to interpret the above claims, reflecting forms of philosophical and spiritual idealism, only as the sacred realities *for* religious and mythical cultures and their believers. This is certainly the case in most of Eliade's studies in his history and phenomenology of religion. However, Eliade repeatedly goes beyond such perspectival limitations and formulations. Throughout his scholarly studies, as well as his literary creations, journals, and autobiographical formulations, he claims that such idealistic views about the sacred nature of reality go beyond the conscious awareness of religious individuals and religious social groupings. They extend to sacred structures of human consciousness and reality in general and finally reveal the true nature of the human being, the human condition and mode of being, and the real nature of the cosmos as such.

What complicates this picture of Eliade's spiritual idealism is the fact that he repeatedly offers evidence of his strong commitment to philosophical realism in most of his phenomenological formulations of sacred reality. This should not be confused with most contemporary forms of naturalistic and materialistic realism that are contrasted with idealism. But Eliade's idealism can be distinguished from the philosophical idealism of Bishop Berkeley, Hegel, and others who focus on human consciousness as constituting experience and reality. Eliade is closer to a position in which the essence of reality precedes humans experiencing and constituting meaningful existence. In this regard, one may note the Platonic tradition in which nonmaterial, metaphysical Ideas or Forms are real and provide the objective basis for our philosophical development, contemplation, and realization. It is not surprising that Eliade interprets the archaic ontology as having a "Platonic structure" (*Eternal Return*, 34–35). Even more central to Eliade's spiritual idealism as philosophical realism are the dominant essentialized mythic and symbolic modes of being in which God or the sacred is real, independent, absolute, supernatural, transcendent, spiritual reality. This is a sacred reality that humans do not create or constitute, but which serves as the essential foundation and exemplary model for our human, sacred, intentional realizations.

In this orientation of philosophical and spiritual realism, Eliade's phenomenology of religion and myth usually involves describing and interpreting how the sacred reality reveals itself, how the sacred cosmos reveals itself through partial disclosures of its structures and meanings, and how the mythic and symbolic sacred reveals our human condition and mode of being. Such a symbolic and mythic sacred reality has ontological and epistemological essentialized status of reality independent of our perceiving and constituting consciousness.

Once again, it is tempting to make the less controversial phenomenological claim that such spiritual realism is true for, and only for, the religious mythic cultures and believers. Of course, they accept that God or the sacred reality is real, independent of their subjective constituting existence, or they would not be religious believers. But, as we have seen, Eliade goes far beyond this phenomenological perspectival interpretation. The sacred reveals essential truths and realities about the structure of the cosmos and its cosmic rhythms; the symbolic structures and meanings of the lunar, solar, aquatic, initiatory, and other phenomena; and the real nature of our human condition and existential crises and so forth. This is why Eliade asserts that modern human beings, secular and even sometimes affirming religious positions, have limited or no understanding of their symbolic and mythic realities, fail to experience the deeper nature and reality of time, history, and the cosmos and cannot solve their contemporary crises without recourse to the symbolic and mythic sacred realities.

It may be possible to present a more adequate philosophical interpretation of the sacred and reality by bringing the above directions and tensions in Eliade's phenomenology of religion and myth into a reformulated, more dialectical, interactive, holistic framework consistent with some twentieth-century and contemporary approaches in phenomenology and other scholarship.[8] In the phenomenological analysis of (religious) experience, human beings experience a reality (the sacred, God, supernatural and mythical beings, nature, the cosmos, other living beings, language, symbolic and ritual structures, economic and political relations, cultural values, etc.) that is revealed, disclosed, or given. Initially, phenomenologically, *homo religiosus, homo mythicus,* Mircea Eliade, and other humans appear as rather passive subjects in experiencing as given a real world of structures and meanings that we have not created.

Nevertheless, this rather passive experience of the sacred, the mythic, or any other reality as given never constitutes religious experience, mythic experience, or any other kind of human experience. There are no religious phenomena without intuiting, sensing, perceiving, imagining, constituting human subjectivity. Religion is always a human construction, a relation expressing how humans relate to what is experienced and evaluated as sacred, transcendent, and real. The sacred always involves a human value relation, a human structure of consciousness and mode of being in the world, a way that humans creatively and actively constitute their worlds.

What this means is that Eliade's phenomenology of religion and myth may be interpreted in terms of a *constituted given*. The sacred, nature, cosmos, symbolic and mythic structures and meanings are given to *homo religiosus*, to Eliade with his literary and scholarly approaches and his personal existential crises, and to other human subjects, but they are always given as partial, hidden and camouflaged, unfulfilled, and in need of our constituting their meanings. When the transcendent sacred reality becomes separated from human subjects with their contextually related existential needs and crises and constituted lifeworlds, then the sacred "dies," as evidenced in modern and premodern "death of god" phenomena. The sacred is no longer experienced as real. In larger phenomenological terms, there is no sacred without the dialectical sacred-profane relation. The sacred realities, with symbolic and mythic structures and meanings and possibilities for creative revalorizations and regenerations, are given to us in limited human experience as offering inexhaustible, contextually relevant possibilities for constituting and reconstituting their meanings.

As informed by the terminology and analysis of Emmanuel Levinas and other existential phenomenologists, in Eliade's phenomenological interpretation of human relational experience, I (the religious being, the mythic being, the modern nonreligious being) always experience an other, which is given and unconcealed in complex, diverse, limited ways. What I experience in authentic relational experience is that the other, disclosed as real and independent of my self-constitution, is always to some extent other. The experienced other always eludes and transcends my attempts to understand, control, and subsume the other within my constituting presuppositions and categories. This is true of the authentic experience of all others, and how much more so in the religious experience of the supernatural, transhistorical, transhuman, transcendent, and sacred other. But this experienced other is not some objectified, relationless, valueless other. The other touches me, moves me, makes demands on me, is given to me in order for me to respond relationally through value-constituting relations that allow one to live a transformed, moral, meaningful, reality-based existence.

This interpretation of Eliade's approach to the relational sacred, incorporating features of philosophical realism, should not be confused with many versions of naive, reductive, physicalist or materialist, neurobiological and other scientific, political, economic, psychological, and philosophical "realism." In such dominant modern versions of realism, the ideal is usually to reduce or completely eliminate biases and values of the subjective self in order to understand and control objective, factual, and verifiable reality.

A more adequate approach, that integrates and reformulates many of Eliade's insights and scholarly contributions, focuses on a more complex, dialectical, and interactive interpretation of philosophical realism that not only allows for, but emphasizes, the essential nature and function of the active, value-constituting, and meaning-constituting self more emphasized in traditional philosophical idealism. This active religious and mythical subject, with its relational ideals and sacred realities, cannot be reduced to, or explained away by, economic, political, scientific, and other "modern" versions of "objective" reality.

In such a holistic approach, expressing how humans relate to dynamic interconnected and mutually interacting phenomena, there is a real given world or reality that exists independent of our human experiences. In my relative, conditioned, and contextualized world, I am situated within a world of real economic, political, cultural, religious, environmental, and other phenomena, with their limiting and enabling structures, that are given and provide the objective contexts for my existence. Poverty and starvation, human suffering, human mortality, war, class exploitation, sexism, racism, climate change and environmental destruction, and religious hierarchical violence and oppression really exist, independent of how I experience and interpret them through self-constituting relations.

But what is experienced as given and real is experienced as there for us to constitute. It is human experience as a constituted given, with its existential crises and contradictions, that allows for the relating of the subjective and objective dimensions of self-transforming, world-transforming, and self-transcending experiences. This allows religious and mythical beings to understand how they are responsible for their indispensable roles in creating and developing structured, meaningful, sacred relations.

This interpretation of religious, mythic, and other relations as constituted givens affirms our experiential realization that nature has value, other human beings have value, other sentient beings have value, and, certainly for religious beings, the transcendent sacred has value as ultimate reality. But this sense of valued givenness is experienced as incomplete, unfulfilled, and partially disclosed but also concealed and hidden. Our human potential for living lives of meaning is revealed in the structures and relations that are presented or given to us. This requires our active engagement in unconcealing, transforming, and developing our moral and spiritual relations in new, existentially meaningful ways.

In this interpretation of phenomenology of religion and myth, there is the complex, mediated, dynamic, dialectical, interactional relation of the subjective and objective. *Homo religiosus, homo mythicus*, or the modern subject is not the insulated, self-sufficient, Cartesian, modern ego-self. The relational religious subject engages and embraces the relational sacred other in its givenness as an integral part or structure of one's transformative process of relational, structured, and meaningful self-constitution and world constitution.

Eliade's phenomenology can be interpreted as offering us an insightful, dynamic, holistic, interconnected and interactional, open-ended approach to constituted and reconstituted values as real human relations. We are constituted by and in turn constitute linguistic, educational, social, cultural, religious, technological, environmental, and other conditions, variables, and structures that may tap into or deny our spiritual and mythic potential for living meaningful modes of existing in the world.

Knowledge of traditional or contemporary, particular, economic, historical, social, linguistic, psychological, technological, religious, mythic, and other contextualization is necessary for understanding human relational responses, whether active or passive, nonviolent or violent, loving or hateful, selfish or egoless, cowardly or courageous, egalitarian or unequal, free or unfree, truthful or untruthful. After all, although Eliade usually ignores or deemphasizes negative features of religious phenomena, the history and phenomenology of religion repeatedly show that religions, with their symbolic and mythic revelations of the sacred as real, often express constituted given, sacred-profane structures and meanings that are integral to violent, intolerant, oppressive, dehumanizing, alienating, untruthful, and life-denying relations.

In Eliade's phenomenology of religion and myth, it is primarily the dominant, modern, secular mode of being in the world, in rejecting the mythic and symbolic revalorizations and structures of the sacred, that is impoverished, threatening, reductionistically provincial, dehumanizing and "inhuman," and meaningless. Lacking in spiritual reality, it cannot provide adequate solutions for our contemporary existential crises.

Although Eliade tends to overemphasize what is insightful and valuable in premodern mythical and religious cultures, while ignoring the progressive insights and contributions of modernity, his phenomenology is significant for relating to our contemporary mode of being with its life-threatening and life-denying existential crises. Despite some of his misleading formulations, Eliade is not advocating some romantic and utopian, nonhistorical, noncontextualized return to some premodern, sacred, and mythic mode of being. He frequently emphasizes the mythic and ritual structure of a "return to the origins" or beginnings as invaluable for periodic regeneration and spiritual renewal, but, for contemporary humans, Eliade intends this as a symbolic and mythic "return" in order to reappropriate what is given as significant and meaningful for contemporary life in new, creatively constituted worlds of meaning.

Here we find Eliade's frequent descriptions, interpretations, and judgments about the most urgent contemporary need for a "cultural renewal," a "new humanism," a "planetary consciousness" and harmoniously and coherently structured cosmos, expressing a qualitatively different paradigm shift in human presuppositions, ways of being in the world, and realizations of sacred realities. For Eliade, the history and phenomenology of religion provide us with indispensable resources for such a paradigm shift with its cultural and spiritual renewal, by uncovering and interpreting the entire symbolic and mythic history of humankind and the buried symbolic and mythic structures within each of us. The contemporary, creative, spiritual project is to "burst open" the limiting, self-imposed, contextualized, modern structures and relations in order to experience the inexhaustible, open-ended, symbolic and mythic possibilities for revalorizing and constituting new expressions of sacred realities.

Notes

1. This essay includes my attempt to formulate a number of key points from my previous interpretations of Eliade's phenomenological approach to religion and myth. I formulate and analyze these points at much greater length, with extensive documentation, in my books, especially *Structure and Creativity in Religion: Hermeneutics in Mircea Eliade's Phenomenology and New Directions* and *Myth and Religion in Mircea Eliade*. In this essay, consistent with phenomenological and hermeneutical approaches, I usually provide sympathetic descriptions, interpretations, and reformulations of Eliade's phenomenology of religion and myth. I do not introduce my criticisms of Eliade's interpretations, including my view that historical and material analyses and explanations of religious and mythic phenomena are not necessarily inadequate and "false," but can be insightful in providing valuable scholarly contributions.

2. I have attempted to analyze the biographical, historical, and scholarly issues involved in Eliade's tremendous status and influence and in his decline in recent decades in various publications, including the following: "Recent Defenders," 333–51; "Prologue," 319–27; "Eliade's Legacy," 15–28.

3. Because of his ill heath, Eliade delayed and then abbreviated the third volume to include religious phenomena through the seventeenth century. A fourth uncompleted volume was to have included the religious creativity of modern secular societies. In my chapters "Eliade's Antihistorical Attitudes," 211–34, and "The Primacy of Nonhistorical Structures," 235–66, in *Myth and Religion*, I provide extensive documentation and analysis from Eliade's writings. I attempt to show that Eliade's herculean project of synthesizing and presenting a universal history of religions is dependent on his antihistorical attitudes and presuppositions and especially on his adoption of a largely nonhistorical methodology and hermeneutical framework of interpretation grounded in the nonhistorical essentializing and unifying structures of the dialectic of the sacred and the coherent structural systems of symbolic associations. Although historically minded critics understandably dismiss Eliade's history as pseudo-history and lacking rigorous historical analysis, I attempt to show that Eliade's phenomenological approach, while largely antihistorical and nonhistorical, must also pay attention to the historical nature of the data, and there is a complex interaction and relation between the historical and the nonhistorical in Eliade's scholarship.

4. The following brief formulation of Eliade's theory of myth is developed at length in my other writings, including *Myth and Religion*, especially "The Structure of Myth," 179–210.

5. I formulate this theme of mythic renewal at great length and with extensive documentation in "Cultural and Spiritual Renewal," *Myth and Religion*, 291–331.

6. Similarly, when it comes to Romanian and other forms of Christianity, Eliade has little interest in dominant formulations of theology, philosophy, and institutionalized ideologies and practices that devalue this worldly existence as essentially sinful and evil and propose an otherworldly interpretation of salvation. Instead, Eliade's subject matter, typically ignored or devalued by other scholars as unworthy, infantile, or superstitious, often focuses on interpreting how Romanian peasants and others live meaningful worldly existences, transfigured and sanctified by concretely living the symbolic and mythic sacred. Thus, he devotes little time to abstract Christian theology, but focuses on uncovering the deep symbolic and mythic structures and meanings in peasant, nature-oriented, ritualized dances, celebrations, and other lived practices of nonhistorical "cosmic religion." For Eliade, the more dominant, historical forms of Judaism, Christianity, and Islam are ossified and increasingly irrelevant and threatening to our contemporary world. In contrast, the ignored or easily dismissed cosmic religion, still rich in lived symbolic and mythic values and structures, can be revalorized in new and unexpected ways. It can be integrated as part of new creative spiritual experiences that are essential for overcoming our contemporary crises and for our future survival and renewal.

7. In my writings, especially the concluding chapter "Descriptive Evaluations and Levels of Meaning," *Structure and Creativity*, 201–46, I distinguish and analyze Eliade's different levels of meaning, with his normative judgments, ontological moves, and levels of generality. I also attempt to formulate an interpretation of how Eliade arrives at and might provide justification for

his most controversial claims about the reality of the sacred as experienced at most "elevated" and "highest" levels of spiritual experience.

8.   I do not maintain that Eliade ever presents such a formulation. As part of his creative genius, Eliade does many things simultaneously. He often includes, within his historical and phenomenological descriptions and interpretations, personal interjections and judgments and nonphenomenological claims. He is not overly concerned with defending his scholarly studies against charges of inconsistency and incoherence or with other criticisms. What I suggest is my own attempt at modifying and reformulating Eliade's phenomenology of religion and myth and developing it in new ways that may render it more adequate and significant for contemporary scholarship and the contemporary world.

Works Cited

Allen, Douglas. "Eliade's Legacy 25 Years Later: A Critical Tribute." *International Journal on Humanistic Ideology* 4.2 (2011):15–28.

———. *Myth and Religion in Mircea Eliade*. New York and London: Routledge, 2002.

———. "Prologue: Encounter with Mircea Eliade and His Legacy for the Twenty-first Century." *Religion* 38.4 (2008):319–327.

———. "Recent Defenders of Eliade: A Critical Evaluation." *Religion* 24.4 (1994):333–351.

———. *Structure and Creativity in Religion: Hermeneutics in Mircea Eliade's Phenomenology and New Directions*. The Hague: Mouton, 1978.

Caillois, Roger. *Man and the Sacred*. Translated by Meyer Barash. Glencoe, IL: Free Press, 1959.

Eliade, Mircea. *The Forbidden Forest*. Translated by Mac Linscott Ricketts and Mary Park Stevenson. Notre Dame: University of Notre Dame Press, 1978.

———. *A History of Religious Ideas*. Vol. 1: *From the Stone Age to the Eleusinian Mysteries*. Translated by Willard R. Trask. Chicago: University of Chicago Press, 1978.

———. *Journal I, 1945–1955*. Translated by Mac Linscott Ricketts. Chicago: University of Chicago Press, 1990.

———. *Mephistopheles and the Androgyne: Studies in Religious Myth and Symbol*. Translated by J. M. Cohen. New York: Sheed and Ward, 1965. Also published as *The Two and the One*.

———. "Methodological Remarks on the Study of Religious Symbolism." In *The History of Religions: Essays in Methodology*, edited by Mircea Eliade and Joseph Kitagawa, 86–107. Chicago: University of Chicago Press, 1959.

———. *Myth and Reality*. Translated by Willard R. Trask. New York: Harper & Row, 1963.

———. *The Myth of the Eternal Return*. Translated by Willard R. Trask. New York: Pantheon Books, 1954. Also published as *Cosmos and History*.

———. *Myths, Dreams and Mysteries*. Translated by Philip Mairet. New York: Harper & Row, Torchbooks, 1967.

———. *No Souvenirs: Journal, 1957–1969*. Translated by Fred H Johnson Jr. New York: Harper & Row, 1977. Also published as *Journal II, 1957–1969*.

———. *Ordeal by Labyrinth: Conversations with Claude-Henri Rocquet.* Translated by Derek Coltman. Chicago: University of Chicago Press, 1982.

———. *Patterns in Comparative Religion.* Translated by Rosemary Sheed. New York: World Publishing Co., Meridian Books, 1963.

———. *The Quest: History and Meaning in Religion.* Chicago: University of Chicago Press, 1969.

———. *The Sacred and the Profane: The Nature of Religion.* Translated by Willard R. Trask. New York: Harper & Row, Torchbooks, 1961.

———. *Shamanism: Archaic Techniques of Ecstasy.* Translated by Willard R. Trask. New York: Pantheon Books, 1964.

———. "Structures and Changes in the History of Religions." Translated by Kathryn K. Atwater. In *City Invincible,* edited by Carl H. Kraeling and Robert M. Adams, 351–366. Chicago: University of Chicago Press, 1960.

———. *Yoga: Immortality and Freedom.* Translated by Willard R. Trask. New York: Pantheon Books, 1958.

Otto, Rudolf. *The Idea of the Holy.* Translated by John W. Harvey. New York: Oxford University Press, 1958.

7

The Magic Fact
and the Mystic Fact:
Eliade's First Encounter
with the Works of Evola

Liviu Bordaş

In his monograph on Mircea Eliade, published in 1978, Ioan Petru Culianu points out that René Guénon and Julius Evola must be taken into account among those authors who contributed to the development of his theories on religion (110, 146). However, the relations between Eliade and the exponents of the so-called Tradition started to be discussed, documented, and analyzed only about a decade later. Although this discussion is now a quarter of century old, we are still far from a common consensus or a clear conclusion on the nature of Eliade's relationship with the works of René Guénon, Julius Evola, and Ananda K. Coomaraswamy.[1]

Both the perspectives from which this question has been approached and the intentions and information of the authors have varied widely. Some commentators are adepts or sympathizers of "Traditionalism" (or Perennialism) and, consequently, interested in laying claim to the work, ideas, and persona of an important historian of religions like Eliade, exaggerating the impact that the reading of the exponents of the Tradition had on him and wrongly attributing to them the origin of some Eliadean texts. At the opposite pole, the presumed influences of the "Traditionalists" upon Eliade are a motive and an additional argument for continuing and amplifying the theoretical and methodological criticism that has been brought to his *oeuvre*. Insofar as Evola was an exponent of the radical right and the thought of Guénon was claimed by the French *Nouvelle Droite* as well as by other new right conservatisms, the two categories of authors described above are doubled by another binary pair: on the one hand, those who try to claim Eliade for the conservative or radical right, and on the other, those who use this thing to denounce a presupposed hidden agenda or toxic ideology in Eliade's thought. Often esoteric and political motivations are assumed, while authors from the first pair (Traditionalists and their opponents) are also found in the second (the right and their opponents).

Besides these two categories, the subject has been approached by authors representing diverse disciplines (especially religious studies, but also literary theory, history, political science, etc.) interested in historically and theoretically reconstructing the relations between Eliade and Traditionalists so as to understand their motives and their impact on his thought and work. Unfortunately, their investigations have remained partial and debatable, not succeeding in explaining the genesis and evolution of Eliade's interest in this current of thought or of discerning the proportion of acceptance/rejection or convergence/divergence. The principal reasons for this failure have been inadequate knowledge of primary sources, lack of familiarity with the context of the younger Eliade's intellectual formation, and contamination by works from the other two categories.

In that which follows, I shall try—on the basis of all the published sources and known manuscripts—to reconstruct the way Eliade's first contact with works of the Traditionalists took place, the motives that brought about their involvement, the way he related to their ideas, and the immediate consequences of this intellectual encounter. The first contact can be localized historically to the years 1926–1928, when Eliade was taking courses in the Department of Philosophy and Letters at the University of Bucharest. It is mainly a contact with the writings of Julius Evola. The way in which Eliade continued to be interested in the works and ideas of the Traditionalists in the Indian period (1929–1931), then after his return to Romania (1932–1940), and during the time of the War (1940–1945) will constitute the object of future articles.[2]

The First Encounters with Exponents of "Traditionalism"

The discovery of authors such as Evola and Guénon in 1926—at the age of nineteen in his first university year—comes as the continuation of a prior interest of Eliade's for parapsychology, occultism, spiritualism, theosophy, and for authors like Edouard Schuré and Rudolf Steiner. The first signs of these preoccupations date from the year 1921, when Eliade was just fourteen. In 1926, he advanced beyond primitive and vulgarized forms of these subjects to an intellectual level as elevated as possible and more scientifically acceptable. Thus, popular and vulgar spiritism is replaced by the "Metapsychism" of Charles Richet, Theosophy with the Anthroposophy of Rudolf Steiner, and magic in conformity with the theories of Vittorio Macchioro and James George Frazer.

In his critique of Theosophism, René Guénon's book *Le Théosophisme. Histoire d'une pseudo-religion* (1921), which Eliade cites in an article devoted to Rudolf Steiner (*Adevărul literar și artistic*, June 20, 1926), played an important role. Although he accepted Guénon's criticism, he considered that the errors committed by contemporary Theosophists did not compromise "true *theosophy*" (Eliade, *Misterele*, 133, 135). The book will be invoked again in another article dedicated to Steiner (*Cuvântul*, April 13, 1927) and in the article "*Teosofie?*" in the series "*Itinerariu spiritual*" (*Cuvântul*, October 22, 1927) (Eliade, *Itinerariu spiritual*, 141, 328).

Eliade paid attention to Guénon after he discovered Evola, and the writings of the latter would contribute to furthering his knowledge of the French Traditionalist. He had met Evola in the pages of *Bilychnis*, which he called then "the best Italian review of history, psychology, ethics, pedagogy, and philosophy of religion" to which "the most distinguished savants or scholars of religious phenomena" contribute. In the January 1926 volume, he remarked upon Evola's study, "*La scolastica dinanzi allo spirito moderno*" ("Scholastics *vis-a-vis* the modern spirit"), to which he promised, in his review in *Revista universitară*, to return on another occasion ("*Reviste*," in Eliade, *Misterele*, 65). He would not return, however, until almost two years later when he would review another study of Evola's in the November 1927 issue of *Bilychnis*, "*Il valore dell'occultismo nella cultura contemporanea*" ("The value of occultism in contemporary culture"). From this review, we learn that he knew Evola's other articles from *Bilychnis*, as well as "its original review, *Ur*" ("*Ocultismul în cultura contemporană*," in Eliade, *Itinerariu spiritual*, 371–374), which—at least in 1928—he will receive regularly in Bucharest (Eliade, *Europa, Asia, America* . . . I, 272). This latter may indicate that there was already contact by letter with Evola, who was director of the review. In those years, however, the Italian did not yet subscribe to the core ideas of Traditionalism but was an esoteric philosopher of "magic idealism." Evola cited Guénon positively on some issues, but also criticized him rather harshly on others. His adherence to Traditionalist ideas, as he understood them, can be dated to 1930 and would become evident in his book *Rivolta contro il mondo moderno* (1934), but he was not—and never became—an (orthodox) member of the Traditionalist or Perennialist school.

Coomaraswamy, on the other hand, seems to have been discovered through the criticism made of him in Henri Massis's *Défense de l'Occident* (1927), a book that Eliade read in the library of the University of Geneva and promptly reviewed (*Cuvântul*, October 2, 1927). But the work to which the French neo-Thomist referred to, *The Dance of Shiva* (1918)—in a French translation backed by Romain Rolland—he would be able to read only in 1928, probably in the latter half of the year. It immediately became one of the books Eliade recommended to his friend Rica Botez, for whom he played the role of a Pygmalion.[3] Obviously, he did not find in it the "anarchy in thought" that exasperated the neo-Thomist thinker. It must be specified again that, when Coomaraswamy published this book and even at the time when Eliade read it, he was not yet influenced by René Guénon's ideas about Tradition. This would happen only in his writings after 1932.

What must have attracted the young Eliade about this book was probably the wide cultural and metaphysical openness of the Anglo-Singhalese scholar, as well as his profound sensitivity to things spiritual. The book refers to ideas and themes that already preoccupy Eliade and to which he will devote attention in later years: the significance and magic power of art, the Hindu conception of the identity between *puruṣa* and *prakṛti*, the fact that *yoga* is a *praxis* rather than a belief, the practice of *yoga* in Buddhism, Śiva as a *yogin*, and so on. But Eliade did not at that time publish a single line about Coomaraswamy. His manuscripts, so far as they are known to date, remain mute about this first book, which revealed to him one of the Indologists who would remain forever in the circle of those he admired.

Between Magic and Mysticism

Until 1925, Eliade's interests in the occult, "metapsychism," and theosophy were based upon a spiritual position close to the "magical pragmatism" of Giovanni Papini, one of his important influences at that time. In his university period, and to a great extent as a result of meeting Nae Ionescu, he begins to discover Christianity, Orthodoxy, and thus tended more toward a spiritual position defined by mysticism.

The series of articles "*Itinerariu spiritual*" ("Spiritual Itinerary"), which he published in *Cuvântul* between September 6 and November 16, 1927, can be considered the synthesis of his thought, readings, and experiences until then. But it also mapped his future course, identified courageously with that of his whole generation. The steps of the "Itinerary" culminate in mysticism, which Eliade distinguishes from Theosophism and which he finds fulfilled in Orthodoxy, as the only authentic spiritual experience accessible in the Romania of those days. Anthroposophy, however, remains an alternative solution in the case of those not prepared for the Orthodox experience.

It is in this period that Eliade's passage from a preponderant preoccupation with the occult to that with the mystical was accomplished. Mysticism, however, was understood as a superior form of the occult and the "metapsychism."

The "*Itinerariu spiritual*" marks the first public adherence to the values of Orthodoxy and the church. This twenty-year-old Eliade considered Orthodoxy to resolve the dynamic antagonism between Jesus and Apollo-Dionysus. His Orthodoxy, however, was not the fruit of a personal experience, but of an ideological choice in the name of a new spirituality. The personal debate between magical voluntarism, which characterized him, and Orthodox mysticism, to which he aspired, was not yet over. He remains close to the "temptation" of magic, which had also a luciferian side (see the obsession of "Sfântul Diavol," "the Holy Devil"). The passage from paganism to Christianity takes place only on the ideological plane, not the existential, on which Eliade wanted to leave himself full liberty for experience. The two *states of spirit* live side by side in an unstable equilibrium.

The transformation of man into God continued to be his objective. Christian life meant for him a "heroic life." Christ was viewed, not as Son of God, but as "the first and greatest hero" of Christianity. This is obvious in the article "*Apologia virilității*" ("Praise of Virility," *Gândirea*, August–September 1928, but written between August 1927 and January 1928). The virile personality is born through the tragic confrontation and synthesis of the Dionysian with the Christic. The restoration of man can be realized through a new virility sprung from the spiritual life. The core idea of this "new humanism" is the "personality," understood as a spiritual organism constituted through a concrete and inner experience, as a *new* consciousness that transcends and survives the physical (Eliade, *Virilitate și asceză*, 227–243).

This is precisely why Eliade would have to deny the position in another article, "*Virilitate și asceză*" ("Virility and Asceticism," *Cuvântul*, October 11 and 17, 1928). Here he recognizes that the ascesis of "*Apologia virilității*" was one of a magical kind: the asceticism of the Ego exalted through reflection upon itself, outside of divine grace, and of anything transcendent. At the end of one year of experiences, he announces that he has left this position behind: definitive ascesis cannot be fulfilled without grace. He preserves his position of ultimate asceticism, but by turning values upside down, that is, introducing grace and eliminating "self-creating personalism" ("personalismul autocreator").

The reconciliation of the two visions remained an intention. Eliade did not then transcend the magical idea or the heterodoxy of his religious conception, anchored not in faith in a Supreme Being but in a religious hero (Christ being the supreme figure). He would do it later, in the 1930s, but in another sense than the Orthodox. For the time being he preferred the debate—very stimulating for his creativity—between Dionysus and Christ, between magic and mysticism, between virility and asceticism, and between adventure and the absolute.

Evola and the Resignification of Occultism

Scarcely finished with *"Itinerariu spiritual"*—in which, for the first time, Eliade discussed Theosophy, Anthroposophy, occultism, and magic from a perspective meant to be Christian—he returned to one last article about this family of spiritual attitudes. After that he no longer treated the subject directly, but just marginally, allusively, with a critical eye—often under obligation—and with visible difficulties of theoretical adaptation to his new ideal.

This article was itself occasioned by an article of Julius Evola published in the review of religious studies *Bilychnis*: *"Il valore dell'occultismo nella cultura contemporanea"* (November 1927). As we have seen, Eliade had already drawn attention to another of Evola's articles, *"La scolastica dinanzi allo spirito moderno"* (January 1926) and stated that was familiar with Evola's criticism of Anthroposophy and Anglo-Indian Theosophy (i.e., the article *"Nuovi... Messia"* ("New ... Messiahs," May–June 1926),[4] as well as with his articles from the review *Ur*, founded that very year.[5] He had not yet read any books by Evola, whom he considered a "thinker" who shows originality, clarity, and prolonged familiarity with the phenomenon of occultism. How Eliade came to know of publications as little-known and inaccessible in Romania as *Bilychnis* and *Ur*, we do not yet have any clue.

In his study, Evola defined occultism as a "transcendental experimentalism," a term paired with "transcendental pragmatism." The fundamental presupposition of this is that it is better to know that you don't know, than to believe. Only that which results from direct, immediate, individual experience is effective knowledge. Occultism is characterized thus by an "experimental radicalism." In distinction from the modern inclination that considers a phenomenon that appears in a direct way, positing behind it an ideal being as the true reality, for occultism "real" is only that which is received directly through experience—not necessarily one of a sensible nature, but perhaps a spiritual vision.

The supreme form of true occultism is magic. Evola institutes a categorical opposition between this and mysticism, identified in the fact that magic preserves and empowers individuality: the universal is not experienced as such, but as a modality higher than the individual.

Through criticism brought against idealist philosophy, religion, and pseudo-esoterisms, but also through his radical ideas about magic and initiation, Evola turns out to be a veritable avant-guardist of the occult. He understood that, in occultism, the problem of survival after death is different from that of immortality, properly speaking. Immortality is not a state gained once and for all, but an infinite burden, a function developed in time, which must be confirmed and renewed at each and every point. It is obtained only by a select few, such us the Indian *muktas*, the Buddhist enlightened ones, the "rescued from waters" of certain Gnostic schools, or the heroes of Greek traditions. In the same way, Evola rejected the doctrine of reincarnation, characteristic to pseudo-occultisms. Like immortality, reincarnation, is obtained only by an elite, by those who have followed the path of perfection to its end—and this road is perpendicular to that of the common man (Evola, *I saggi di Bilychnis*, 67–90).

Evola accepted fully the evidences brought by modern "metapsychism" in support of the reality of spiritual and supernatural phenomena. His study makes frequent references to Indian philosophy, which is clearly the "tradition" preferred by the Italian occultist. He refers to his new book, *L'Uomo come Potenza. I tantra nella loro metafisica e nei loro metodi di autorealizzazione magica* (1926), and to the review, *Ur–Rivista di indirizzi per una scienza dell'Io* (1927), which aimed to establish occultism as a positive science, conscious of itself and intentionally methodical, free of any dogmatic creed and any ethical system. The final section—titled *"Nostalgia"*—cites the recent volume of René Guénon, *Le roi du monde* (1927).

From the very beginning of his article, Eliade seeks to give a definition of occultism more adequate than those he had proposed in the past. This is "a tested setting of practical methods aiming at a re-elaboration of consciousness, a fulfillment of spiritual functions (together with logic—an esthetic or religious experience; together with a timid will—a will transfigured, previsions, clairvoyance, psychometrics, etc.)" (Eliade, *Itinerariu spiritual*, 371). The fundamental trait of occult science is, therefore, experience.

With this, Eliade begins to point out the correspondences between Evola's conception and the steps of his own *"Spiritual Itinerary."* The first one is, thus, the "experimental radicalism" of the Italian occultist. All the occult experiences converge toward the same end: "the reconstruction of consciousness on the true spiritual plane, its detachment from the so-called laws of psycho-physical correlation (long since annulled for clairvoyant minds through some results of metapsychism)" (371). Thus, possibilities of knowledge of reality, lost through atrophy, develop in consciousness. The term "knowledge" means, in the occultist vocabulary, an "attachment" to reality that can lead to its modification. Occultism, thus, meets with "magical pragmatism" (372).

In the final section of his study, Evola evokes primitive times when humans were not dominated by "representations" or ideas of good and evil, but possessed "powers" through which they could modify reality. Primitive is not thus a prelogical mentality. Eliade affirms with conviction that the reality of the relations of sympathetic magic has been proved experimentally by one of Charles Richet's pupils, Dr. Eugène Osty (373).[6]

Eliade agrees with Evola that, in occultism, everything becomes an object of experience, even the problem of immortality. This is not a given for all, because consciousness that acts only according to physiology cannot survive death. It (immortality) must be constructed. Immortality—"the actual one and [not] in the Buddhist sense, of a structural non-entity of consciousnesses, *discontinuous through death*, nor in the Unamunian sense of glory" (373)—is a reality reserved for an elite. Death of the pure organic consciousness and rebirth to an enlightened consciousness, polarized around the transcendent, is a phenomenon that can be ascertained beginning from the mysteries of Antiquity until contemporary cases of apparent death. "Through a continuous magical effort, the I is reborn little by little into true spiritual cadres, independent of the functional unity which is named *man*" (374).

Eliade draws attention, not without pride, that he arrived at the same conclusion as the Italian occultist through his own investigations in the last three years. He refers to his articles on Orphic Mysteries published between May 1926 and February 1927—under the influence of Vittorio Macchioro—and the article *"Magie și metapsihică"* (*Cuvântul*, June 17, 1927). He also makes this specific because he did not want his assertions to be confused with the "esoteric biscuit of Schuré" (374). (Obviously, the developing young scholar endeavored to forget the bad books he had read in adolescence.)

Nevertheless, he cannot share Evola's position to its end. The latter counterposes simplistically the magical attitude (the Dionysian and dynamic moment) to the theosophic-contemplative (the Apollinian and esthetic). He forgets, however, the third possible attitude, the Christic, realized through the irruption of the spirit (374). The position of Evola is valid only for "occultists who practice the detachment of the personal consciousness from physiological functions through everyday work, and not through experiences of the type that can be found in Christian mysticism" (371–372). Not being a religious spirit, but a "methodologist," Evola misses the concrete of mysticism, the actualization of Christ through active contemplation.

As he did with Anthroposophy in *"Itinerariu spiritual,"* Eliade accepts the validity of the occultist experience for those who have not arrived at Christianity. As for himself, he is situated beyond the theosophic-contemplative and magic attitudes, in the Christic spirit, which he considers to be the most sublime and concrete fact.

The other article mentioned by Eliade, *"La scolastica dinanzi allo spirito moderno,"* contains, in summary, the fundamental ideas of Evola's philosophy. It is, in fact, an extensive discussion of Louis Rougier's book, *La scolastique et le thomisme* (1925). Evola agrees fully with the criticism of scholasticism raised by the French empiricist, but he turns against him when he emphasize its "positive" aspects and especially when he sustains an anti-metaphysical position (Evola, *I saggi di Bilychnis*, 39–61).

The article raises not only a criticism of the return to scholasticism, proclaimed by some contemporary currents like neo-Thomism, but also of the Christian theology, even of Christianity itself, as a religion that institutes an irreducible difference between man and God. Combating the "Thomist pseudo-synthesis," Evola exposes in the final part of his article, ideas sketched in his book *Saggi sull' Idealismo magico* (1925) and developed in *Teoria dell'Individuo assoluto* (1927) and *L'Uomo come Potenza* (1926), whose future appearance he announces. The first is an introduction, the second an exhaustive exposition of his doctrine, and the third represents a practical illustration.

The same ideas constitute the substance of Evola's booklet *L'individuo e il divenire del mondo* (1926), which consists of two lectures held in 1925 at Lega Teosofica Indipendente (The Independent Theosophical

League) in Rome. The first of them, "*L'individuo e il processo del mondo*" ("The Individual and the Process of the World"), approaches the theme of the passage from knowledge through explanation to knowledge through action. The second one, "*Nietzsche e la sapienza dei misteri*" ("Nietzsche and the Knowledge of the Mysteries"), insists upon the opposition between knowledge through action (illustrated by Dionysian mysteries) and the religious attitude (identified with Christianity). The key terms of Evola's philosophy—*atto magic* (magic act), *idealismo magico* (magical idealism), *individuo assoluto* (absolute individual), *potenza* (power)—are already specified here.

The opposition between occultism, esoterism, and initiation on the one hand and religion, faith, and devotion on the other appears even more categorically in these lectures. For Evola, the sense of any true realization through initiation is magic. But the science of (Dionysian) mysteries finds its culmination and fulfillment in the doctrine of Nietzsche. The world is that which any man wills it, transcendentally, to be. The absolute individual is the end and the perfection of the universe. Evola's notion of the "self-realization of the Ego" philosophically conceptualizes the idea of salvation through the self (Evola, *L'individuo*, 31–95).

However, there is no proof in Eliade's published writings or manuscript archive that he ever knew this volume, just as he did not, very probably, know the earlier one. The essays gathered in Evola's first book, *Saggi sull'Idealismo magico* (1925), deal with the following themes: the surpassing of idealism, the concept of power, the supernormal Ego, the construction of immortality, and the essence of magic development. The last one, "*Esigenze contemporanee verso l'Idealismo magico*" ("Contemporary Trends toward Magic Idealism"), discusses critically the works of Carlo Michelstaedter, Otto Braun, Giovanni Gentile, Octave Hamelin, and Hermann von Keyserling.

For Evola, idealism is the philosophical idea that is imposed inevitably in the wake of any criticism of the fundamentals of knowledge. However, the truth or falsity of idealism cannot be demonstrated theoretically, through an intellectual act, but only through a "concrete realization." As a consequence, he develops a critique of the "transcendental ego," postulated by classical idealism. In his view, abstract idealism can be surpassed by occultism as magic idealism.

Evola subordinates the gnoseological problem to the principle of power. Absolute knowledge has power as its condition of existence. But power and, together with it, freedom occur not in action determined by desire, but in autarchic action. It is not possible to speak of power as long as the priority of any law or norm is accepted. Morality and liberty are two absolutely incompatible dimensions of the conscience. The spirit is beyond any morality. Spirit exists only as liberty, and liberty exists only as its own cause: *causa sui ex nihilo*. The obtaining of power through the exploitation of natural forces is an illusion and a gesture that turns against the Ego: making use of nature means to recognize it. Nature is a complete denial of the principle of individuality. Power is not obtained by accepting laws, but by imposing them, dominating them, and violating them. In the same way, technology is the servitude of the Ego.

The essays *"L'Io supernormale"* ("The Supernormal Ego") and *"La costruzione dell'Immortalità"* ("The Construction of Immortality") return to the problem of occultism ("fakirism," Yoga, "mantrism," theurgy) and Metapsychism (Richet and Osty are cited). Evola distinguishes between two kinds of the supernormal: one prior to the value of the individual, the other expressing the absolute concrete and perfection of this. Men of science who have examined supernormal phenomena have been more concerned with the first. For the Italian occultist, this represents a regressive and degenerate process.

Evola criticizes Christianity for its belief in the generality and the naturalness of immortality. In reality, says he, in all the other religions and religious doctrines, immortality is the privileged gift of a few select who have known how to construct it through effort (power) and will. In what way? The Ego creates in its own body (physical, emotional, psychic) a life that is independent of the body and of all the impressions that come from it. It creates a body that is not made of matter, but of liberty and power. This immortal body is the body of the magical Ego. The methodology of obtaining it is illustrated with *kundalī yoga* [sic] of the "Indian system," *Śakti tantra*, described by John Woodroffe, whom Evola connects with the Platonic theory of the Androgyne. It is a matter of surpassing heterogenesis through autogenesis: man becomes sufficient to himself and obtains the power to create from himself his own body.

Metaphysics aside, for Evola, magic idealism harmonizes completely with "oriental gnoseology." To know does not mean to think, but *to be* the object that you know. Diverse transcendental functions do not exist before the act of integration that institutes them. *The real* existence of a spiritual world comes forth only from the process of auto-liberation or purification of the Ego. When the individual obtains the power to externalize his own Ego, he has the possibility of experiencing the real as a sum of subjective entities or as inner centers of liberty. This is the state of intuition or cosmic consciousness. To know means to project the Ego inside beings, to transfer one's own interiority from one individuation to another, *intus-ire*. This way of knowing is the sign of the complete realization of that which is absolutely detached. The final phase of magic realization consists in the actualization of an absolutely indeterminate principle in a concrete and mediated body.

Magic idealism is distinguished from other doctrines by its essentially practical character. Its fundamental exigency is not to substitute one intellectual conception of the world for another, but to create in the individual a new "dimension" and a new depth of life. That which exists outside the Ego appears as such only because it exists likewise within it (the *saṃskāras* of Indian philosophy). The fundamental principle of magic is that the way in which the world appears does *not* constitute an extreme instance. It is not an inconvertible *in itself*, but a phenomenon depending on the pure power of the Ego. Acting transcendentally on *saṃskāras*, one can supersede the conditions under which reality appears and, consequently, the concrete experience of the world. The magic or individual Ego is the principle of the absolute, unconditioned substantiation. As can be seen, Evola draws again upon the technique and terminology of yoga. Besides the books of Woodroffe, *The Serpent Power* (1919) and *The Garland of Letters* (1922), he cites the *Yoga Sūtra* of Patañjali, suggesting its confrontation with *Geheimwissenschaft im Umriss* of Rudolf Steiner or with the *Esercizi spirituali* of Ignatius Loyola (Evola, *Saggi*, 92).

In the last chapter of the book, Evola endeavors to deduce the doctrine of magic idealism historically. The fact that this doctrine is a historical necessity does not contradict its fundamental principle (unconditioned self-determination), given the fact that time is an ideal reality: this is a way through which the Ego orders the material of representations. History, consequently, is nothing but a mode in which the Ego projects on the canvas of time that which it wishes, what is both inner and atemporal.

The problems of these books are taken up again in 1927–1929 in the articles published in the review *Ur/Krur*—of which Evola was editor-in-chief—often verbatim, but with many additional details and clarifications. They mark his transition from an esotericizing philosophy to a philosophic esotericism.

Gruppo di Ur (The Ur Group), the editorial board of the review, was a magical society formed in Rome that declared itself independent of any and all societies or esoteric movements of the time. Its members came, nevertheless, from the ranks of older schools such as Anthroposophy, Pythagorean Masonry, and the *Schola Philosophica Hermetica Classica Italica* of Giuliano Kremmerz. Differences of esoteric affiliation are not totally effaced by the pseudonyms with which these signed their contributions in *Ur.* Under such rubrics as *Dottrina, Practica, Esperienze, Testi, Glosse,* the review published theoretical articles, expositions of methods and techniques, reports of inner experiences, translations of rare or little-known texts stemming from Western as well as Eastern traditions, and diverse commentaries on points of detail. The dominant themes are magic, hermeticism, and alchemy—while, through Julius Evola, there exists a serious openness toward Indian and Buddhist doctrines. The notion of "magic" is invested with an active and functional connotation, close to Roger Bacon's concept of "practical metaphysics."[7]

The first article by Evola, *"Come poniamo il problema della conoscenza"* ("How Can We Pose the Problem of Knowledge"), maintains, against the gnoseological democratism of the modern epoch, the possibility of a direct form of knowledge in which "to know" means "to be," more precisely, to transform one's consciousness into the object known. What is known in this way is real; the rest is unreal. Put under the form of this "experimental radicalism," the problem of knowledge becomes a practical matter, even a technical one: namely, how is it possible to realize that form of perception whose object has the character of absolute reality? That which Evola describes is initiatory knowledge: a realization that is, at the same time, objective and purely individual (i.e., subjective). The problem of knowledge merges with the problem of power, while the fact of knowledge becomes a magical state. Ancient Sanskrit texts are invoked in support of these positions (Evola et al., *Ur 1927*, 196–204).

The second article, *"Come poniamo il problema dell'immortalità"* ("How Can We Pose the Problem of Immortality"), is concerned with the nature of what survives death, distinguishing the "psychic cadaver," the "living consciousness," and the "samsaric Ego." Moreover, it points out that conscious survival after death is not identical with immortality. This pertains only to the "individuating individual," which is not a given but must be constructed. The idea that everyone possesses an "immortal soul," conceived as a facsimile of the living consciousness or of the individual terrestrial ego, is a true ideological aberration for Evola, who nevertheless recognizes its utility as an opiate for the masses. At the same time, the article intends to dissipate both the equivocal idea of reincarnation and the effort in the opposite direction: "liberation" (Evola et al., *Ur 1927*, 143–152.)

The discussion is continued on another level in the article *"La dottrina del 'Corpo Immortale'"* ("The Doctrine of 'The Immortal Body'"). The state of confusion and absentmindedness that people call *life* is nothing but a complex of organic and psychic conditionings of the human body. This is why whoever wishes to live must first *die*, that is, to enucleate an *individuated* life, independent of these influences. Man is immortal insofar as he knows how to construct himself in a self-subsistent life. Immortality is not only, however, a making permanent of consciousness, but it extends over its forms of action and expression, over what is called the *magic body* or *body of resurrection*. It is a matter of recreating the human body, from the top down, from the principle that has conquered death and exists through itself. The immortal body is simple, uncompounded; it is made of consciousness and power, not of matter. (Matter, for Evola, is not a distinct principle, coexistent with the spirit, but a form or state through which the *one* reality, the spirit, experiences itself.) In distinction from the ordinary body, the magic body is supported by the Ego and not the reverse (Evola et al., *Ur 1927*, 196–204).

In the article *"Sul senso dello stato di Potenza"* ("On the Meaning of State of Power") Evola polemically rejects several common preconceived ideas about the meaning of magic and of magical power. Power is not an instrument exterior to the Ego. The condition of "to be able" is "to be." The magus does not seek *to do* but *to be*, to be another man, absolutely free, full, cosmic. The magic act (*atto magico*) is the opposite of the miracle; it is a "state of evidence" of a real, direct causality, in which the *Ego* is the one who acts, who provokes a given effect, an effective state of power that coincides with the very sentiment of inner life.

The magic discipline endeavors to sever the system of relations in which man is a specter or an unconscious instrument. The state of power, the magic act, manifests itself in pure action that is not subordinated to any other instances, which is signification and value in itself. Pure action shines often in the activity of the common man, too, in a moment of heroism, of sacrifice, of invention, of play, of free sympathy.

Magic cannot be considered an instrument. It is the realization of a state of spiritual *possibility*, completely free, the realization of the feeling, unceasingly wider and increasingly evident, that *I can* do.

Evola cites the Sanskrit maxim according to which the gods' principle of existence is play (*līlā*), while that of men is law (*dharma*). Law is necessity, a state of adhesion, of being linked to a certain nature, of passion, of identification, of seriousness. Play is liberty, levity, irony, a state of detachment, of active spiritual spontaneity, of agility. The law of a creature is the play of a god. Like magic, the aim of power is power itself: it is the supreme state in which the ultimate nature of reality is revealed (Evola et al., *Ur 1927*, 254–261).

All these articles in *Ur* are characterized by a special attention to the practical, technical aspect of the subjects discussed, illustrating the assertions with numerous examples from diverse traditions, Western and Eastern. Among them, *yoga* and *tantra* enjoy a privileged position.

Finally, the article "*Sulla visione magica della Vita*" ("On the Magic View of Life") puts the principal ideas of Evola's philosophy in another stylistic register, offering a dense lyrical prose closely related to that of a man he admired in youth, Giovanni Papini, in his *Maschilità* (1915). Although it has not been seen explicitly from what has been said so far, there exists a subtle filiation between Papini's magic pragmatism and Evola's magic idealism, which the later influences of Stirner and Nietzsche on Evola fail to overshadow completely. This article merits a comparative analysis in relation to several texts of Eliade, such as "*Apologia virilității*," "*Ura oamenilor și eroilor*," "*Faptul magic*," and the novel *Lumina ce se stinge*—an analysis we will undertake in a future study.

According to Evola, the principal qualities needed by those who aspire to the magical realization converge in a renewed, heroic, and rugged *feeling* of the world—a sense of the world as power, as sacrificial act, as the rhythmic and agile dance of Śiva. The magic act is calm action, inhuman as liberty, as play, as dance; an action willed because it is pleasure in itself and not for its object; an action ready anytime and any place to decisively assume any direction, superior to winning or losing, to success or failure, pleasure or pain, egotism or altruism; an action liberated from "thought," from "compassion," and from "soul." The magi are reduced to spirit and body—with the second as an unconditioned instrument of the first.

Magic affirms only the individual. God is left behind. He is a thing for which only the degenerate can have nostalgia. Magic philosophy eventually becomes an extolling of wild forces of the superman, of the race of Masters, beyond good or evil, beyond humanity. Heaven is deserted; light has become earth, while among the beings made of earth, only from those of the "race of the Magi" could be expected the resurrection of Earth. In support of this poetic vision, Evola cites Novalis and Nietzsche, the *Bhagavad Gītā*, the Mythraic ritual, and the image of Śiva the destroyer (Evola et al., *Ur 1927*, 153–157 and 299–304).

Besides the sources from which he draws, Evola cites in his *Ur* articles all his books published up until then and several other studies published in reviews. Likewise, he mentions several times René Guénon's little booklet *Le roi du monde* (1927), which had been translated into Italian by Arturo Reghini. *La crise du mode moderne* (1927) will be cited in the 1928 issues of *Ur*. References to these books of the French traditionalist are likely to have rekindled Eliade's interest in Guénon.

In 1928, the number of articles of Evola in *Ur* multiplied. Beside the pages of pure doctrine, no longer as dense as in the previous year, he approached various particular themes, such as the Tibetan ideas about the afterlife, the philosophy of hermetic traditions, and feminine initiation.

The review of *The Tibetan Book of the Dead* (1927)—the first translation of the famous text, by the monk Kazi Dawa-Samdup, a collaborator with John Woodroffe on the series *Tantrik Texts*—gives Evola the occasion to return to the problem of survival and immortality. What must have been of much interest to Eliade here are the short comparative references to Egyptian rituals in the cult of Osiris, to Orphic and Pythagorean funerary rites, the Isis initiation and the Mithraic liturgy (Evola et al., *Ur 1928*, 111–122.)

The article *"Sull'arte dei filosofi d'Ermete"* ("On the Art of the Philosophers of Hermes") is devoted to alchemic Hermeticism. Evola approaches alchemy as a "spiritual science" and polemically rejects the historians of science who consider it a simple infancy of chemistry. In reality, he says—citing Guénon's *La crise du monde moderne*—it is not a matter of a process of "evolution" of "progress" from alchemy to chemistry but on the contrary, of a degeneration: modern chemistry is a teratological excrescence of alchemy.

Evola maintains that, in order to understand all the obscure and apparently absurd things from alchemical literature, one needs a similar approach to that of Luigi Valli in his then recent book *Dante e il linguaggio segreto dei Fedeli d'Amore* (1928).[8] Alchemy, substances, operations, and transmutations must be interpreted in three senses: literary, magical, and symbolic-initiatic. Alchemy interests Evola first and foremost as an *art* of palingenesis and of magical reintegration. For him, the "hermetico-alchemical tradition" is one of the purest forms through which the Tradition manifested itself in the West, especially in the "dark age" brought by the "good news." It is important to state like-wise, that in understanding these traditions, he accords primordiality to "symbol" and "myth" (Evola et al., *Ur 1928*, 148–152 and 167–176).

Two other articles have as their subject the overcoming of the ideas of Providence and ethical norms. In *"Superamento della 'Provvidenza'"* ("Overcoming 'Providence'"), Evola develops a critique of the belief in Providence, which he considers a pale larva of the religious world that continues to oppress the heart of man even after the death of God (in different historicisms, evolutionisms, and optimisms). Its overcoming means a return to "the absolute immanence," that is, to the magic state, the primordial state of the individuated consciousness, a return to pure action, which is pure causality. Evola calls this attitude "active realism" and proclaims it the principle of a "new order" of purity, dignity, and inner liberty that has a single criterion: neither "good" or "evil," "true" or "false," but what is real and what is not. Fear of conceiving liberty makes man presuppose relations of finality, intentionality, or signifi-cation where nothing exists except facts: free, original, noninferable (Evola et al., *Ur 1928*, 136–144).

In *"L'esoterismo e il superamento della morale"* ("Esotericism and the Surpassing of Morals"), Evola radically detaches occult science from any kind of moral conditioning. Science is beyond morals; furthermore, the tradition of occult science is a "non-human" tradition, which is justified from the point of view of *reality*, not "humanity." Magic, be it white, black, or gray, has the same autonomy toward morals as chemistry. In distinction from "moralism," the norms that must be respected in occultism do not derive from a law of good or evil, but are "technical conditions" for the satisfaction of natural and objective laws.

In the "Mediterranean tradition," especially the Hellenic, good is synonymous with reality: the state of perfect, completely realized activity. Evil, consequently, is uncertain possibility, chaotic, incapable of being actualized: unreality. For Evola, the "sacred science" does not intend to make man "good," except in this pagan sense. It wants, that is, to "realize" him. The realized man, whom Evola equates with the *siddha* of Indian tradition, emanates "good" naturally. But he does it in the same way toward good or evil people, without selection, as the sun shines without desiring or choosing. For the realized man, the "others" do not exist (Evola et al., *Ur 1928*, 228–239).

The article *"Sulla metafisica del dolore e della malattia"* ("On the Metaphysics of Pain and Illness") illustrates a case of applied meta-physics (Evola et al., *Ur 1928*, 176–181). Practical considerations in the article *"Alcuni effetti della disciplina magica: la 'dissociazione dei misti'"* ("Some Effects of the Magic Discipline: 'The Separation of Mixtures'") give Evola a chance to discuss the psychogenesis of three possible attitudes toward the spiritual world: mystical (devotional), magical, and intellectualistic. They stem from identification with one of the three energies—sentiment, will, and thought—that become dominant in man (Evola et al., *Ur 1928*, 278–286).

Evola's articles in the last two numbers of 1928 of the review *Ur*, sent to Bucharest, were read by Eliade only in Calcutta, where they were forwarded (Evola et al., *Ur 1928*, 321–357).[9] It is important to know the contents of all these articles and early books of Evola because a part of their themes, ideas, and images are present in Eliade's writings, dating before and after he read them. Some can be found in identical form, some in a similar or adapted one, and others as positions against which he argues. The same thing can be said about some articles written by other members of the Ur Group, as we shall see—especially in the Indian period.

Knowledge of the Magic Fact

Although Eliade was tending more and more toward an intellectual position close to mysticism, in 1928 he was also preoccupied with "the magic fact," probably because he had to redefine himself in relation to it and to reintegrate it into his new spiritual synthesis.

The notions *"faptul mistic"* ("mystic fact") and *"faptul magic"* ("magic fact") are the Romanian equivalent of the French *"fait mystique"*[10] and *"fait magique."*[11] They differ from *"acte mystique"* and *"acte magique"* and were coined on the model of the older terms *"fait religieux," "fait métaphysique," "fait moral,"* and so on. Eliade—and also Nae Ionescu— used them as referring generally to two different forms of *religious experience*, and by extrapolation, to two ways of thinking and relating to reality.[12]

Toward the end of October 1928, in the article *"Chemare la ordine"* ("Call to order")—written for *Cuvântul* but refused by Nae Ionescu on the pretext of "ferocious egotism"—Eliade took an overview of his work up until then and the innovations it has brought to Romanian culture. Among other things, he attributes to himself the introduction of "the knowledge of the magic fact" into the philosophical discipline. This was found in five different registers: in the origins of aesthetic emotions, in the origins of philosophy, in alchemy, in *tantra*, and in occultism (Eliade, *Virilitate și asceză*, 392–393). For the first, however, he offers no bibliographic reference, and it is not easy to discover to what text he is referring. The most probable is the review of Ion Marin Sadoveanu's *"Pe urmele dramei"* ("On the Traces of Drama," *"Foileton bibliografic,"* *Cuvântul*, July 7, 1927), but the idea of arts being rooted in magic is mentioned in other successive texts. The other four registers refer to the following articles: *"Cuvinte despre o filosofie"* ("Words about a Philosophy," *Gândirea*, June–July 1928), *"Marcelin Berthelot şi alchimia"* (*Cuvântul*, February 14, 1928), *"Varnamâlâ sau 'Ghirlanda literelor'"* (*"Varnamâlâ* or 'The Garland of Letters,'" *Cuvântul*, July 11, 1928), and *"Faptul magic"* ("The Magic Fact," planned to be written for the projected review *Duh şi slovă*). Very soon he will add observations about the magic fact in a new register, the medical, in the article *"Institutul de istorie a medicinei"* (*Cuvântul*, October 31, 1928).

In the essay *"Cuvinte despre o filosofie"* ("Words about a Philosophy"), Eliade asserted that there are only three means of survival: insensitivity, magic, and mysticism (Eliade, *Virilitate şi asceză*, 212–215). Any activity that suppresses the impetus of the spirit toward its own worlds leads to insensitivity: "the valorization of sexual life, the dogmatization of collective mediocrity, the limitation of the spirit to pathetic 'ideals' of social and family life" (212). Spiritual brutalization preserves fresh in the body the desire to be attached to life. Not only sterile souls are tempted by this path, but also elite spirits lacking the courage of "magical self-creation" or of "subordination in a spiritual economy of mystic origin" (212). In distinction from these two "roads to salvation," brutalization is spiritual suicide.

For the first time now, Eliade configures with clarity the meaning of the two concepts, mysticism and magic, which will become the cardinal points of his thought in the following years. Mysticism (*mistică*) is identified with religious experience and characterized by "dualism and transcendentalism, equilibrium of spiritual economy through a point of support *outside*; the meaning of existence: assimilation of divine virtues and the realization of the man-of-God" (212–213). The magic attitude implies

> monism, imanentism, self-creation and creation of the World through personal effort, the absence of ethical function, the point of support *in oneself*, the denial of *effectively objective* existences [. . . ,] the cosmos understood as a feud of impersonal forces, and the *meaning of existence* as a magical realization, an actualization of inner powers and of cosmic possibilities disciplined and led through a labor that ends by affirming oneself God. (213)

The first attitude has its supreme incarnation in the type of the saint, the second in that of the magus. But authentic magi are found more and more rarely in history. The magic attitude has become "mediocre," ending in philosophy. As examples, Eliade refers to Indian and pre-Socratic philosophies, "phases of decomposition of a magic mentality and of recomposition on a rational plane." Likewise, magic as "the necessity to create the world, from us and for us" is identifiable not just in idealism, but in the whole history of philosophy (213).

Philosophy realizes a transposition of magic onto the "ideological" plane. If this latter creates effectively in the cosmos, philosophy creates meanings in consciousness. It attempts to reconstruct the relation between the Ego and the world, with the aim of balancing the individual consciousness and conferring a meaning to existence. The valorizing of a philosophy is not quantifiable in categories of true or false, but only according to its coherence and self-consistency. Still, not every philosophy coherent with itself entails a spiritual process. On the contrary, the majority of philosophies will remain a matter of indifference to a given individual; they will not draw him into spiritual attitude because they cannot be actualized in personal experience. Authentic philosophy is the experienced: the systemization of the results of spiritual crises, the valorization of personal sympathies and antipathies, the spiritual creation of the world, and salvation.

Unlike the previous articles in which he had outlined the magic attitude, Eliade now refrains from naming it "pragmatism." The reason is probably the attempt to extrapolate it to the entire young generation and to root it in the "heritage of the nation" as a fact of experience, an attempt through which he aims to integrate himself into two larger selves: the generation and the nation. The article ends with a rhetorical question concerning the magic "heritage" of the latter: "What if the magic of our ancestors passed too quickly into the religious phase (by projecting into space the personal potentialities), preparing thus— through the tragic sense of life—Christianity?" (215). This is an implicit endorsement of the evolutionist schema of J. G. Frazer. Otherwise put, the magic of the Dacian (or Thracian) priests did not stop in the phase of philosophical "mediocrizing," but was transformed immediately into mysticism, paving the way for religiosity of a Christian type.

The article "*Marcelin Berthelot și alchimia*" contains a single paragraph about the "magic" of alchemy. Eliade observes that the alchemical mentality introduces into the "universal dynamism" new elements of "magic of a primitive pragmatism." The alchemist accepts universal causality as well as the possibility of its annulment (Eliade, *Virilitate și asceză*, 54–58).

The same thing is observed in *"Varnamâlâ sau 'Ghirlanda literelor,'"* in connection with tantric mentality, which displays a "pure and universal form of magic." In its center lies the conception of the "creative, magical power" of the word. Any reality has its own sound, perceptible only to the yogin. Knowing the sound, "the name," and repeating it in a ritualistic, magical way, one obtains power over the corresponding reality, which can be actualized or annulled (Eliade, *Virilitate și asceză*, 194–197).

But in a contemporary text published posthumously, Eliade proved to be aware of the danger of the "self-realization of the magic mentality," which is met always on "the road to the transcendent," that is, on the road of the soul toward another spiritual infinite (390). As in the case of the heroic attitude, which rejects the non-Ego, in another article, *"Soliloquiu,"* Eliade considers that the essential structure of thinking is the monologue. Perfect dialogue is perfect monologue. But precisely by virtue of its nature, the absolute soliloquy is attended by a great danger: "Thought which grows from itself, without receiving verification and justifications from outside, risks *enchanting* itself, of living a dream, of becoming *magic*" (302).

With this reflection, Eliade was approaching the content of the last article announced in the series of the "knowledge of the magic fact." The series was, however, constituted *post factum*. In reality, each of these five articles had its own meaning. Thus, *"Faptul magic"* itself was part of a cycle of articles with other objectives: *"Theös éghènou,"* *"Apologia virilității,"* and *"Virilitate și asceză."* Already in the last of these, Eliade announces *"Faptul magic,"* where he would explain the surpassing of the magic conception of asceticism by an overturning of the values to which he had adhered until then: that is, by the introduction of grace into the economy of the human effort to become divine (277–278). *"Faptul magic"* was, thus, supposed to be a reconciliation of "magic pragmatism" with mysticism and, especially, with Christian theology. Not by chance it was destined to be published in a review of Orthodox orientation.

In his autobiography, Eliade presents the new review, *Duh și slovă* (*Spirit and Letter*), as a continuation of the defunct *Logos*, edited by Nae Ionescu. If this is indeed true, it means that the end of *Logos* was already known by close friends of the professor before the appearance of its second and last number.[13] This came out in the first days of October

1928, almost at the same time as the announcement of the publication of *Duh și slovă* ("*Confesiuni și semnificații*," Eliade, *Virilitate și asceză*, 272). Barely a month later, Eliade spoke about "the *Duh și slovă* Group" as having a distinct profile in the framework of the young generation ("*Spiritualitate și ortodoxie*," 294).

Together with the editorial team of the review *Kalende* (Șerban Cioculescu, Pompiliu Constantinescu, Vladimir Streinu, and Tudor Șoimaru), the *Duh și slovă* group represented the binary ideological landscape of the generation. In a programmatic article, Mihail Polihroniade attached to the youth of *Kalende* group the label of radical socialism (rational, scientific, anti-mystic, anticlerical, antinationalistic) and considered that the "manifestations of humanists and extremists of the left are so rare and so qualitatively inferior that they do not count." For him, the most remarkable personalities of the generation are those of the *Duh și slovă* group (that is, the young people from the reviews *Gândirea* and *Cuvântul*). If we are to believe his declaration, with the possible exception of Stelian Mateescu, this group was openly hostile to nationalism: "The youth grouped around *Duh și slovă* are possessed by the rage for the absolute: they despise the temporal, the contingent; they subordinate the ethnic to the spiritual" (Polihroniade, 26–27).

The first number of the review was supposed to appear on Christmas Eve and was dedicated to "the mystic life." Eliade had the duty of presenting "the structures of magic philosophies" and of showing "to what extent magic constitutes one of the greatest temptations of the spirit." Stelian Mateescu followed by demonstrating the invalidity of magical philosophy, whereas Mircea Vulcănescu presented the specific characteristics of the Christian religious experience (Eliade, *Memorii*, 154–155). We do not know the subject of Paul Sterian's article, but we can surmise it was in the area of Orthodox spirituality.

Hence it is clear that "*Faptul magic*" was not an apology for magical individualism, but an exposition—very clear, as Vulcănescu assures us ("*Carte pentru* Isabel")—of "magical experience," with the aim of demonstrating the superior distinction of Christian mystical experience. This should have enlisted him into the Orthodoxy of Nae Ionescu's school, for whom magic was, in the last analysis, a failure of the spirit.

Eliade worked at the article on board the steamer *Hakone Maru*, on which he had embarked from Port Said on the first of December. Upon arrival at Colombo on December 12, he immediately sent it to Mircea Vulcănescu. He realized that the article was rather negligently written—even a "sorry manuscript"—and that it probably will not satisfy everyone, but he could not do better in the circumstances in which he had written it (Eliade, *Europa, Asia, America* . . . III, 243, 244, January 23 and July 23, 1929). Unfortunately, *Duh şi slovă* never appeared, and Eliade did not succeed in recovering the manuscript of this article, which marked the end of his Romanian phase and the beginning of his Indian one.[14] Only a draft of it survived (Eliade, *Jurnal* I, 228), but it was not preserved in his archive at Bucharest.

Seven years later, in reviewing Julius Evola's book *Rivolta contro il mondo moderno* ("Revolt against the Modern World," 1934), Eliade would write: "In the year 1928 I composed a whole study about his philosophy of magic, which has remained in manuscript" (Eliade, "*Revolta contra lumii moderne*"). This statement can only refer to the article "*Faptul magic.*" In the absence of the text, we have no way of knowing how Eliade related to Evola's philosophy: whether he had truly followed his initial intention to correct the magical position with the Christic or had changed his mind at the last moment.[15]

We also do not know which of the Italian occultist's writings were used as references: the articles from *Bilychnis* and *Ur*, which he knew, or some of his books published by then—*Saggi sull'Idealismo magico* (1925), *L'Individuo e il divenire del mondo* (1926), *L'Uomo come Potenza* (1926), *Teoria dell'individuo assoluto* (1927*)*, and *Imperialismo pagano* (1928)—which we have no proof that Eliade knew. The publication of the last two volumes was announced by Evola himself, in a letter he sent to Calcutta along with his earlier book dedicated to tantra (*Mircea Eliade şi corespondenţii săi*, I, 276, May 28, 1930). The fact that he did not send Eliade the first two books could be considered evidence that he had already read them.[16]

Indeed, some recent studies have maintained that the subject of the article "*The Magic Fact*" would have been either *Saggi sull'Idealismo magico* (Țurcanu, 90–93) or *L'individuo e il divenire del mondo* (De Martino, 146, 262–299), which Eliade would have read in 1928. This could have happened only in the course of his second sojourn in Italy in April–May 1928 or after his return to Romania. We do not, however, have a direct testimony about their reading, not one single mention of them, and in those years Eliade had no reason to hide his consultation of the Italian writer's works.

These facts plead for the articles from *Bilychnis* and *Ur* as the only sources about the thought of Evola that Eliade could have used in "*Faptul magic.*" They contained, nonetheless, all that the Italian occultist had said in his first two books and somewhat more. As for the way in which Eliade related to the magic attitude, it will remain unknown until the possible recovery of the article's manuscript. We are inclined to believe, however, that he held to the initial intention: to illustrate the overcoming of the magic position through the Christic position and the "self-creating personalism" through grace. Although Evola's terminology—"magic idealism," "absolute individual," "transcendental I," "absolute self-realization," "autarchy," "liberty and power," and so on—was known to him from the two reviews, it is not found, except partially, accidentally, and critically, in Eliade's texts of the second half of 1928.[17]

Likewise, one cannot speak at this moment of Evola as a major influence in Eliade's thought, but rather of a convergence of ideas, those of the Italian thinker being already synthesized in a theoretical construct. The themes of magic, the heroic, the superman, and the fascination with "metapsychic" powers are present in Eliade's writings well before his encounter with the works of Evola. Furthermore, at the moment of that encounter, he was already in the process of surpassing the magical attitude, which led him to take a critical distance from Evola.

Other questions of his relation with Evola also remain unclear. In the first letter sent to Eliade in India, the former assures him: "I recall you perfectly" (*Mircea Eliade și corespondenții săi*, I, 275, May 28, 1930). But what did he remember: the face of a person or the letters of a correspondent? Can this be a sign of a meeting between the two? Unfortunately, the letters from Eliade to Evola have been destroyed. Some authors, even among his contemporaries, have presumed that he met Evola on the second of his two trips to Italy (Acterian, 78).[18] Indeed, the occasion for a meeting could have been the first *Congresso nazionale di studi romani* held at Rome from April 21–26, 1928, with a large number of scholars from Italy and other parts of the world attending.[19] Evola did not participate with a paper, as he would do at the third session of the Congress in 1933, but it is not impossible that he may have been among the auditors, like Eliade. Both have declared, however, that their first meeting took place only ten years later, in Bucharest. Does this mean then that they carried on a correspondence, however short, before Eliade left for India? Very probably, but it remains for the time being mysterious, like other aspects of the relationship between the two scholars fascinated by the occult, magic, and the supernatural.

"*Faptul magic*" and *Soliloquii*

Just before leaving for India, Eliade published in *Gândirea* (November 1928) the article "*Soliloquiu*." It came instead of the announced "*Cântări pentru pustnic*" ("Chants for a Hermit") or "*Cântece pentru singurătate*" ("Songs for Solitude"), which were to continue the series consisting of "*Theös éghènou*" (December 1927), "*Cuvinte despre o filosofie*" (June–July 1928), and "*Apologia virilității*" (August–September 1928). The last had been corrected with "*Virilitate și asceză*" (*Cuvântul*, October 1928). Here Eliade announced the article "*Faptul magic*," which was to complete the surpassing of the magical conception of asceticism. As we have seen, the manuscript of that article sent to Bucharest was lost.

Eliade did not have the habit of leaving texts unpublished, even the less important. It is hard to believe that he did not recycle, in one of his later writings, the draft of "*Faptul magic*," an article that had an especial theoretical value for him. Indeed, there exists a text that presents striking coincidences with what we know he wanted this article to be: part two (of four) of the little book *Soliloquii*, published after his return from India in 1932. The hypothesis we propose is that *Soliloquii* uses the draft of "*Faptul magic*," preserved by him, or at least the most important part of it.

It was not at all unusual for Eliade to publish or reuse a text years from the time it had been written. A large part of his articles in adolescence had been drafted long before their publication. Some of those that appeared when he crossed the threshold of university date from three or even four years earlier. His journal notes about Maitreyi are used almost verbatim in the novel that bears her name, some three years after the events. The travel impressions in India and a part of the Indian journal were published in volumes after a period that extends two to six years from their being put to paper. A large part of the thoughts published in *Soliloquii* come from the notebook "*Monstrul nr. 1*," containing notations from June 2 to September 5, 1930.[20]

Another argument pleads strongly for the validity of this hypothesis. The text of the second section of *Soliloquii* is, both as to ideas and style, a continuation of the above-mentioned articles from *Gândirea*. Unlike the following two sections of the book, it did not require contact with India in order to have been written. Its comparison with these articles on the one hand and with Eliade's writings from India on the other proves that it belongs to the first period.

These pages from *Soliloquii* commence with meditation on asceticism. We recall that "*Faptul magic*" and *Tratatul de asceză* ("Treatise on Ascesis," announced in "*Apologia virilității*") were parts of the same theoretical project.[21] Eliade observes that man is given only two existential options, just two "roads of integration of human life into eternity": glory and asceticism. The rest of the ideals and aspirations satisfy only biology: instincts, curiosities, and weaknesses. But the two roads are not entirely separate. Asceticism can be magical or religious. That of a magical type is a rare species of glory (*Solilocvii*, 25–28). We have thus, on the one hand, the type of hero and on the other that of the magus or the saint.

The final part of section two of the book compares pagan and Indian asceticism with the Christian (34–42). Christianity has aspects that represent an implicit asceticism, such as love of your neighbor and submission to the community of faith (the church). But the true Christian asceticism is imitating the drama of Christ and the supernatural assimilation of the sufferings and humiliations of the Savior. Its success is possible only through the double miracle of Christ: the resurrection and grace. Eliade insists on the necessity of grace in the religious life, for that here "asceticism is a dramatic imitative act, and, left to his own powers, man will never coincide with God" (34). Without the presence of grace, such an attempt is ineffectual from the religious point of view and invalid from a theological perspective.

Christian asceticism is not possible without prayer, which is the "hope for and humble invocation of Grace." This "exercise," which installs the same living relationship between man and Christ, tends increasingly to replace asceticism, properly speaking. It does not originate from a negation, like asceticism, but from an affirmation: "the victory of the Savior over agony, life, and death" (40).

If in religious asceticism man needs the help of divinity, magical asceticism on the contrary is a force that can be oriented, even against this one. "The relations of the magus with the god are relations of invocation and conjuring, never of adoration. He coincides with the god through his will and the power of ritual, without the help of the god" (35).

There are other differences between the two types of asceticism: The Christian ascetic suppresses passions, while the magus exalts them to the point of transfiguration, integrating them as instruments of his consciousness. Then, play, the magic instinct of individual freedom, "unrestrained and lawless," irresponsible, the impulse to creation and to dream, is called Satan by Christian theology. But this, maintains Eliade, does not pertain to Satan because it isn't personal, nor personified in man. It is beyond good and evil, in the very nature of the universe, inborn in man as part of creation. "Certain men have taken knowledge of these things; they participate in that which we have called, throughout this book, the magic attitude" (39). But this term, "magic attitude," no longer appears in the following two sections of the book, although magic continues to be the principal subject. This could be more evidence that the text is taken from the draft of "*Faptul magic.*"

Not surprisingly, a contemporary critic well-acquainted with Italian culture wondered whether the "magical solution" in *Soliloquii* was not due to the "influence of the Italian philosopher Evola and of those of his group" (Călinescu, 868), that is, to the *Ur/Krur* review.

Nae Ionescu and the Mystic Fact

Magic was also an old preoccupation of Eliade's professor, probably linked to his inclination to occultism in his young years. Both in his university courses and in articles, Nae Ionescu dwelt often on the passionate interest of Renaissance men and of Goethe's Faust for magic as a way to knowledge. He would recall that the "whole of modern science has its origin in such fantastic interests: magic, alchemy, astrology, geomancy, etc."[22]

Nae Ionescu admitted that some men are gifted with "extraordinary spiritual powers" and even the possibility of inducing in a material way "special powers" that permit access to "certain realities which are out of the ordinary."[23] Time and again, he recognized the reality of miracles, however, from the perspective of Christian theology, not from that of the occultist paranormal, although he admitted the possibility of the appearance of stigmata through autosuggestion.[24] The preoccupation with magic does not therefore imply an approval of it. On the contrary, the professor considered that occultism has an "obviously dissolving action" on the church.[25] He pronounced categorically against magic practices "consisting of witchcraft and superstition," which he identifies—and combats—even within the church.[26]

But only in 1929 would he speak specifically, in an extensive and systematically argued way, against the magic mentality and occultism. This relationship of temporal succession with "*Faptul magic*"—which, as mentor of the *Duh și slovă* group and review, we have every reason to believe that he had read it—raise the suspicion that Nae Ionescu reacted to his disciple's position toward magic.

In the month of February, his course, *Theory of Metaphysical Knowledge*, began to take another turn. Today we know that this was, at least in part, the result of reading Evelyn Underhill's *Mysticism* (1911), which had just been translated into German. Far from being a plagiarism, as some have accused him on the basis of tendentious comparisons, the last eight lectures are, in fact, a polemical dialogue with the author of that book, whose name—for reasons that are to be clarified—was not recorded by the stenographer of the course.[27] In addition to attacking Underhill, Nae Ionescu polemized against other positions on mysticism, among which is that of the author of "*Faptul magic.*"

A first and evident proof of this is the repeated use of the expressions "*fapt magic*" and "*fapt mistic*," while Evelyn Underhill uses only "mystic fact," and only once, in the title of the first part of her book. In his Lesson XII, "*Mystic Type, Logical Type, and Mixed Types,*" Nae Ionescu characterizes active and contemplative types in the same way Eliade had described the magic and mystic types in "*Cuvinte despre o filosofie*" (Eliade, *Virilitate și asceză*, 212–213). On the other hand, his positioning in Lesson XXI, "*The Bridegroom Type,*" with regard to the two possible interpretations of "The Song of Songs," is a tacit polemic against Eliade's conclusions in his review of Paul Vuillaud's book *Le Cantique des Cantiques d'après la tradition juive* (1925).[28] His pupil accepts as possible both interpretations: literal (physical love) and allegorical (spiritual love). Nae Ionescu inclines toward Vuillaud's side and his Kabbalistic interpretation. He asks if it is permissible to give the "Song" only a spiritual interpretation and reaches a positive conclusion.

But the most important implicit reference to Eliade happens in Lesson XVI, "*Mysticism and Magic.*" For Nae Ionescu, the magic fact is a "moment of the pantheistic evolutionism," inaugurated by the Renaissance, the ultimate point of it being illustrated by the Kabbalah, Rosicrucianism, Freemasonry, Theosophy, and New Thought, but also by democracy, liberalism, and individualism. "In the magic fact there exists, on the one hand, an identification of the universe with myself and, on the other hand, a sort of transformation of myself into a center of action" (Ionescu, *Opere* II, 107).

Fundamental axioms of magic—the existence of the astral plane, the existence of an analogy between it and the sensible plane, the possibility of its control by the disciplined will of man—are taken from the book by Underhill, who in turn took them explicitly from *Dogme et rituel de la Haute Magie* (1856) by Eliphas Lévi. Underhill, proceeding descriptively, does not present them in this order. Nae Ionescu expounds them in a logical way, deducing one from another and adding a fourth fundamental principle: egocentrism. Eliade had written about the three characteristics of magic (implicitly, not as a didactic typology) in an article about Rudolf Steiner, in *Cuvântul*, two years earlier (Eliade, *Itinerariu spiritual*, 140, 152).[29]

The therapy by autosuggestion of Dr. Coué, about which Eliade had written—again in *Cuvântul*—is cited by Nae Ionescu as an example of a magical method. The professor specifies:

> I have absolutely nothing in common with the magical viewpoint and with all the tribulations of Freemasonry, Theosophy, etc.; I have no sympathy with this point of view; but this does not keep me from accepting that there is something serious in this attitude, and what is usually called the swindle of magi or of magicians, is not swindle at all, but simply a kind of special therapeutics which can take weird forms, but whose weirdness is part of the very method. (Ionescu, *Opere* II, 110)

For Nae Ionescu, between the two spiritual attitudes there exists a clear demarcation. The fundamental source of the magic fact is will, while that of the mystic fact is love. As a criterion of identification, he states that "all that which is egocentrism is magic, and all that which is theocentrism is mystic" (110). Magic is correlated with immanentism, pantheism, and idealism, and is manifested as a creative attitude. Mysticism is correlated with emanatism, dualism, and realism, and is manifested as a contemplative attitude. The magic fact is a position characteristic of the West, while the Christian East has totalized all the components of religion in the mystic life.

> The mystic attitude is, consequently, the identification of the subject with the object through the conscious dissolving of the subject into the object, while the magic attitude is, on the contrary, the taking of the object into the subject. The accent of reality falls, in the magic case, on the subject; in the mystic case, on the object. (112)

Plato is given as an example of mystic attitude, while Hegel one of the magic. There exist, however, some mixed forms, which Ionescu illustrated with Plotinus or, later, through shamanism and Brahmanism (283, 286).

Thus, the fundament of the mystic attitude is the postulate of transcendence, whereas its principal instrument is love. Love is not only an instrument of knowledge, but a law of the existence of man, a constituent element of his being. Its exercise does not stem from the imperative of knowledge, but from his very being. Like love, mysticism is not determined pragmatically—not even by the need for salvation—but it is a natural function of the human spirit. This means that no one can avoid it, not even in profane life, much less in the problem of salvation,

141

an assertion whose consequences are dangerous for the Orthodox—as Nae Ionescu observes himself—because it leads to the conclusion that "the absolute is a point of arrival of an activity which exists in us, of a faculty that exists in us" (114). Another perilous conclusion is the independence of mysticism—and implicitly of the religious life—from morality. Probably without realizing it, Nae Ionescu brings the mystic fact very close to the magic fact.

This is seen better in Lesson XXII, "*The Type of the Saint.*" Nae Ionescu places the saint in the register of "pure life." In this same pure life come together the two opposite spheres, the mystic and the magic. "The saintly life represents, therefore, a danger inasmuch as it can be modeled after or grafted onto a magical attitude, that is, an attitude through which we believe we participate ourselves, in one way or another, in divinity" (139). Pantheism, Theosophy, and occultism cultivate the same attitude. But not alchemy—says Nae Ionescu, contradicting what he had said a few lessons before (111, 140). It pertains, without doubt, to occultism, but it is a "mystical operation" of occultism. Alchemy is a therapy, while magic is a technique. Alchemy creates an instrument for perfecting the self, while magic creates instruments for the mastery of external reality. Alchemy is situated on a transcendentalist position, while magic is on a demiurgic one.

These new ideas about magic will be framed in his theologico-metaphysical worldview in a public lecture, "*Creațiune și păcat*" ("Creation and Sin") delivered on December 11, 1929. One of the ideas repeated often by Nae Ionescu is that the purpose of human life is not creation, but spiritual salvation, whether by the metaphysical path (equanimity through ultimate knowledge) or by the religious path (salvation of the soul). He already discussed about the possibility of salvation through knowledge and through action in one of his first courses preserved in stenographic transcript, *The Problem of Salvation in Goethe's "Faust"* (1925).

In this public lecture, he begins from the idea that work is not and cannot be an ideal; it is a punishment for man. The ideal of work, which dominates the contemporary *ethos*, is a product of Anglo-Saxon provenience, as foreign to the Eastern Christian mentality as it is to human reality in general (Ionescu, *Teologia*, 85). Nae Ionescu adopts a position radically opposed to this ideal. Given that in certain moments in history the means has been transformed into the end, man has become slave not only to his needs, but to his creations, too, to his very creative action. "The original sin of the entire present conception which makes of work an ideal" is "the tendency to autonomize the idea" (85). The creativist ideal develops from the analogy that man establishes between God and himself. At the basis of the ideology of work lies the concept that, for God, the act of thinking is equal to the act of creation. It is an old current of thought, so-called *Gnosticism*, which "continues today under the name of *idealism* and I don't know what else" (87).

God, however—continues Nae Ionescu—creates from nothing, while man creates out of preexistent matter, independent of himself. Consequently, the creative action of man is limited by the laws of substance. "Which means that our initiative is not, properly speaking, ours, but is the result of certain realities exterior to ourselves" (88).

The fundamental elements of Western thought carry in them—through their Mediterranean, Egyptian, and Greek origins—the possibility of identifying, in one way or another, man with God. "All European thought—with Mediterranean roots which are not necessarily European—all this thought has been falsified, if not poisoned, by certain underlying veins of ideas which go in a totally opposite direction from considerations of good sense" (88). It is precisely the idea fundamental to magic:

> Today, in 1929, we are living in a period of continuous magic. All that the ancient occultists of Hermes Trismegistus' lineage did is identical with our spiritual structure and with what we are thinking and doing in the present moment. That is, we imagine, as the magi did, that we could *substitute ourselves for God*; and we imagine this because we imagine indeed that we have the power to know. [. . .] There has not existed, for three hundred years, a period more ready to fall victim to magic and occultism than the one in which we live today. It is a horrible mess, in which the lack of discipline and self-control are ravaging. All that is happening in contemporary life, call it what you will: occultism, Christianity—that is, authentic religious life, authentic mysticism—, the Bible of health, the new American movement "Christian Science," and so on, they are all trends which go in the same direction: toward *the conquest of the absolute*. [. . .] Consequently, in the contemporary epoch, *this trend to know equals the trend to substitute ourselves for God, to exclude God from our calculations or to merely affirm our identity with God*. (*Teologia*, 88–89)

The sin of man consists therefore in *superbia animi*, in the pretention to create, and thus to take the place of God. And the punishment for sin is sterility, to which the result of man's creative actions is condemned. For Nae Ionescu, man does not invent anything; he can at most "catch the fundamental structures of reality." His creation is reduced to "orienting, systematizing, and developing the real powers, out of the chaos in which, many times perhaps, they would succumb without his intervention" (91). This is even a duty: to fulfill the law of reality, which is also the law of man. Otherwise said, the duty of man is to know himself and be what he is. A metaphysical goal formulated by the most ancient thinkers. But Nae Ionescu does not say how it can be attained. After he had excluded the path of magic, nothing else remained from his point of view but that of mysticism—a fact that he did not find it necessary to reiterate.

In the absence of *"Faptul magic,"* we cannot know the exact points in it with which Nae Ionescu took issue. Nor could Eliade know the reaction of his professor. Only after his return from India, in December 1931, would he be able to read the three courses on metaphysics that the latter had held in the meantime. It would be, from all points of view, too late to engage in a dialogue. Unless, perhaps, the publishing of *Soliloquii*, in May 1932, was Eliade's rejoinder.

Magic and Tantrism

In the summer of 1928, Eliade wrote to John Woodroffe to share with him his "intuitions about the structural correspondences between *tantra*, Mithraic liturgy, certain formulas of the Kabbalah, and the Dhāraṇī sect." This letter was not found, but he mentioned it in another letter sent to Jakob Wilhelm Hauer.[30] We know more about his "intuitions" from the article *"Varnamâlâ sau 'Ghirlanda literelor,"* which is devoted to the works of the British scholar. Eliade had just read some of his writings, along with others by J. H. Hauer, and discovered in them the Hindu and Buddhist practices of verbal "ritual" formulas (*mantra, dhāraṇī*) used as an instrument of concentration or a psychic talisman (Eliade, *Virilitate şi ascezǎ*, 194–197).

Eliade knew Hauer through his "extremely interesting brochure" *Die Dhāraṇī im nördlichen Buddhismus und ihre Parallelen in der sogenannten Mithrasliturgie* (Stuttgart, 1927). The booklet dealt with the practice of *dhāraṇī* in Mahāyāna Buddhist meditation—which Eliade hastened to praise as "the most authentic and magic" Buddhist school (194)—and with its parallels with Mithraic liturgical formulas. For the latter, Eliade cites the works of Albrecht Dieterich and Franz Cumont. Causal relations between the two "magical and mystical rituals" being hard to admit, Hauer concluded that it is a matter of a correspondence of methods in following the same experiences (contemplation, ecstasy).

Later, however, in his letter to Hauer, Eliade would acknowledge that, in that moment, he did not know about *dhāraṇī* except from hearsay. It is possible, therefore, that the information about the little book of Hauer came from another work or from a book review. It was some time later—says Eliade—that an Italian friend drew his attention to the writings of the German Indologist. If true, we wonder who that friend might have been. Judging from his correspondence, it is not Carlo Formichi or Aldo Mieli or Arturo Farinelli. It might be Giuseppe Tucci, but his letters prior to the year 1929, if they existed, have not been preserved. Or Evola, but the existence of a pre-Indian correspondence with him remains, for the time being, an unproven possibility.

From the work of John Woodroffe, "one of the most accomplished English Indologists," Eliade claims to know the "magnificent" collection *Tantrik Texts* (fourteen volumes between 1913 and 1928), *Shakti and Shākta: Essays and Addresses on the Shākta Tantra-shāstra* (1918, 1927[3]), *The Serpent Power: The Secrets of Tantric and Shaktic Yoga* (1919, 1928[3]), and *The Garland of Letters (Varṇamālā): Studies in the Mantra-shāstra* (1922). But it is obvious that, despite the fact that he promises to publish a review of the entire collection of Tantric texts, he knew directly only the last of the above-mentioned books. Eliade was not even aware that "Arthur Avalon" is a pseudonym of Woodroffe (which covered his collaboration with several Bengali pundits), so he refers in several places to "scholars like Avalon and Woodroffe." The ignorance of Arthur Avalon's identity is proof that he had not read *Shakti and Shākta*, since, in its preface, Woodroffe acknowledges the pseudonym.

What must have immediately attracted Eliade to *tantra* was its philosophy of "a magism pure and universal" (but also the "rehabilitation" of sexuality). In distinction from the way the word is understood in the West, says he, in the dynamic-energetic view of the cosmos specific to tantrism, *mantra* has, besides the physical body and a content of consciousness, a third dimension: a magical, creative power. Every object has a "natural name," which is the sound produced by the forces inherent in it, accessible, however only to the "infinite ears" of the yogin. Mastering sound, pronouncing correctly the "name" of a thing (that is, having a psychic attitude appropriate to it), the yogin obtains power over it (Eliade, *Virilitate și asceză*, 196).[31] An ancient conception, Eliade observes, which is found from primitives to the Bible and the Kabbalah (197).

"Words are *magic acts*, acts through which existences are controlled or postulated." Eliade is fascinated by the universal domain of sounds, which he sees as a vast ocean that awaits the explorer. This conception of universal dynamism appears to him to be completely scientific. Moreover, he writes, science proceeds from magic, while philosophy returns to magic when it encounters a crisis, as in the case of idealism or pragmatism (197).

Most probably, Eliade's first meeting with *tantra* was mediated by the review *Ur*, where he could have read, in the translation by "Arthur Avalon" (retranslated into Italian by Evola), the first chapter of *Kulārṇava tantra*—a text dating from the eleventh to the fourteenth centuries, very popular in Bengal.[32] In the same place he could read a translation of the Mithraic ritual from the so-called Great Magical Papyrus of Paris. It was done by the Neo-Pythagorist Giulio Parise, directly from the Greek original, but collated with the German translation of Albrecht Dieterich (*Eine Mithrasliturgie*, 1903). Evola also published, on the basis of John Woodroffe's book *The Garland of Letters*, an article on the general theory of the *mantra* ("*Sulla dottrina generale dei 'Mantra'*"), while Parise contributed one about "the names of power" ("*Opus Magicum*").

The introduction and notes to *Apathanatismos*—the only ritual of the ancient mysteries preserved intact—make references to the practice of *mantra*, to the "letters of light" in Kabbalah, and draw parallels with various traditions: *yoga*, Buddhist *tantra*, Orphism, Gnosticism, Hermeticism, Neo-Platonism, the Bible, Kabbalah, and so on, while citing Franz Cumont's *Les mystères de Mithra* (1913) and Arthur Avalon's *The Serpent Power* (1924[2]) (*Ur 1927*, 90, 91, 103, 106, 107, 108, 113, 115, 116). In Evola's notes to the translation of the *Kulārṇava tantra*, comparisons are made between the Mithraic ritual and the Kabbalah (65, 68). And in his study about the theory of *mantra*—which does not resemble that of Eliade—the Italian esoterist refers to the possible correspondences between this and the Kabbalist tradition (332, 339).

The intuitions about which Eliade writes to Hauer and Woodroffe have, undoubtedly, their origins in these four texts in the review *Ur*, which oriented him toward new readings. The only new thing he brings into comparison is *dhāraṇī*, after J. W. Hauer's work, which, however, he knew only indirectly, probably from a review.

On the Tracks of "*Faptul magic*"

Although the Indian period is the object of a future article, some of the immediate consequences of the ideas presented in "*Faptul magic*" must be dealt with here.

Two weeks after he had sent the article to Mircea Vulcănescu, Eliade wrote to Vittorio Macchioro about his discoveries:

> Do you know that I have found a counterpart to the ideas of R. Otto? It is a "magic" element, opposed to his *Heilige* and which is not the minimal creature feeling, but the sentiment that results from the contemplation of a human creation. I compare the dream and the aesthetic emotion to magic. In *Mantra Shastra*, more precisely in the tantric translations of Avalon (Sir John Woodroffe), I have found dazzling texts about the other side of the sacred, about the creative power through human magic. (*Mircea Eliade și corespondenții săi* II, 162, December 26, 1928)

We cannot say for certain from these lines whether Eliade was informing Macchioro about the ideas expounded in *"Faptul magic"* or about some ulterior development of them. The very short distance from the conclusion of the study combined with its hurried dispatch to Bucharest argues for both possibilities. However that may be, this letter shows that Julius Evola was not the only reference of his mysterious lost opuscule.

For Eliade, magic is opposed to the sacred, in the sense in which Otto uses the term, but not in an absolute way, because it remains part of it—its "other side." What defines magic is its creative, demiurgic power. On the same plane he puts dream and aesthetic emotion. The strategic author in maintaining his point of view is John Woodroffe, more precisely, his translations of tantric texts like *The Garland of Letters*, a book to which he had already devoted an article before leaving Romania. Both the authors and the ideas invoked belong to the pre-Indian period.

In an Indian article, *"Fragmente"* ("Fragments"), dated January 13, 1929, one of Eliade's meditations dwells upon tiredness as a discontinuous moment of creation. It is that tiredness that springs from the ideas and sentiments themselves, not from their conflict with mental physiology. "Natural tiredness of the soul, manifesting through loss of critical acuteness, through the abandonment of the meanings of the great coefficients that nourish the conscience, through the involuntary sympathy toward those forms of life born from dream (art, love, etc.)." Specifying this, Eliade makes a very significant parenthesis:

> I note here in passing, that dream is the great enchanter and support of earthly life, helping us to forget or to veil the cruel isolation of the humane. Through dream we believe that we can become another,

that we can become the other. Magic (the most organized form of dream) incites us to believe that we can leap over the threshold of our isolation, by creating effectively through a will channeled into ritual, by becoming demiurges. (Eliade, *"Fragmente,"* 1)

These attitudes—dream, magic, art, love—become sympathetic to man in the state of spiritual weariness. Positions of courage, of *avant-guard*, of danger—like living metaphysics or religious experience—are abandoned, because they demand "continuous intellectual effort, continual humiliation of simple human values, intense and shrewd analysis of the data of consciousness" (1).

As can easily be seen, these observations continue the ideas that Eliade communicated to Macchioro some two weeks earlier. Magic and religion are found again in opposite positions, while dream and artistic creation are put in sympathetic correspondence with magic.

These observations and ideas are found also in the third section of the book *Soliloquii*, published after Eliade's return from India. Along with them, the book includes notations from the miscellaneous notebook "*Monstrul nr. 1*" (June 2–September 5, 1930). Eliade amalgamated in this booklet notations spread over a period of three years: from the journey to India (the draft of "*Faptul magic*") to the return to the homeland.[33]

These pages precisely refer to Otto's *creatural*, the sentiment of dependence on God, to which Eliade opposes the sentiment of the *Creator*, that of being a demiurge resembling God. Here, however, magic is put on the same plane as dream, art, and dance, while mysticism is aligned with love (Eliade, *Solilocvii*, 47).

Around the same time, Eliade informs Mircea Vulcănescu about his continuing interest in the problem approached in "*Faptul magic*." Meanwhile, he is gathering material with the aim of explaining magic as a form of dream, but he is thinking that, in several years, he will be able to write a study titled *Essai sur l'histoire et la signification de la magie* (*Europa Asia, America . . .* III, 243, January 23, 1929).

In an article written February 19, whose title, "*Schiță pentru un îndreptar*" ("Outline for a Guidebook"), announced a rather ambitious program similar to "*Itinerariu spiritual*," Eliade distinguishes two ways of relating to life: the impulse to live it and the impulse to understand it (an activity to which he confers a spiritual content, different from simple knowledge). He is almost exclusively interested by the first of them: *trăirea*, the Romanian equivalent of the German *Erlebnis*.

As contemporary examples of authors or currents that find the solution to life in the very experience of it, he cites Bergsonism, Futurism, H. von Keyserling, A. Gide, and M. de Unamuno. Eliade warns against considering these attitudes as "mystic" because they have nothing in common with mysticism except the intuitive element situated beyond reason. He prefers to call them "esthetic," the esthetic having its roots not in religion but in magic (Eliade, "*Schiță pentru un îndreptar*," 1).

If before leaving for India he foresaw only two roads in the spiritual life—magic and mysticism ("*Cuvinte despre o filosofie*") or adventure and the absolute ("*Aventura*")—now Eliade finds three classic solutions of life as *trăire*. The first is the heroic solution: to make of your own life a masterpiece. A magical, autocratic, adventurous attitude, entailing the illusion of vastness, of superman, of the creative act. A youthful solution, superb but tragic. The hero suffers cruelly, without reason, only because it is "beautiful" to do it. It is the solution of the artists of genius. But they do not realize anything, except for their own lives. Even this is a value only inasmuch as it is seen by others: their lives are great exclusively from the outside.

At the end of the hero's road, there are two possibilities: either he will realize the illusion in which he finds himself or he will recognize that he has failed to make of his life a masterpiece. Both lead to suicide. "The hero who has not met on his road the temptation to commit suicide is a false hero," declares Eliade. Inasmuch as he had followed the heroic road himself (it becomes obvious also from the amount of space he devotes to it here compared to the other two), we could be justified in taking these lines as a confession. In fact, he speaks about suicide from the very beginning of the article. The examination of life, leading to "the lucid experience of time"—that is, the taking conscious-ness of becoming, the invading of consciousness by the sentiment of becoming[34]—may release a convulsion of the soul so deep that it leads to the suppression of life itself.

The second solution is that of the actor: to play his role in the cor-rect way. This means not to "intervene in the creative imagination of the author, but to respect it, realizing it." Finally, the third is the solution of the absolute: to transcend the categories of life. That is, to renounce becoming, to suppress terrestrial existence in order to live like a saint or a metaphysician (a "true" one). "In a certain sense, this is equivalent to an anticipation of Heaven or Nirvana, depending whether the one who experiences it is a European (positively) or an Asian (negatively)" (2).

But the multiplication of options continues. Eliade discerns a fourth solution, accessible to any mortal, which seems to be the choice of his own spiritual itinerary. It is the solution of the creating of life, which—says he—becomes a duty for those who cannot make one of the three classic choices. His reflections about this new attitude are still in the magmatic form; their meaning must rather be guessed. For the time being, Eliade has not found a suitable name; he calls it "the concentration of the attention upon the vital phenomenon." The sense he gives here to the word "attention" is not that of dissociation (between subject and object), but to "*presentify*" a fact, to make it alive and immediate.

The attitude that he proposes is a continuous exercise: to take knowledge of life, to intervene into it in a lucid and calm way, to create it. The road begins through "the obsession with *construction*." Man has the power to create his own life. He can exercise his freedom not only through heroic gestures, but also in humble, mediocre moments. This is verified in troubled circumstances, contrary to the instantaneous instinct. We really master only those fragments of life that are lived in opposition to physiology and society, those whose foundations reside in one's own will. "Living one's life begins by contradicting life."

Eliade warns against confusing this exercise with the *je-m'enfichisme* ("I don't give a damn" [Fr.]), cultivated by Futurism, or with "the humble heroic life" of Romain Rolland.

"The awakening of the attention" (*deșteptarea atenției*) means to eliminate the self-forgetfulness in the flux of life. In this way, the process of living is reversed: life starts from the thought, desire, and imagination of man. Eliade writes without blinking: Everything lies in the power of the individual, except grace. The exception gives him the occasion to open a parenthesis about this notion, which, we recall, played the key role in the surpassing of the magic conception of asceticism in "*Faptul magic*": "But Grace is an extramundane element, and it would be better to remain silent about it. Those who have it, belong to another world. They experience other relations. They lose the meaning of existence. They are the resurrected dead, born to a new light, feeding on other foods" (2).

Through a continuous daily practice of this exercise, life becomes an unceasing revelation. It does not exclude, however, and does not diminish the rational faculties. The exercise of reason begins only here: "I can judge only in the *real*, in that which I feel *exists*." Problems are either gratuitous or else insoluble if the soul who raised them has not awakened in himself this "sentiment of existence."

The article "*Schiță pentru un îndreptar*" closes with an explicit confession: "I am a man who has learned to live, and all I have written is of no value for those who have not apprehended existence, for those who have not realized that they are alive" (2). Thus, Eliade had learned to live in the sense revealed here by the term "*trăire*": concentrated permanently on the present moment, in a state which excludes projection into the past or the future, and constructing his life moment by moment through the exercise of his own will. It is easy to see that it is still a magic solution, of self-creation, even if it shifts from the heroic register into the ordinary everyday. It seems to correspond to a metaphysical reorientation toward "realism," which Eliade will acknowledge soon.

It could be believed that Eliade had already begun to experience some Indian psycho-physiologic techniques. The two exercises to which he refers in the first part of the article—"the lucid experience of time" and "the concentration of the attention on the vital phenomenon"—evoke the well-known Buddhist meditation technique *vipaśyanā*, on the impermanence and momentariness of existence. In Buddhism, however, the orientation is in the direction of what Eliade called "the solution of the absolute," that is—according to his distinctions—the mystic way. However, he himself did not surpass his old magical predispositions.

Probably these exercises were the result of his neurasthenic attacks, like the one recorded in his journal a little while before the article:

> I feel, with a mighty sensibility, lucidity, attention, and clarity how time is racing around me, how each moment buries another, how all that fascinates us or troubles us is nothing but an ephemeral flash.... The attack continues even now, when I write. Time, time—it obsesses me to the point of neurasthenia. Why can't I find stable points, absolute, eternal? When I gain the consciousness of time that flows without any power that can stop it, I tremble. It seems to me that either I'll go mad, or else I must do, urgently, a great *deed* [*faptă*]. (Eliade, *India. Biblioteca maharajahului. Șantier*, 265–266)

The new spiritual guidebook remains, however, in the phase of this sketch. Not one of the texts he wrote in the following months continues the lines penned here. Only a few reflections on the "sentiment of presence" and a "new sense of time" will be ascribed to "the Doctor" in the novel *Isabel și apele Diavolului*, while the attitude called "*attention* to life" will be attributed to Fräulein Roth (Eliade, *Opere* I, 41–42, 64–65, 96–97).

Nevertheless, a passage from a strange short story, *"Carnaval"*—dated March 1929—deserves being brought into this context for its value as a possible confession:

> The fantastic and the mystery of my life lie in a violent state of cerebral tension, passion, and will. Crime does not satisfy me, perversion disgusts me, adventure *outside of ourselves* perished with the Middle Ages. I was conscious of my inner life when I reached twenty. What could I do? Freedom and foolish actions could not become a purpose. I proposed, then, to become God [Zeu].
>
> I specify: not I am God [Dumnezeu], but a god [zeu], a simple pagan god, with the soul of a god and, of course, his powers. Indications about such beings—which the ignorant call mythic—we have preserved, in abundance. The purpose of my life was to follow step by step these indications and to realize them. The first deed which I was supposed to accomplish you know: I must kill my father and swallow my children. But as it happens, I have no children. I had thus to begin the palingenesis from the second step. I have begun the deification of my soul. I believe my methods are the best. Endowed with an almost morbid sensibility, with a painful elasticity of thoughts, with a robust will, and a rich effusion of instincts, nothing remains but to activate with intensity all these qualities, preserving nevertheless *a stone-like indifference*, a stupid calm. Not a *mask*, but a soul calm in the frenzy, as were the souls of the gods. I cannot express the strangeness of those first attempts. I remember that I succeeded in recognizing, after a few years, a strange and clear element, immutable and inaccessible to the self-knowledge of other men. It was *the soul*. Gentlemen, it was the soul of a god! [. . .]
>
> In order to try the powers of my soul, I submitted myself to the rack. Not the body, not the senses, but I sought temptations for my vast inner life. These were my tortures, which I endured smiling, tumultuous and indifferent. I told myself that the soul of a god must receive a joy or an unhappiness with the same tension of an everyday event. Joys first: I sought and I found them. And in the passion that tortured my soul, the true soul contemplated itself lucidly, serenely, clearly. (Eliade, *Maddalena*, 143–144)

Eventually, the character in the short story commits suicide because, he says, only the one who cuts off his life without reason is master of it. Only the one who dies as a man becomes a true god. It is not difficult to recognize in this text the Evolian idea of magical deification, to create an immortal soul through will and self-effort. It also contains other evident traces of the influence of Giovanni Papini; however, here is not the place to insist on that.

Probably the writing of the short story had a compensatory function in the economy of Eliade's spiritual life. At the end of March, the encounter with a young Indian professor who was living a "complete spiritual itinerary" made him realize that lately he was trapped between intellectual work and satisfaction of the senses. He does not feed his soul with any spiritual substance, nor does he practice a rigorous meditation technique. The first step he will take is bodily purification, the renunciation of sensuality, the return to asceticism.

> Otherwise, why have I come here? Solitude, meditation, study I could find, in the same conditions, anywhere in Europe. But here there exists a certain atmosphere of renunciation, of effort toward inner fulfillment, of control over consciousness, of love—which is more propitious for me. Not Theosophism, not Brahmanic practices, not rituals; nothing barbaric, nothing historically created. But an extraordinary belief in the reality of truths, in man's power to know them and to live [trăi] them through an inward realization, through purity, and recollection especially. This belief is also mine. The belief that, in spite of all demons and lusts, there exists a straight bridge on which I can walk anytime, from any infernal region where I may find myself. (Eliade, *India. Biblioteca maharajahului. Şantier*, 279–280)

Nevertheless, this meeting did not have any consequence (277). Eliade did not return to the ascetic life and the practice of spiritual exercises. The explanation could be found in one of the pages from the largely autobiographic novel *Isabel şi apele Diavolului*, on which he will begin to write: "I have not returned to my old faith; I have not become again medieval. I have not ordered self-discipline, because the freedom that I enjoyed for too long has annihilated my organized will. My will was now spasmodic, interrupted by vast arid or penitent periods, and capricious" (Eliade, *Opere* I, 37).

On the contrary, other encounters, like that with André Gide's book *Si le grain ne meurt . . .* (1924), stirred up a desire to live the extremes of life, of wanderings, of vice, of demonism (Eliade, *India. Biblioteca maharajahului. Şantier*, 289). The "magic fact" continues to be an intellectual preoccupation, but—until the end of the year—it remains far from his personal life.

* * *

Thus, in the years 1926–1928, the impact which his—limited—reading of Guénon and Coomaraswamy had upon the intellectual formation of Eliade was minor. More important was the impact of Evola, even if only through articles in *Bilychnis* and *Ur*. But, as we have seen, the positions of Evola with which Eliade was in accord he gained by himself, independently, through his own "spiritual itinerary" and through the frequenting of other authors (Macchioro, Frazer, Otto), whereas with other positions of the Italian occultist he found himself in explicit disaccord. He wrote it in black and white: "I don't accept all of Evola's conclusions," but "this doesn't mean that a certain part of his thought is not valid" (Eliade, *Itinerariu spiritual*, 371). That which he accepts from the thought of the Italian is the result of a convergence, not of an influence. In the best case, his writings helped Eliade to explicate his independently achieved position. The theories he developed, starting from there, are not only different, but even opposed to those of Evola.

A new encounter with these authors would take place in Calcutta, after the experience of what Eliade will call "the first six months in India." When his understanding of the Indian spiritual phenomenon gained depth, Eliade seems to return toward them with a new perception of their thought. In June 1929 he received Guénon's books *L'homme et son devenir selon le Vedânta* (1925) and *La crise du monde moderne* (1927), which he had ordered through a friend in Paris (Eliade, *Europa, Asia, America...* I, 265, April 17, 1929).[35] At the same time he wrote to Bucharest that the new issues of *Ur/Krur* and *Bilychnis* should be forwarded to him in India (272, June 13, 1929). To Evola himself, he would write only in the spring of 1930, to request his recent books. This new stage in the encounter with the writings of the Traditionalists and the dialectics of acceptance/rejection through which he relates to them will be dealt with elsewhere.

Translated from the Romanian by Mac Linscott Ricketts

Notes

1. See a presentation of the most important texts published in the period 1986–2003 in Spineto "Eliade e il 'pensiero tradizionale.'" Since then, however, a considerable number of new publications have appeared.
2. On this point I have referred already in Bordaş, "*Secretul doctorului Eliade*"; "*Istoria doctorului Honigberger*"; and "*The Secret of Dr. Eliade*." I have treated the postwar period in Bordaş, "*The Difficult Encounter in Rome*."
3. The manuscript list of books is preserved in the Romanian Academy Library, A 3412c, f. 5.
4. Very probably, he also knew his older articles in this review: "*E. Coué e l' 'agire senza agire*'" (January–February 1925) and "*Della 'purità' come valore metafisico*" (June 1925); rep. in Evola, *I saggi di Bilychnis*, 11–38.
5. In 1927, Evola published in *Ur*, under the transparent pseudonym "Ea," six articles (see below). Probably the articles signed "Iagla" ("*Saggezza serpentina*" and "*La legge degli Enti*") and the unsigned glosses belong to him too.

6. The article has as its motto a citation from Dr. Osty's book *La Connaissance supranormale. Étude expérimentale* (1923), taken from the text of Evola.

7. A well-documented historical view of the group and its review in Del Ponte. An interesting discussion about the psycho-physiological techniques practiced in the group in Cardinale.

8. See also the article published earlier on the same theme by Reghini.

9. In the month of October 1928, Arturo Reghini and Giulio Parise broke with the group "Ur," after which, from 1929, the review was renamed *Krur*.

10. "*Fait mystique*" is different from the Latin expression "*factum mysticum*" as employed by Hugo of Saint-Victor, William Perault, and other medieval authors. Apparently the first modern author who used it as a concept was Fr. Jérôme-Édouard Récéjac, in a book that enjoyed some influence at that time: *Essai sur les fondements de la connaissance mystique* (1897; translated into English as *The Basis of Mystic Knowledge*, 1899). He defined it as "a *naïve* and non-methodical attempt to apprehend the Absolute" and as "a *symbolic* and not a dialectic mode of thought" (4). The expression was adopted in German ("*die mystische Tatsache*," Rudolf Steiner, 1902) and also in English ("the mystic fact," Evelyn Underhill, 1911), where it already existed with a common meaning ("act" or "deed"). However it did not enjoy the same circulation as in French, where it was taken up by other scholars of mysticism (e.g., Henri Delacroix, in 1921, for whom ecstasy was the "mystic fact" *par excellence*), and it is still commonly used today.

11. "*Fait magique*" seems to have been used for the first time at the beginning of nineteenth century in the circle of Émile Durkheim (Marcel Mauss, Henri Hubert, Paul Huvelin, etc.). See, for example *L'année sociologique*, 10 (1905–1906): 1–47 (2–3). "Magic fact" entered into English but could not impose itself—probably because of the older "magical fact," meaning "act," "deed"—as it will succeed later on in Italian ("*fatto magico*," Ernesto de Martino, 1948, but used already by others in the 1930s). In his book *From Religion to Philosophy: A Study in the Origins of Western Speculation* (1912), Francis Macdonald Cornford defines the primitive "magical fact" (*sic*) as an "intense emotional activity, collectively experienced by a group" (73).

12. In French, "*fait mystique*" is found more often than its twin. Actually and quite strangely, I couldn't find them used as a couple in the way Eliade and Ionescu do it. "*Fait magique*" is sometimes used in contrast with "*fait religieux*." For Eliade's earlier use of the term "mystic fact," see his articles "*Misticismul orfic al lui Heraclit*" and "*Ernesto Buonaiuti*," rep. in Eliade, *Itinerariu spiritual*, 51–54, 59–62 (52, 60).

13. The correspondence of Eliade from the first half of the year 1929 shows that the third number of the review was in preparation. See letters from G. N. Mallik, February 5, and R. Otto, March 9 (*Mircea Eliade și corespondenții săi*, III, 123, 240–241), and letters to J. W. Hauer, January 26, May 14 (see below), R. Pettazzoni, February 19, April 8 and 25 (Spineto, *L'histoire des religions* 103, 109–110), and M. Vulcănescu, July 23 (Eliade, *Europa, Asia, America . . .* III, 245).

14. Mihail Polihroniade lets him know on January 15, 1929, that the manuscript has arrived. *Mircea Eliade și corespondenții săi*, III, 332. It has not been found in the archive of M. Vulcănescu. It is possible that it remained among the

papers of P. Sterian, the other editor of the review, but the fate of his archive is unknown.

15. A neurotic dream in a "vagotonic" moment in January or February 1929 suggests that the article could not be precisely to the liking of Vulcănescu: "M.V., whom I recognize at once behind me, tries to squeeze me in his arms, at first smiling, and then with a grotesque expression, his face bloated, decomposed. 'Why did you write *Faptul magic?*' he screamed in my ear." Eliade, *India. Biblioteca maharajahului. Şantier*, 260.

16. In a later journal entry, on the death of Evola, Eliade recalls the discovery of his first books in the university years. Eliade, *Jurnal* II, 164–165 (July 1974).

17. In June 1928, in his examination paper for the course Encyclopedia of Philosophy, titled "*The Problem of Natural Death and Its Ontological Significance*," he refers to the "self-realization" characteristic of magic mentality, as a danger that is met on the "road to the transcendental" (Eliade, *Virilitate şi asceză*, 390.) In October, in one of his papers for the BA examination, "*The Intuitionism of Spinoza*," he uses, in a parenthesis, the expressions "the magic conception of self-realization through self-affirmation" and "magic idealism"—the last one however "post-Kantian," that is, that of Novalis, sympathizer of Spinozism (Romanian Academy Library, A 3907, Fond Nae Ionescu, Vol. II, ff. 358–362). In the article "*Virilitate şi asceză*," published the same month, he characterizes his surpassed position, as a *magic* attitude, distinguished by a "presumptuous impulse toward self-realization." For the Ego exalted through magic, fellow men exist as a simple excitant and catalyst of one's "self-realization" (Eliade, *Virilitate şi asceză*, 272, 278.)

18. Evola is mentioned, however, alongside R. Pettazzoni and G. Tucci, whom Eliade had not yet met.

19. Eliade, "*Contribuţiile românilor la Congresul de studii romane*," rep. in *Virilitate şi asceză*, 138–139. It is interesting to add here that, in the spring of the same year, through the intermediary of Claudiu Isopescu, who lived in Rome, Eliade published several articles in *L'Impero* and *Il lavoro d'Italia*, newspapers to which Evola also contributed. (Isopescu could be the common friend to whom Evola refers in his letter of May 18, 1930.)

20. Eliade, "*Fragmentarium*," 100. Integrated into the third section of the book. A single note, that of August 24, was blended into the second section; Eliade, *Solilocvii*, 33–34.

21. A manuscript page with a sketch of the future *Tratat* is reproduced photographically in Handoca, *Mircea Eliade*, 85.

22. Ionescu, "*Horoscopul religiilor*," rep. in Ionescu, *Opere* VII, 359–361 (360). See also *Curs de metafizică, 1928–1929*, in Ionescu, *Opere* II, 111.

23. *Curs de filosofie a religiei. 1924–1925*, in Ionescu, *Opere* I, 126; *Curs de metafizică. 1928–1929*, in Ionescu, *Opere* II, 101, 104, 105.

24. Ionescu, *Opere* I, 284, 288, 297–298; *Opere* VI, 263; *Opere* VII, 210.

25. Ionescu, "*Horoscopul religiilor*."

26. Ionescu, "*Duminica*," rep. in Ionescu, *Teologia*, 337, 353.

27. See Bordaş, *Apaşul metafizic şi paznicii filozofiei*, from which I extract some ideas and passages in what follows.

28. Eliade, "*Paul Vulliaud . .*"; published by Nae Ionescu in his review *Logos* (but a rewriting of the article "*Cântarea Cântărilor*," rep. in Eliade, *Misterele*, 185–193).

29. Eliade refers to "the occult science," particularly to Anthroposophy, but also for Eliphas Lévi magic and occult science were one and the same thing. See likewise his earlier article about Steiner, in Eliade, *Misterele*, 131–141 (138).
30. Letter of January 26, 1929, preserved in Bundesarchiv Koblenz, Nachlass J. W. Hauer, T (courtesy of Horst Junginger and F. Țurcanu).
31. See a more recent approach to the subject, which reexamines in detail the analysis of Woodroffe, in Padoux.
32. Woodroffe, "*La conoscenza quale liberazione*." Although the English version of the *Kulārnava tantra* had been announced by Woodroffe a short time after the Sanskrit edition appeared in the series *Tantrik Texts* (1917), it was never published. The translation belongs, in fact, to Atal Behari Ghose, Woodroffe's principal collaborator. An incomplete manuscript of it was found with his heirs. See Taylor, 205, 225–226.
33. Eliade, "*Fragmentarium*." Cf., for example, the fragments for June 25, 1930; July 29, 1930; August 8, 18, and 24, 1930; September 15, 1930; and *Solilocvii*, 47, 63, 61–62, 50, 51, 65–66, 33–34, 66–67.
34. About this, see also *Isabel și apele Diavolului*; Eliade, *Opere* I, 65.
35. The two books bearing Eliade's signature and the date, "Calcutta, 18 June 1929," become part of Ieronim Șerbu's personal library (Șerbu, 207).

Works Cited

Acterian, Arșavir. "Un secret al lui Mircea Eliade." *Caiete critice* 1–2 (1988):77–80.

Bordaș, Liviu. "Secretul doctorului Eliade." *Origini. Journal of Cultural Studies* 1 (2002):72–87.

———. "Istoria doctorului Honigberger și secretul unei nuvele eliadești." *Origini. Journal of Cultural Studies* 1–2 (2003):20–30; 3–4 (2003):129–158.

———. "The Secret of Dr. Eliade." In *The International Eliade*, edited by Bryan S. Rennie, 101–130. Albany: State University of New York Press, 2007.

———. *Apașul metafizic și paznicii filosofiei*. Bucharest: Humanitas, 2010.

———. "The Difficult Encounter in Rome: Mircea Eliade's Post-war Relation with Julius Evola—New Letters and Data." *International Journal on Humanistic Ideology* 2 (2011):125–158; also in Italian, *Nuova Storia Contemporanea* 2 (2012):79–96.

Călinescu, George. *Istoria literaturii române de la origini până în prezent*, Bucharest: Fundația Regală pentru Literatură și Artă, 1941.

Cardinale, Pasquale. "Il Training autogeno di J. Schultz e le tecniche psicofisiologiche del Gruppo di Ur. Un raffronto e alcune considerazioni." *Vie della Tradizione* 12 (1983):114–136, 168–187.

Coomaraswamy, Ananda K. *La danse de Çiva. Quatorze essais sur l'Inde*. Translated by Madeleine Rolland. Foreword by Romain Rolland. Paris: Rieder, 1922.

Culianu, Ioan Petru. *Mircea Eliade*. Assisi: Cittadella Editrice, 1978.

Del Ponte, Renato. *Evola e il magico Gruppo di Ur. Studi e documenti per servire alla storia di Ur-Krur*. Borzano: Sear, 1994.

De Martino, Marcello. *Mircea Eliade esoterico. Ioan Petru Culianu e i "non detti."* Rome: Settimo Sigillo, 2008.

Eliade, Mircea. "Reviste." *Revista universitară* I.2 (February 1926):72–76.

———. "Rudolf Steiner." *Adevărul literar şi artistic* (June 20, 1926):5.

———. "Cântarea Cântărilor." *Adevărul literar şi artistic* (October 24, 1926):5.

———. "Misticismul orfic al lui Heraclit." *Adevărul literar şi artistic* (January 23, 1927):5–6.

———. "Ernesto Buonaiuti." *Cuvântul* (January 28, 1927):1–2.

———. "Rudolf Steiner." *Cuvântul* (April 13, 1927):1–2.

———. "Itinerariu spiritual, VIII. Teosofie?" *Cuvântul* (October 22, 1927):1–2.

———. "Ocultismul în cultura contemporană." *Cuvântul* (December 1, 1927):1–2.

———. "Theös éghènou." *Gândirea* 7.12 (December 1927):355–357.

———. "Marcelin Berthelot şi alchimia." *Cuvântul* (February 14, 1928):1–2.

———. "Fragmente." *Cuvântul* (April 1, 1928):1.

———. "Paul Vulliaud, «Le Cantique des Cantiques d'après la tradition juive» (Paris, 1925)." *Logos* 1.1 (April 1928):141–143. Signed "X.Y.".

———. "Contribuţiile românilor la Congresul de studii romane." *Cuvântul* (May 13, 1928):1–2; (May 15, 1928):2.

———. "Cuvinte despre o filosofie." *Gândirea* 8.6–7 (June–July 1928):299–300.

———. "*Varnamâlâ* sau «Ghirlanda literelor»." *Cuvântul* (July 11, 1928):1–2.

———. "Apologia virilităţii." *Gândirea* 8.8–9 (August–September 1928):352–359.

———. "Confesiuni şi semnificaţii." *Cuvântul* (October 6, 1928):1–2.

———. "Virilitate şi asceză." *Cuvântul* (October 11, 1928):1–2; (October 17, 1928):1–2.

———. "Aventura." *Cuvântul* (November 4, 1928):1–2.

———. "Spiritualitate şi ortodoxie." *Viaţa literară* (November 10, 1928):1–2.

———. "Solilocviu." *Gândirea* 8.11 (November 1928):453–454.

———. "Fragmente." *Cuvântul* (February 16, 1929):1–2.

———. "Schiţă pentru un îndreptar." *Cuvântul* (March 21, 1929):1–2.

———. "Carnaval." *Viaţa literară* (April 27–May 11, 1929):2.

———. "Revolta contra lumii moderne." *Vremea* (March 31, 1935):6.

———. "Fragmentarium [Notaţii fugare din India]." Edited by M. Handoca. *Manuscriptum* 3 (1987):95–102.

———. *Solilocvii.* Bucharest: Humanitas, 1991.

———. *Jurnal,* I–II. Edited by M. Handoca. Bucharest: Humanitas, 1993.

———. *Mircea Eliade şi corespondenţii săi,* I–V. Edited by M. Handoca. Bucharest: various publishers, 1993, 1999, 2003, 2006, 2007.

———. *Opere, 1. Romane.* Edited by M. Dascal and M. Handoca. Bucharest: Minerva, 1994.

———. *Maddalena. Nuvele.* Edited by M. Handoca. Bucharest: Jurnalul literar, 1996.

———. *Memorii (1907–1960).* 2nd revised edition. Edited by M. Handoca. Bucharest: Humanitas, 1997.

———. *Misterele şi iniţierea orientală. Scrieri de tinereţe, 1926.* Edited by M. Handoca. Bucharest: Humanitas, 1998.

———. *Europa, Asia, America… Corespondenţă,* I–III. Edited by M. Handoca. Bucharest: Humanitas, 1999, 2004.

———. *India. Biblioteca maharajahului. Şantier.* Bucharest: Humanitas, 2003.
———. *Itinerariu spiritual. Scrieri de tinereţe, 1927.* Edited by M. Handoca. Bucharest: Humanitas, 2003.
———. *Virilitate şi asceză. Scrieri de tinereţe, 1928.* Edited by M. Handoca. Bucharest: Humanitas, 2008.
Evola, Julius. *Saggi sull'Idealismo magico.* Todi and Rome: Atanòr, 1925; 4th edition. Rome: Ed. Mediterranee, 2006.
———. *L'individuo e il divenire dell'mondo. Due conferenze.* Rome: Libreria di Scienze e Lettere, 1926; reprint, Carmagnola: Arktos, 1990.
———. "La scolastica dinanzi allo spirito moderno." *Bilychnis* 15.1 (January 1926):1–18.
———. "Il valore dell'occultismo nella cultura contemporanea." *Bilychnis* 16.11 (November 1927):250–269.
———. "Come poniamo il problema della conoscenza." *Ur* 1 (1927):20–25; 2 (1927):26–29. Signed "Ea."
———. "Come poniamo il problema dell'immortalità." *Ur* 5 (1927):143–152. Signed "Ea."
———. "Sulla visione magica della Vita." *Ur* 6 (1927):153–157; 11–12 (1927): 299–304. Signed "Ea."
———. "La dottrina del «Corpo Immortale»." *Ur* 7–8 (1927):196–204. Signed "Ea."
———. "Sul senso dello stato di Potenza." *Ur* 9 (1927):254–261. Signed "Ea."
———. "Sulla dottrina generale dei «Mantra»." *Ur* 9 (1927):331–339. Signed "Ea."
———. "La coscienza iniziatica nel post-mortem." *Ur* 3–4 (1928):111–122. Signed "Ea."
———. "Superamento della «Provvidenza»." *Ur* 3–4 (1928):136–144. Signed "Ea."
———. "Sull'arte dei filosofi d'Ermete. Introduzione." *Ur* 5 (1928):148–154; 6 (1928):167–176. Signed "Ea."
———. "Sulla metafisica del dolore e della malattia." *Ur* 6 (1928):176–181. Signed "Ea."
———. "L'esoterismo e il superamento della morale." *Ur* 7–8 (1928):228–239. Signed "Ea."
———. "Alcuni effetti della disciplina magica: la «dissociazione dei misti»." *Ur* 9 (1928):278–286. Signed "Ea."
———. "Sul «sapienziale» e l'«eroico» e sulla Tradizione Occidentale." *Ur* 11–12 (1928):321–337. Signed "Ea."
———. "Appunti sulla morfologia occulta e sulla corporeità spirituale." *Ur* 11–12 (1928):339–347. Signed "Ea."
———. "La donna e le modalità dell'iniziazione." *Ur* 11–12 (1928):349–357. Signed "Ea."
———. *I saggi di Bilychnis.* Padova: Edizioni di Ar, 1987.
Evola, Julius et al. *Ur 1927.* Rome: Tilopa, 1980.
———. *Ur 1928.* Rome: Tilopa, 1980.
Handoca, Mircea. *Mircea Eliade: o biografie ilustrată.* Cluj-Napoca: Dacia, 2004.

Ionescu, Nae. "«Horoscopul religiilor»." *Cuvântul* (October 25, 1926):3.

———. "Duminica." *Cuvântul* (June 20, 1927):1; (June 4, 1928):1.

———. "Creațiune și păcat." *Buna Vestire* (December 31, 1940):2.

———. *Opere*, I–IV, VI–VII. Edited by M. Diaconu and D. Mezdrea. Bucharest and Brăila: various publishers, 2000, 2005, 2010, 2011, 1999, 2002.

———. *Teologia. Integrala publicisticii religioase.* Edited by D. Mezdrea. Sibiu: Deisis, 2003.

Padoux, André. *Vāc: The Concept of the Word in Selected Hindu Tantras.* Translated by Jacques Gontier. Albany: State University of New York Press, 1990.

Parise, Giulio. "Opus Magicum. I nomi di Potenza e i Segni degli Enti." *Ur* 3 (1927):79 sq. Signed "Luce".

———. "Apathanatismos. Rituale mithriaco del «Gran Papiro Magico di Parigi»." First translation directly from the Greek by Luce. Introduction and commentaries by Ea, Leo [= Giovanni Colazza], Luce, P. Negri. *Ur* 4 (1927):89–120.

Polihroniade, Mihail. "Criza naționalismului." *Acțiune și reacțiune* 1 (May 1929):15–28.

Reghini, Arturo. "Il linguaggio segreto dei «Fedeli d'Amore»." *Ur* 1–2 (1928):71–80. Signed "Pietro Negri."

Șerbu, Ieronim. "Generația ezoterică." In *Idem, Vitrina cu amintiri*, 203–211. Bucharest: Cartea Românească, 1973.

Spineto, Natale, ed. *Mircea Eliade and Raffaele Pettazzoni. L'histoire des religions a-t-elle un sens? Correspondance. 1926–1959.* Paris: Cerf, 1994.

———. "Eliade e il «pensiero tradizionale»." In *Idem, Mircea Eliade storico delle religioni*, 133–163. Brescia: Morcelliana, 2006,.

Taylor, Kathleen. *Sir John Woodroffe, Tantra, and Bengal: "An Indian Soul in a European Body"?* Richmond: Curzon Press, 2001.

Țurcanu, Florin. *Mircea Eliade, le prisonnier de l'histoire.* Paris: La Découverte, 2003.

Vulcănescu, Mircea. "Carte pentru *Isabel*" (I). *Cuvântul* (September 26, 1930):1–2.

Woodroffe, John. *Shakti and Shākta: Essays and Addresses on the Shākta Tantra-shāstra*, London: Luzacs, 1918; 2nd edition, 1920.

———. "La conoscenza quale liberazione (Dal primo capitolo del *Kulâranava-Tantra*)." Translated for *Ur* from the Sanskrit by Arthur Avalon. *Ur* 3 (1927):62–70.

Contributors

Douglas Allen is professor of philosophy and the former chairperson of the Department of Philosophy at the University of Maine. A recipient of Fulbright and Smithsonian grants to India, he served as president of the Society for Asian and Comparative Philosophy, 2001–2004, and is series editor of Lexington's Studies in Comparative Philosophy and Religion. His Eliade books include *Structure and Creativity in Religion, Mircea Eliade: An Annotated Bibliography* (coauthor Dennis Doeing), *Mircea Eliade et le phénomène religieux*, and *Myth and Religion in Mircea Eliade*. His most recent books are *Mahatma Gandhi* (2011) and *Mit și Religie la Mircea Eliade* (2011).

Nicolae Babuts is emeritus professor of French at Syracuse University, where he taught French language and literature for more than thirty years. He obtained his BA in French and English from the University of Toronto and a PhD in French from the University of Michigan in Ann Arbor. In the spring of 1968, he was director of the Syracuse University Program Abroad in Poitiers, France. He has been doing research in nineteenth-century French literature and in the field of cognitive approaches to literature. Babuts is the author of numerous articles on Baudelaire, Hugo, Flaubert, and Balzac and of the following books: *Mimesis in a Cognitive Perspective: Mallarmé, Flaubert, and Eminescu* (Transaction Publishers, 2011); *Memory, Metaphors, and Meaning: Reading Literary Texts* (Transaction Publishers, 2009); *Baudelaire: At the Limits and Beyond* (University of Delaware Press, 1997), and *The Dynamics of the Metaphoric Field: A Cognitive View of Literature* (University of Delaware Press, 1992).

Liviu Bordaș holds a PhD in philosophy from the University of Bucharest and is currently completing a PhD in Sanskrit at Jawaharlal Nehru University of New Delhi. He studied philosophy and Indology at the Universities of Bucharest, Vienna, Rome, Pondicherry, Delhi, and Heidelberg and has done research work in Romania, France, Italy, the United States, India, and Pakistan. He has been a fellow of the Institute of Oriental Studies (Bucharest), Institut Français d'Indologie (Pondicherry), Centre de Sciences Humaines (New Delhi), Centre for the Study of Traditional Culture (Zalău), Accademia Romena a Roma, New Europe College (Bucharest), and Institute of South-East European Studies of the Romanian Academy (Bucharest) and is currently a Fulbright visiting scholar at the University of Chicago Divinity School. Besides many articles and book chapters, he published a volume on Romanian cultural contacts with India during the period 1780–1860 (*Iter in Indiam*, 2006), one on the debates around Nae Ionescu's philosophical originality (*Apaşul metafizic şi paznicii filozofiei*, 2010), and has a forthcoming book on Mircea Eliade (*Eliade secret*).

John D. Dadosky is an associate professor at Regis College in the University of Toronto where he teaches philosophy and theology. He is author of *The Structure of Religious Knowing: Encountering the Sacred in Eliade and Lonergan* (SUNY Press, 2004). Recent essays include "Merton's Dialogue with Zen: Pioneering or Passé?" and "Sacred Symbols as Explanatory: Geertz, Eliade and Lonergan," both in *Fu Jen International Religious Studies* (2008, 2010); "Sacralization, Secularization and Religious Fundamentalism" in *Studies in Religion/Sciences Religeuses* (2007); "'Naming the Demon': The 'Structure' of Evil in Lonergan and Girard" in *Irish Theological Quarterly* (2011); and "Is There a Fourth Stage of Meaning?" in *Heythrop Journal* (2010). He is author of *The Eclipse and Recovery of Beauty: A Lonergan Approach* (University of Toronto Press, 2014).

Robert Ellwood is distinguished emeritus professor of religion at the University of Southern California, where he taught for thirty years after receiving the PhD in history of religion from the University of Chicago in 1967 and a master of divinity from Yale Divinity School in 1957. He has served as an Episcopal clergyman and navy chaplain. He is the author of a number of books, including *The Politics of Myth: A Study of C. G. Jung, Mircea Eliade, and Joseph Campbell, Introducing Japanese Religion,* and of studies in Japanese religion, American religion, and myth. Robert Ellwood now lives in Ojai, California.

Mac Linscott Ricketts was born in 1930 and reared in Ohio and Florida. He studied for the Methodist ministry at Emory University. After five unhappy years in that profession, he sought a place where he could prepare to teach comparative religions on a college or university level. A friend of his recommended the Divinity School of the University of Chicago where a faculty member in that field named Mircea Eliade had recently been hired. That was in 1959, and from then on, Ricketts's life was to be centered increasingly upon Professor Eliade. Awarded a doctorate in December 1964, he taught at Duke University Department of Religion (1965–1971) and subsequently at Louisburg College, Louisburg, North Carolina, until his retirement in December 1994. Among his numerous writings and translations, he considers most important *Mircea Eliade, The Romanian Roots: 1907–1945*; the English versions of Eliade's *Autobiography* (two volumes), *Journal* (volume I, volume IV), and *The Portugal Journal*. Add to these Eliade's great novel, *The Forbidden Forest,* cotranslated with the late Mary Park Stevenson. Mac Linscott Ricketts resides in Independence, Virginia, with his wife of sixty-two years and continues to write and translate.

Robert A. Segal is Sixth Century Chair in Religious Studies, University of Aberdeen, where he has taught since 2006. Previously, he was professor of theories of religion at Lancaster University, England. Prior to his relocating to the United Kingdom in 1994, he taught in his native United States at Reed College, Stanford University, the University of Pittsburgh, and Tulane University. He is the author or editor of, among other works, *The Poimandres as Myth* (Mouton de Gruyter, 1986), *Joseph Campbell* (revised edition, New American Library, 1990), *The Gnostic Jung* (Princeton and Routledge, 1992), *The Myth and Ritual Theory* (Blackwell, 1998), *Jung on Mythology* (Princeton and Routledge, 1998), *Theorizing about Myth* (Massachusetts, 1999), *Myth: A Very Short Introduction* (Oxford, 2004), *The Blackwell Companion to the Study of Religion* (Wiley-Blackwell, 2006), and *The Hero's Quest* (coedited) (Salem Press, 2013).

Eric Ziolkowski is the Helen H. P. Manson Professor of the English Bible at Lafayette College in Easton, Pennsylvania. He is author of many books, articles, and book chapters on religion and literature, an area in which he has lectured widely in the United States and Europe, as well as in China and Australia. Formerly the North American general editor of the journal *Literature and Theology* (2004–2012), he is also a main editor of the *Encyclopedia of the Bible and Its Reception*, a prospective thirty-volume resource published by De Gruyter (Berlin) and coeditor of the book series Religion and the Arts, published by Brill (Leiden).

Index